THE LAST AMERICAN ROAD TRIP

Also by Sarah Kendzior

They Knew

Hiding in Plain Sight

The View from Flyover Country

THE
LAST
AMERICAN
ROAD
TRIP

A Memoir

SARAH KENDZIOR

FLATIRON
BOOKS
NEW YORK

www.flatironbooks.com

Title spread illustration by Sergii Tverdokhlibov / Shutterstock

Designed by Donna Sinisgalli Noetzel

Library of Congress Cataloging-in-Publication Data

Names: Kendzior, Sarah, author.
Title: The last American road trip : a memoir / Sarah Kendzior.
Description: First edition. | New York : Flatiron Books, 2025. |
    Includes bibliographical references.
Identifiers: LCCN 2024043197 | ISBN 9781250879882
    (hardcover) | ISBN 9781250879899 (ebook)
Subjects: LCSH: Kendzior, Sarah—Travel—United States. |
    United States—Description and travel. | United States—
    Social life and customs—1971–
Classification: LCC E169.Z83 K3895 2025 | DDC 917.304—
    dc23/eng/20240925
LC record available at https://lccn.loc.gov/2024043197

Our books may be purchased in bulk for promotional,
educational, or business use. Please contact your local
bookseller or the Macmillan Corporate and Premium Sales
Department at 1-800-221-7945, extension 5442, or by email at
MacmillanSpecialMarkets@macmillan.com.

First Edition: 2025

10 9 8 7 6 5 4 3 2 1

For my beloved family, and our elusive dreams

There's no Riviera in Festus, Missouri.

—TAMMY WYNETTE AND GEORGE JONES,
"(WE'RE NOT) THE JET SET"

So we grew up with mythic dead
To spoon upon Midwestern bread.

—RAY BRADBURY, "BYZANTIUM"

Contents

THE LAST AMERICAN ROAD TRIP

Introduction

An American Family

I drive the highways of America like I'm reading its palm.

I set out each time from the same place: my home in Missouri, a state in the center of an America that does not hold. I travel with the same people: my husband of twenty years and our two children. We started taking family road trips in 2016, when I felt compelled to show our children the entire United States, in the event of its demise.

A lot has changed since we first hit the road. My daughter went from being a fourth grader to a twelfth grader, my son went from being a kindergartner to an eighth grader, and the United States went from being a flawed democracy to a burgeoning autocracy.

We drove past the point of no return—and kept on driving. Road trips are storied American avenues of escape, but that romance looks different in the rearview. I search for truth and justice and wind up on the American Way, a path of pain and violence that permeates from past to present. Yet even in the worst of times, I refuse to believe our nation's fate is preordained. There is no inevitable autocracy or inevitable democracy. There are no red states or blue states. There are only purple states, purple like a bruise, and people trying to survive in a broken-promise land.

I want my children to see it all and see it plain.

We are Midwesterners, so we do not fly. We drive long distances, an approach advantageous for understanding a vast and varied land. When you start from the center, you see America from all sides. The plains that turn into mountains that turn into desert when we go west. The farmland that turns into forests that turn into beaches when we head east. The Mississippi River we follow south until it empties into steaming swamps and north to lakes that look like oceans. We travel famed highways and byways. But we prefer the back roads because that's where the secrets live.

Over the years, we developed a routine: pack the car before dawn, load up on coffee and snacks at the gas station, and hit the highway, my husband and I belting out songs of our twentieth-century youth as our twenty-first-century children cover their ears. What changes each time is our destination: we never make the same trip twice. We are a regular family traveling on a budget on school breaks, so we have not yet succeeded in seeing everything. But we're getting there.

My children have been to thirty-eight states, twenty-one national parks, and dozens of monuments and museums. But we've learned the most in the small, strange places: relics and ruins, truck stops and tourist traps, graveyards and ghost towns. We frequented the homes of presidents and the hideouts of gangsters. We saw where state crimes were plotted and where the victims are mourned. We visited sacred Native American sites and centuries-old Spanish churches and withered Americana shrines. We explored our home terrain of the Midwest and the South, regions that are often misunderstood or ignored.

Above all, we embraced nature. We traveled up mountains and over plains, across lakes and down rivers, inside caves and through lava tubes, to the tops of dunes and the depths of canyons. We hiked and kayaked and canoed and climbed. We saw comets and supermoons and the Milky Way. We found glittering rocks in the earth and roamed the remains of abandoned mines.

We road-tripped through eight of the most turbulent years of American history. Two chaotic presidential elections, one global pandemic, massive technological change, severe new legal restrictions, and climate catastrophes that followed us wherever we went. We fled floods and outran fires. We kept a wary eye on the man-made threats of surveillance and violence, too.

I published three books during this eight-year period, all of which documented the dark side of the United States. The first, *The View from Flyover Country*, is a collection of essays on economic exploitation and institutional rot. The second, *Hiding in Plain Sight*, tracks the tandem erosion of America and rise of Donald Trump from the 1970s to the present. The third, *They Knew*, examines real government conspiracies and argues for an honest reckoning about corruption, painful as that may be.

My nonfiction horror stories prompted many questions. The one I got most was, "How are you raising kids in America, knowing all of these terrible things?!"

I answered, "I love America with all my heart and would never live anywhere else. I write about problems in the hope that we can fix them, so that our kids won't have to."

Folks would ask what I told my children about our national plight, and I would say, "The truth." I never hold back when my kids have questions. But it was not enough to tell my children about America: I wanted them to experience it.

This book is not about one continuous journey but multiple

trips through a country falling apart. We traveled where we could when we could. Then we returned to work and school, much as you likely do, and waited for the day we could roam free once more.

This is a book about time as much as place and the fragile nature of both.

In an era when empathy is demonized, my love for America has come to feel like defiance. Powerful operatives want to destroy this country, and they want ordinary Americans to think it was their own idea. They smear states with stereotypes and preach partition. They push us to shrug off the plights of the marginalized. They bank on us not having enough compassion for our countrymen to see what all corners of America are like. They want us to stay in our places, literally and figuratively.

They want to crush curiosity. But the wonderful thing about children is that they keep you forever curious. You see your country through their wide eyes, its wonders and flaws, while keeping watch like a parent. You study how prior generations of Americans survived their own dark times. You pay tribute to their sacrifice.

Every time my family would leave for a new adventure, I wondered if it would be the last. I vowed to make every road trip special and perfect. What I learned is that it already was because the people I loved most were with me.

I feel the same way about my country, even when it breaks my heart.

I drive the highways of America like I'm reading its palm because I know the only way to put things back together is to see how they fell apart. I trace the past in roadside ruins, period pieces in a national puzzle. I read billboards and bumper stickers like they are prophecies. I study slogans scrawled in rest stops and graffiti spray-painted in alleyways. I am searching for answers about an uncertain future because I am a mother, and I can't help but worry.

But the future is behind me in the back seat, asking me where we're going next. Our last American road trip was only the beginning. We are an American family, and we are staying that way—no matter what. This is our story.

1

The Great River Road

In June 2022, I took a canoe trip to an uninhabited island to see the supermoon.

My husband and I had booked the trip as a wedding anniversary gift to ourselves. The temptation of an uninhabited island was impossible to resist. Like everyone who lives in Missouri, we shared the Mark Twain fantasy about getting on a raft and floating to wherever the Mississippi River takes us, letting life's problems drift away. Like anyone who has actually read Mark Twain, we knew the Mississippi River was an emblem of America's crises as much as it was an escape from them.

That night was the first time I paddled the Mississippi River, though I had lived in St. Louis for sixteen years. My memories are tied to the river like a backdrop in an undated photo, marking seasons and the passage of time. I had watched it flood and wither, driven its bridges and byways, waded in it with my children until we were knee-deep in mud, but never navigated it myself. I wanted to be part of the river, buoyed by motion of my own making. I wanted nothing around me but the darkness of night and the laps of the waves and the silhouettes of the rusted monoliths that line the industrial landscape I call home.

It is impossible to be a twenty-first-century romantic about the Mississippi River, and I know because I tried. But it is possible to love something that has long lost its luster. Obligatory, even, these days.

Our trip began in a parking lot near the Mural Mile, a floodwall in downtown St. Louis decorated with graffiti. KISS THE WEEDS, THE FLOWERS MAY NEVER RETURN, one panel warned, and I walked on, asphalt burning beneath my feet. It was the hottest day of 2022, the beginning of a drought that would soon engulf the region, but we did not know that yet. We knew that it felt cooler on the water, that it was a crystal-clear night, and that the supermoon—a rare event when the moon is both full and in close proximity to Earth— would guide our way.

Our long voyageur canoe was parked on a riverbank across the street from an abandoned cement plant. The plant had been in the process of being transformed into a playscape called Ce- mentland when its creator, artist Bob Cassilly, died in what was at first reported as a bulldozer accident but was later deemed a murder.[1] Like many St. Louis stories, Cassilly's 2011 death had no resolution. His killer was never found, his vision never fulfilled. His death was shocking but not surprising: St. Louis is the most dangerous city in America.[2]

Cassilly is a St. Louis legend. In 1997, he created City Museum, a multistory playhouse where children climb on artistic renderings of repurposed industrial wreckage. He rejected the idea that our wastelands are worthless: you just have to learn to see them in a new way.

Cassilly's unexpected demise ended Cementland, which now looms over Riverview Drive like a monument to lost potential. You gaze at it wondering what secrets remain unearthed. There is a man-made geology to St. Louis that Cassilly understood, one that rewards anyone with an imagination powerful enough to dig through the layers of hell we call history and find the beauty within. It's a necessary quality in a city of ruins, a place where everything feels a little broken, a bit too apt to leave you no matter what foundations are laid.

Everything, that is, except for the Mississippi and the moon. That's what drew me outside in record heat: I wanted one night of comfort in the chaos. No matter what happened to the rest of the world, I thought, the Mississippi and the moon would stay the same.

My husband and I shared our canoe trip with a dozen strangers, a mix of locals and tourists. Our guide was Michael "Muddy Mike" Clark, a canoeist who had navigated the Mississippi for decades and founded the company Big Muddy Adventures. When covid hit in March 2020 and St. Louisans were ordered to shelter in place, Muddy Mike filled his canoe with supplies and paddled to an uninhabited strip of land in the middle of the river. He dubbed it Quarantine Island. He camped there for months in a tent with his dog, occasionally receiving supplies from his sons on the mainland. He was waiting for the world to return to normal, he told me, but it never did.

In June 2022, I was a novice canoeist but an avid kayaker. I paddled a local lake so frequently that I had come to recognize individual birds and deer that lived in the woods by the shore, and I liked to pretend that they recognized me too. I welcomed the freedom of a kayak in an era of endless shifting regulations about how to stay alive on land. I had long found peace in the woods—I am an experienced hiker, albeit the kind that wanders off the trail—but now I preferred the water because it had no trail at all. There was a route in my mind, but it had to do with how the sunlight hits the lake at certain times of day and where animals would emerge if I approached them with care. I could discard this mental map whenever I wanted. On a quiet lake, there is no current to confront, no ships to pass, no one in the kayak but me.

This was not the case with the Mississippi River. From the moment we set off, we faced multiple obstacles: the propulsion of the current, the debris in the water, and our own inexperience. We needed to paddle as one, battling the elements in the way that, Muddy Mike reminded us, travelers had done on this river for millennia. He expounded on the perfection of the canoe, unaltered since its invention by Native Americans, as we found our rhythm and the city faded away. The sun was at its late afternoon peak and it was over one hundred degrees, but I didn't mind. We were on an ancient trajectory, and the water was its own reward.

We passed islands, some barely intact, and I kept a watchful eye. I had a dark obsession that even the rhythm of the river could not cure. For years, I had wandered the old cemeteries of St. Louis counting the number of local celebrities killed in duels on a Mississippi River sandbar. The sandbar was named Bloody Island, and the victim list was long. In the nineteenth century, Bloody Island was where bureaucrats and bankers went to blow each other's brains out.

In 1817, Missouri senator Thomas Hart Benton, the architect of Manifest Destiny, killed lawyer Charles Lucas on Bloody Island after Lucas demanded a duel for the indignity of Benton calling him a "puppy."[3] The year before, Lucas had dueled on Bloody Island with Joshua Barton, Missouri's first secretary of state. Barton survived that duel only to be killed on the island in 1823 by Thomas Rector, the surveyor general of Illinois. In 1831, Thomas Biddle, the director of the St. Louis branch of the Bank of the United States, had a Bloody Island duel with Spencer Pettis, Missouri's fourth secretary of state. The nearsighted Biddle suggested that they shoot each other from five feet away, and both men died as a result. In 1856, Missouri state representative Benjamin Gratz Brown and St. Louis district attorney Thomas Caute Reynolds got in a spat over the merits of slavery and headed to Bloody Island to battle it out. Emerging with flesh wounds, they went on to serve as concurrent Missouri representatives on opposite sides of the Civil War: Reynolds as the governor of Confederate Missouri and Brown as the senator of Union Missouri.

The penchant for dueling on Bloody Island nearly cost America a president. In 1842, a self-described Illinois prairie lawyer arrived on Bloody Island to battle Illinois state auditor James Shields, whose lack of prowess with the ladies the lawyer had mocked. Both men withdrew at the last minute and called a truce.[4] That prairie lawyer was Abraham Lincoln.

In the nineteenth century, Bloody Island was considered a "field of honor": a fair and normal way to resolve disputes.[5] It was halfway between Missouri and Illinois and therefore belonged to neither a slave state nor a free state. It belonged to the Mississippi River, and the river claimed it as its own, pulling blood and bodies into its depths. Though the respectable thing to do at the time was to accept state officials killing each other on a sandbar as a normal part of Midwestern life, a few voices decried this mode of diplomatic resolution. "Bloody Island, in the midst of the rushing stream, stretches out its barren, sandy shores, and gloomy as the graveyard! ah! a graveyard! and when the associations connected with its dark history are permitted through the mind, the appellation is no misnomer. A graveyard!" cried the editorial team of the 1838 *Iowa News*.[6]

But Bloody Island was the rule, not the exception. The decades before the Civil War were marked by extreme regional violence: the hangings of Black Americans in Missouri's east, the murderous exile of Native Americans on the Trail of Tears that crossed Missouri's south, the state-sanctioned massacre of Mormons in Missouri's west. Bloody Island was the way things were, and remain, in the American borderland known as Missouri. It is a reminder that nothing here has ever been normal, including the people in charge.

Even those who denounced Missouri's violence ultimately fell into its pull. In 1839, one year after Iowans wrote an editorial condemning Bloody Island, the governors of Missouri and the Iowa Territory dispatched militias armed with pitchforks, swords, and, in one case, a sausage-making machine[7] to the state line to battle over beehive-bearing trees. This event is known as the Honey War. (In 1849, the Supreme Court resolved the border dispute in favor of Iowa, and the matter faded into obscurity.)

In the end, Bloody Island was destroyed by a feat of engineering. In 1837, the US federal government hired an engineer to restructure the western channel of the Mississippi River and ensure St. Louis maintained adequate shipping space. The engineer, an up-and-comer in the army, created a plan to divert the river and wedge Bloody Island into the Illinois shore. Promoted to captain for his innovative work, he returned home to Virginia. Two decades later, he declared war on the United States of America. The man hired to end Bloody Island was future Confederate general Robert E. Lee.

No trace of Bloody Island remains today. I went looking for it after our canoe trip and found the remnants of its shoreline: a gravel strip by the railroad tracks down the street from a casino in East St. Louis, Illinois. People avoid this area because impoverished, majority Black East St. Louis—the site of 1917 white mob violence so intense, locals mistook the sound for a stampede of wild animals[8]—routinely lands on lists of the most dangerous cities in the United States.

There is no plaque to mark that Bloody Island existed because

Americans are not supposed to remember that statesmen acted like gang members and got away with it.

The island we visited on the night of the supermoon was free from the history haunting its neighbors. Mosenthein Island is one of few islands near St. Louis that look largely the same as they did two centuries ago. The thousand-acre island, home to wild turkeys and deer, had been the quarantine refuge of our guide. I imagined future historians writing about the island: *And in 2020, it became a hideout from the plague.* I wondered if the future would have historians and if historians would have a future, and then pushed those thoughts away like an oar beating back the current. This was not the night for that.

When we reached the shore, I stepped out of the canoe warily, having sunk deep into sound-seeming Mississippi mud more times than I could count. I climbed the mudbank until it became sand, and the sand became grass, and the grass became a lush and tangled forest. I wandered until humanity faded from view and all that remained were trees, scrawnier and younger than the towering oaks of the mainland. Life felt new in this vulnerable place, hopeful. This was an innocent land and I had not seen anything innocent in a long time. I let the mosquitoes feast on me—it seemed the least I could do, given my trespass—and walked back to check out the action on the water.

Other canoers were using their portable flotation devices as miniature inner tubes, entering the water beer in hand and letting the current swirl them around the island like a natural lazy river. They were taking part in the great athletic pastime of Missouri: floating. Missourians need our state sport to be floating because we have endured too much to exert ourselves voluntarily. Floating is democratic, something everyone can do, and since we are deprived of democracy in law it is nice to find some in nature. On a Missouri float trip, you are not expected to paddle hard but coast along, often with a cooler tied to your vessel, gazing at the world through blurred and boozy eyes. I had planned to dedicate the summer of 2022 to float trips, drifting through the rivers in a beat-down reverie. But it was not to be.

My husband joined me at the shore, and we wandered down the beach to a pile of driftwood. We sat down and I told him I wanted to be alone. He understood because we have been married for over two decades, and he knows not to take my need for isolation as an insult. He knows he's a central character in the real story, the one no one else can decode. I do not believe in an "average" American family any more than I believe in a "real" America, but I check the boxes of both like an extra in a right-wing campaign ad. When I was twenty-four, I married, Dusty Springfield–style, the son of a preacher man. We left our life in New York City behind and moved to Missouri, *Road House*–style—kidding, kidding— and had two children, a girl and a boy, with whom I stayed home until they were old enough for public school. My husband and I stayed together as a couple and played together as a family, taking the kids to state parks on the weekends, watching TV and reading books with them at night. We loved the Fourth of July, when we'd grill a mound of meat midday then head to the riverfront in the evening for fireworks and fried food and a Ferris wheel from which we would wave our flags from the exploding sky and love every person on the ground waving back, our fellow Americans— our fellow 'muricans!

I would be the model of the Midwestern housewife the right wing claims to revere had I not spent my spare time writing books about plutocratic plots to strip my country down and sell it for parts.

The French writer Gustave Flaubert said that one should be regular and orderly in one's life so one can be violent and original in one's work. When I was younger, I would quote this to pretend I had made a choice instead of being a collection of contradictions I could not control. Now that I am older, in an America lurching toward autocracy, I can see there was never a paradox in my love for day-to-day American life and my loathing for our rotted institutions.

I want to be a good mother, a good writer, and a good American. I want my children to love our country out of conviction instead of out of delusion or obligation. I want them to know the truth about America, but I want the truth to be less painful, which means that crises must be exposed so they can end. I want my predictions to sound less like eulogies.

You can leave your children home for a night, but they never leave your mind. You are always looking for a better way, a stable reprieve, and this longing filled me as I traced the outline of the shore. Mosenthein Island looks like a teardrop. You can see its shape only from a distance, but when you are there, you feel it: in the sand under your feet, in the pangs inside your heart, in the bittersweet release it lends you. An honest land will make you weep. Later, you understand why.

I don't want my children's generation to inherit the hell I inhabit. That hell needs to be defeated instead of functioning as it has, devouring everything I encounter. Over the past two decades, as one institution after another collapsed—the economy, the media, the government, long-standing conceptions of facts and faith and freedom—and I was tasked with explaining why, I found myself searching for something, anything, that was sure to last.

I've been alive in the twenty-first century longer than I was in the twentieth, and I don't like it.

There is a map of the Mississippi River on my living room wall. It was drawn by Harold Fisk, a geologist for the Army Corps of

Engineers. Tasked with illustrating a 1944 government report on the river's course, Fisk instead depicted millennia of transformation in a region called the meander belt. He used dozens of colors to highlight pivotal years in the river's development. The result is an image that looks more like a Jackson Pollock painting than a bureaucratic document, with multicolored strands of history looping and intertwining across the page. Each color represents a change in the river, a rejection of the path it was supposed to take. Fisk's map shows how the arterial pathway splitting the heartland was never as steady as people wanted to believe. Its only reliable quality was its formidable nature. The best you could do, as Mark Twain knew, was respect the river, hope it wouldn't kill you, and enjoy the ride.

On Mosenthein Island, I watched the sun sink until the St. Louis lights became visible. The Gateway Arch emerged, a silver sliver on the skyline. I joined my husband because it was time to wait for the supermoon, and that wonder is best shared. My husband and I have spent our marriage seeking light in the dark. Astronomy, the religion of the ancients, is the contemporary comfort of the anxious and insolvent. No matter how our situation changes, the cycles of the moon stay steady. It costs nothing to look up and watch the celestial show. When people on a budget ask me for recreation tips, that is what I recommend. I've been broke; the sky is free.

It is easy to see the stars in Missouri. I have spent decades driving to spots with low light pollution, letting phrases like *Bortle scale* enter my vocabulary and feeling sad that a dark sky site was the exception instead of the rule. But I had never seen the moon from an isolated island in the Mississippi River. It rose, blazing and enormous, as if emerging from the water itself. It was yellow with orange-red craters, like it was borrowing from its neighbors: the stature of the sun, the colors of Mars. The supermoon shone like a spotlight singling us out in approval. It lit up our route back, but we did not want to go. There was nothing we needed more than that moment, and we did not want it to end. We hadn't known there would be a supermoon when we'd booked the trip. We just got lucky like that.

But it was time: we were guests on no-man's-land, and now we would paddle home in the dark.

I had seen the Mississippi many times from many angles, climbing bridges to watch bald eagles or hiking cliffs to spot vistas or simply passing it on the highway, where we noted its presence with a dutiful "hey, there's the Arch!" (Everyone says this when they pass the Arch, no matter how long they've lived in St. Louis.) But I had never *felt* it, not in the way you feel without your sense of sight. At night, the Mississippi came alive in a new way. The river had become a glistening black-brown mass, choppy and thick, like rowing through oil. I could feel it pulsating beneath me, moving me in ways I could not control. I thought of all the travelers who had made this trip in darkness, from the Native Americans of Cahokia—a twelfth-century metropolis near St. Louis that was once the largest city in North America—to Twain, who wrote in *Life on the Mississippi* of his terror of navigating in the night.

We passed landmarks, and with each one it was like we were returning regretfully to our current plight, edging a little closer to the mistakes of modernity. We paddled under bridges and passed by barges, one of which came so close that our canoe nearly toppled. Drenched in dirty water, we drifted under the Eads Bridge, the oldest surviving bridge on the Mississippi River. Built in 1873, the Eads Bridge was so novel that the *New York Times* had declared it "the World's Eighth Wonder" and lamented that New York City could not match the architectural majesty of St. Louis.[9] The final spike of the bridge had been hammered into place by Union general William Tecumseh Sherman, Robert E. Lee's great rival. I watched the supermoon shine through its ornate arches, faint from land but clear from the water, lit up by an orb of the night.

"We need to come back here. We've got to show this to the kids," my husband said, and I agreed, with the bittersweet heartache that accompanies twenty-first-century plans.

I don't remember when I started mourning the future more than the past. There were milestones—9/11, the 2008 financial collapse, the pandemic—but no singular moment of revelation. It just crept up on me, the realization that if someone with a time machine asked me whether I wanted to live in the past or the future, I would instantly answer "the past"—not because the past was wonderful but because the past was *there*.

I am not afraid of the unknown. I am haunted by the *known*: climate catastrophes and political bloodshed and the unbearable ambivalence with which the powerful greet both. Like many in my generation, I'd long ago ditched the pursuit of happiness in favor of the pursuit of survival, and it was not a choice. We didn't have American Dreams; we had American Circumstances. And the circumstances we had inherited, the circumstances my children would inherit, were unforgivable.

But as much as I longed for stability, the truth was I could never choose the past. From the day my daughter was born, my heart belonged to the future we would share together. Raising children in a world running out of time means contending with two clocks ticking at once: the moments you spend with them as they grow up and the years left—for your country, for the planet, for everyone. The first clock is a marvel of memory, the second a countdown to doom. You cannot live your life by these clocks, only alongside them. You forge ahead regardless of the odds because that is your obligation as a parent. Your job is to navigate the twenty-first-century nightmare world, to teach your children how to see in the dark.

I don't want my children to chase American illusions marketed as American dreams, but I want them to understand why things went wrong. To appreciate everyday miracles and not think them small. To have reverence for the good that endures and work to protect it. A republic, if you can keep it. A family that would remain American whether or not America remains. We would love America out of defiance and defy America out of love.

The moon was high as we neared the St. Louis shore. Mosenthein Island was miles away, and water flowed as far as we could see. If we followed the river in either direction, we would reach the end of America.

My arms were aching when the Gateway Arch appeared, towering in the floodlights like it was competing with the supermoon for grandiosity. The Arch is the tallest monument in the United States, and its ninety-acre grounds are the smallest national park in the United States. In the first half of the twentieth century, historic buildings on the St. Louis riverfront were destroyed for its construction, displacing the local population in the process. That dual legacy of creation and destruction made the Arch a symbol not only of St. Louis but of America. The Arch was a triumph and a tragedy, a gateway and a memorial, a monolith with no practical purpose that looks dramatically different depending on where you stand.

I've taken hundreds of photos of the Arch, striving for one that captures it so I can show people who have never been here what I see. But you can't capture the Arch. I have photos of my children from the first time they each saw it: my daughter laughing at her distorted face in its mirrored curves, my son in his stroller, squinting at the shimmering slope in the sky. Later they wondered about the point of this 630-foot metal monument to nowhere. But they didn't wonder when they were there, and neither did I. The Arch makes sense when you're under it.

We dragged our canoes on shore as gunshots and laughter rang out in the night. We were back in St. Louis. We were home.

Before the Arch was created, the most famous building in St. Louis was the Old Courthouse. Built in 1828, seven years after Missouri had become a state, the Old Courthouse is no longer active but is part of the national park, a neoclassical museum over which the Arch expands like a silver rainbow. This is where the Dred Scott case was tried.

In 1842, Scott, a Black American born enslaved but who had lived for years in the free territories of Illinois and Wisconsin, sued for his freedom after being forced to return to Missouri. Scott and his wife, Harriet, argued that as prior residents of free states they were not bound to slave state laws, particularly since their daughter had been born on a steamboat on the Mississippi River and ostensibly belonged to no state. Though the number of enslaved Black Americans in Missouri was much lower than in the Deep South, Missouri's entry into the United States was predicated on the condition that slavery be allowed. The result was that Missouri—and St. Louis in particular—became a central rhetorical and legal battleground in the decades before the Civil War.

Inside the Old Courthouse, trials and retrials of the Scott case went on for a decade until, in 1852, the Missouri Supreme Court overturned twenty-eight years of legal precedent. They decreed that the Scott family's prior residence in free states was irrelevant, and Missouri would no longer defer to it.

Dred Scott took his case to the Supreme Court only to receive an even more devastating result. In 1857, Chief Justice Roger Taney ruled that anyone descended from Africans, whether slave or free, was not a citizen of the United States. He declared that Black Americans "had for more than a century before been regarded as beings of an inferior order . . . so far inferior that they had no rights which the white man was bound to respect."[10] Taney proclaimed that this was the way it would be because this was the way it had always been. He was lying. He rewrote the past to control the future because that is what authoritarians do.

Dred Scott, along with every Black American, lost his right to full citizenship. The Missouri Compromise—the 1821 trade-off that Missouri would be admitted as a slave state to balance out Maine's entry as a free state—was nullified in favor of broader repressive rule. Black Americans lost the right to petition for their freedom in a trial because property—which the Scotts had been legally declared—could not sue.

Dred Scott died in 1858 and was buried in St. Louis. Near his gravestone is a plaque saying "in memory of a simple man who wanted to be free." The plaque is covered in flowers and pennies from visitors paying him the respect he was not afforded in life. Scott is buried in Calvary Cemetery, in a simple plot down the hill from the elaborate crypts of the wealthy bureaucrats who had shot each other to death on Bloody Island, crypts so neglected that trees have grown out of their domed roofs.

One week after our canoe trip, the Supreme Court overturned *Roe v. Wade*, leaving the fate of women's reproductive rights and privacy in the hands of state governments. We'd known it was coming. In 2021, multiple states had passed new repressive laws, including a law in Texas that offered bounty hunters ten thousand dollars for proof that a woman had an abortion or that someone had helped her get one. In 2022, a Mississippi case, *Dobbs v. Jackson Women's Health Organization*, reached the Supreme Court, and the court had been packed with so many right-wing extremists that the outcome was predictable. That court was no longer for debate but for commands, and we had been commanded to stop being hysterical. For years, women who had warned that their autonomy

was in jeopardy had been derided as paranoid. We'd been told that
Roe was "the law of the land," that the United States was "a nation
of laws," that the Supreme Court would never overturn decades of
legal precedent. As if it had not happened before, as if courts had
not always been the cage bars of American autocracy.

Missouri is a trigger state, which means that bans on abortion
prohibited by *Roe*'s 1973 passage would become law once federal
protections were struck down. At some point, I knew, I would
become a second-class citizen. One morning, I would wake up and
legal protections I had known my entire life would be gone. One
day, everything would be the same except my husband and son
would have more rights than me and my daughter, and I would
have to explain to my children why. I have never had an abortion and have no intention of getting one, but that is true of many
women who end up getting abortions. The perverse pain of the
Roe reversal was how it made me feel like a failure, above all, as a
mother: the very identity the state prescribed. I could not protect
my daughter from the government. Our bodies were state property
now.

When the day came—June 24, 2022—I knocked on the door
of my husband's makeshift pandemic home office, said "they
overturned *Roe*," and left before he could respond. I got in my
car and drove to Creve Coeur Lake, an offshoot of the Missouri
River where I go kayaking in the summer. *Creve Coeur* is French
for "broken heart" but I didn't know that because no one knows
how to pronounce or interpret Missouri French. "Creev Core," we
say, we unsophisticated rubes whom the Supreme Court had made
cattle—cattle that so many different forces wanted to corral.

I kayaked until my hands blistered and bled, and while I was
out on the water the attorney general of Missouri signed away my
bodily autonomy. I don't know the exact moment it happened,

whether it was when I saw a duck shielding her ducklings and started to cry, or when I passed an elderly woman drifting under a highway bridge, her face streaked with tears, and she put on sunglasses so they would not show, or when the clouds darkened the lake with the threat of rain and I thought, *Bring it. You cannot do anything worse to me today. Show me some action. Give me a battle I can fight.* And then the clouds parted, and in the light of the sun I saw the blood on my palms like a stigma, like stigmata. I knew God did not want this and that state officials did not care about God because they had decided to replace him with themselves.

In the car I wrapped my hands with old covid masks to stop the bleeding and started the drive home. I had lived through enough catastrophes to know that I would pass stores and schools and playgrounds and it would look normal, that life would seem un-altered while everyone fought an internal war, and that in the era of cell phones and viral videos you wait until you get home to cry. I flipped through FM radio because I wanted to pretend it was the Before Time, the time when I had a constitutional right to my own body, and radio was the soundtrack of that era. A local rock station was playing "Falling Away from Me" by Korn, a song by a band that I used to think was terrible, a band that, like my reproductive freedom, had peaked when I was in college.

The singer screamed about powerful forces beating him down, beating him down into the ground, and I heard a horrible laugh and realized it had come from me. This was going to be the soundtrack to the day my uterus became Missouri state property, I realized. This was going to join the canon of metal songs I had determined were secretly about women's problems—Metallica's "The Unforgiven" (rape), Black Sabbath's "Over and Over" (men-strual cramps, obviously)—because I would forget this was a man's world and delude myself into thinking the world was mine, too.

This ludicrous, perfect song was going to be what drowned out the blather of politicians feigning shock and women expressing agony and coastal power brokers declaring that "red state women" deserved it, that we were *asking for it* because then they could pretend this could never happen to them.

This cruel reaction always occurred when my state government did a terrible thing that most everyone living here deplored, with our views disregarded by the far-right legislature. Residents of other states taken hostage by dark money and gerrymandering—Texas, Ohio, Wisconsin, and so on—got the same sneering dismissal. We must *want* corruption, *want* deprivation, *want* the government to control our bodies, otherwise we would "just move," liberal pundits crowed. They ignored that money, or lack thereof, is why many of us live here in the first place.

Our lives are cheap to them because we don't have enough wealth to buy our freedom. Instead of wealth, we have an inheritance, but it is the wrong kind. Our inheritance is ignominy ordered from the top down, state murder marketed as collective suicide. We are human trading cards for the political overclass. Neither political party cares about our actual views or our actual bodies or our actual daughters. No one understands the pain of this dehumanizing, multifaceted abandonment except other ordinary people who lost their own rights in their own hostage states.

Well, and Korn, I thought maniacally as I pulled up to my house, *don't forget Korn*. I silenced the engine and wiped blood off the wheel and studied my face in the rearview mirror, my new second-class citizen face. I was a rearview woman with rearview rights and objections closer than they may appear. I entered my home quietly, not wanting to talk to anyone, not ready for the gut punch of social media confirmation. I opened my laptop and found I had a new email. It was from Speaker of the House Nancy

Pelosi. The email said the Democrats would maybe, *maybe*, get me my bodily autonomy back if I gave them some money. I stared at this ransom note and slammed my computer shut.

The next day, I woke up needing to do two things: go to the Mississippi River and get out of Missouri. The first urge was out of a desire for comfort, the latter out of dark curiosity: would I feel different if I crossed into Illinois, a state where my right to bodily autonomy was guaranteed? I had always dismissed *red states* and *blue states* as a dangerous fallacy, and I still do. The boundaries contrived by pundits during the 2000 presidential election make neither geographic nor political sense. America is a diverse nation held together by disillusionment, not by binary categories that correspond to state lines. Most Americans don't vote, and most of those who do vote don't belong to either party. America is purple: purple like a bruise.

In the past, when I left St. Louis for Illinois, I would go from a liberal city in a state with a conservative government into a conservative county in a state with a liberal government. The entire exercise felt like proof of how illusory partisan designations are. But suddenly states' rights mattered in a way that directly impacted my life. The Mississippi River border was no longer the purview of the nineteenth century, the distant domain of Dred Scott and *Huckleberry Finn*, but a living boundary that determined how much of a human being I was allowed to be. Whether I was a person or just a woman.

"What can I do to help?" my husband had asked when I had woken in the dead of night in a helpless rage that I could not process and he could not feel. We both knew the answer was "nothing," so when I said, "I want to go to the Loading Dock and look at the river," he was relieved. That was something he, a Midwestern man, could do. And I, his chattel bride, could maybe find some relief or at least a distraction from my newfound obsolescence.

The Loading Dock is one of my favorite places. All of my memories of it are good, including the ones attached to terrible days. The first time I heard live music after the pandemic closures was at the Loading Dock. It was a run-of-the-mill Lynyrd Skynyrd cover band, and as I held up an invisible lighter to "Free Bird," my eyes flooded with tears of gratitude, while my children rolled theirs at my drama and bad taste. The Loading Dock is a sprawling outdoor restaurant on the shores of the Mississippi River in Grafton, a town that advertises itself as "the Key West of the Midwest." The restaurant is attached to a flea market where I have spent years acquiring useless treasures. My family has a Grafton routine: order lunch, usually brats and fries, and, for the adults, a potent concoction called Dock Lemonade; play cornhole on the lawn while we wait for our meal; walk to the lighthouse to see how high the Mississippi River is; hit the flea market; and head home. We have had this routine for sixteen years.

To get to Grafton, you cross the Mississippi River and exit St. Louis ("Hey, there's the Arch!"); drive through the haunted town of Alton, home to the Underground Railroad, Martin Luther King assassin James Earl Ray, and antifeminist fanatic Phyllis Schlafly; pass a casino and a factory; and enter the Great River Road, one of the most spectacular stretches of American highway I have seen, and I've driven through all forty-eight contiguous states. It is a two-lane winding road with tree-topped white cliffs on one side and the Mississippi River on the other, endless and blue, like I had imagined it from books before I'd seen it in life.

On the Great River Road, it is impossible not to feel free. But now I felt a new sort of freedom: the transitory freedom of arbitrary law.

There are no stops between Alton and Grafton except for a pull-off where a hideous grinning beast, winged and fanged, is painted on the walls of a roadside cave on a limestone bluff. A plaque proclaims it is a portrait of the Piasa, "the bird that devours man": a re-creation of an alleged seventeenth-century Native American painting. The Piasa is a creature that started hunting people in war. Because the wars in this region never stopped, it developed a taste for human flesh and scours for victims to this day. The wings of the Piasa are red-and-white striped. From a distance, the monster looks like an American flag.

We arrived in Grafton early and hungry, having left the house in a frenzy prompted by my urge to flee. The restaurant was not open but the flea market was, so we sampled some alligator jerky and banana bread and started wandering the aisles. My children love the flea market. They have grown up attacked by algorithms, but in the flea market, they are free. Nothing is tailored to them, no machine molds them, no step leaves a trace. What they find is serendipitous, surreptitious: *someone else owned this once, and now it's mine, and I paid with paper money, and the internet can't find me!*

I have tried explaining to my children that when I was a kid in the 1980s, many considered the great crisis of American life to be consumerism: people wasting time roaming malls buying things they did not need with the extra money they had, which was called disposable income. *Extra money?!* my daughter would say with a laugh. *No pandemic?!* my son would exclaim, for this was an America they did not recognize. The closest approximation of what seemed to them an enchanted age devoid of surveillance or plagues were the flea markets or antique malls that we frequented. (*Antique mall* is Missourian for a year-round flea market held inside.) You never knew what would happen to you at the flea market, and the flea market didn't keep track.

It was hot that morning, so I paid an amateur blacksmith

two dollars for a piece of twisted iron and wrapped my long hair around it, piling it on my head. I looked at myself in the mirror: was this the face of someone who had just lost control of her body? I was seeing if I looked different. It was an impulse I recognized from past violating events, and I put the mirror down. I glanced at the women around me, vendors selling quilts or paperback novels or objects shaped like Elvis. These ladies still had their legal rights—unless they had driven in from Missouri like I had. It was pointless, this speculation, and it went against the spirit of the flea market. In Grafton, the analog era ruled. My cell phone got terrible service, everything was from the twentieth century or would fit in there fine, and outside was the Mississippi, that reliable river as old as time.

We stood under a giant poster of Donald Trump that said MISS ME YET? and tallied our wares. My husband had bought hot sauce, my fourteen-year-old daughter had spent three dollars on what she excitedly informed me was a "rare manga," and my eleven-year-old son asked if he could buy a "future history simulation game" he had found while crawling under a table covered in knives. This game turned out to be a training exercise produced and intended for use by US government officials to prepare for annihilation by the Soviet Union. We had no idea how this 1980s training game had wound up in the Grafton flea market, but it fit the mood, so I told him yes. "The Nuclear Devastation of America: Recovery and Reunification," I read on the cover, which was decorated with mustard-yellow mushroom clouds. I thought about how quaint the premise of this game was, that after disaster America would reunify and recover.

We walked to the Grafton lighthouse, a red-and-white-striped tower with a bright blue top, and noted how shallow the river had become in the week since our canoe trip. Usually our worry was the opposite: floods. Grafton had been devastated by the

Great Flood of 1993, and the memory of that year looms over everything—the new houses built on stilts, the watermarks on the stone buildings that survived. In 2019, the Mississippi had flooded again, dangerously high, and Grafton had held steady while other river towns struggled to survive.

I have sweet memories of all these river towns—Kimmswick, Clarksville, Louisiana—like I do of Grafton, and I was furious at the dismissal of pain that often came from outsiders when this region faced a catastrophe: false assumptions that residents do not believe in climate change, that they deserve sneers instead of sympathy. I felt protective of Grafton because it held my memories and my reprieve, even if my reprieve was a ruse that ended the instant that I crossed the Missouri border.

"The river is too low," I said to my husband. "I wish it would rain."

One month and one day later, I woke to the staccato beat of water and wind. At first, it seemed like nothing notable: Missouri often had dramatic summer storms that came out of nowhere. In the summer of 2006, I had gone to Kyrgyzstan for graduate school research and lived in a yurt while my husband lived in a scorching apartment with no electricity for weeks, thanks to a derecho that toppled trees and slashed power lines. He spent his days charging his phone at a Church's Chicken and his nights drinking beer from a cooler while listening to Art Bell on a transistor radio. Halfway across the world, I rode horses on a bucolic mountaintop, oblivious to his travails. Central Asia was a breeze compared to Middle America.

I listened to the rain, feeling relief at a break in the drought, which had stretched all summer long and had been declared an emergency by the governor the week before. Then I heard an explosion, and another, and then the air-conditioning creaked to a halt and all I heard was the roar of the Thing Outside. Our neighborhood had lost power. I walked to the front door and tried to open it only for it to slam in my face because the wind was too strong. It was a new kind of wind, a new kind of rain, different from any I had felt before: straighter, harder, unearthly. I smelled smoke.

"Transformers blew," said my husband, who had come downstairs to survey the damage. We lit candles and sat in the living room, light flickering off the framed map of the Mississippi River meander belt on the wall. The kids came down and we gave them flashlights, promising them it would be okay. We waited for the tornado alarm to go off, for surely this could be nothing else. But it wasn't. The sun had not yet risen, and based on internet commentary, no one else in St. Louis understood what was happening either, but it was no tornado.

At dawn I stepped outside, unable to see far; I waded (*why was I wading?!*) into the road and looked down the hill and screamed. The lower half of my street was an ocean of submerged porches and floating cars. It had flooded in a way that had never happened in the history of this area, for we do not live near a major river. This was pure rain, a record seven inches in five hours, accompanied by relentless wind. A garbage can flew by my head and landed on the downward slope, drifting with the debris of my block.

I am usually good in a crisis. One of my worst qualities is that I can envision the most nightmarish outcome of any situation. But in an emergency, everything flips. Paranoia becomes preparedness, impatience becomes quick thinking, my flaws become my strengths. My utility had risen in the twenty-first century with its unending series of disasters.

During a crisis, I try to stay strong in front of the kids. But that morning, I crumbled in a corner and cried because it was too much. We had already lost too much. The city, the country—we had lost too much, yet every day brought a reminder that there was more to lose. I live in an old house with stained-glass windows built during the pandemic of 1918. I had spent years gazing at their red and yellow and green designs when I felt sad, reminding myself that a century of people had looked to these windows for comfort during their own periods of hardship. Now I stared into that colored glass because it blocked the view outside.

My sister-in-law called to tell us that she and her husband and children had swum out of their submerged street and climbed to elevated ground. They were safe, but their house was flooded, their car swept away, and they had nowhere to go. My family was lucky, I realized with horror; we were only witnesses. We offered my in-laws our home, our car, whatever they needed because it wasn't fair and because we could.

In the afternoon, the rain slowed to a trickle, and my children and I decided to go for a walk. We navigated a trail of trash past the dollar store and the truck lot until we arrived at the local park—their old stomping ground, where they had played on the swings and attended summer camp and swum in the public pool since they were small. The pool was an unusually nice feature of a neighborhood in decline because it had been built in the 1930s, when people cared about St. Louis and St. Louis cared about the public good.

I loved the pool so much I had written about it, briefly, in the book I had just completed, *They Knew*, describing it as an oasis from a national nightmare, a place where I could disappear underwater and feel free. The pool was now destroyed along with much of the park, and my thoughts spiraled to an irrational place: *Did this happen because I wrote about it? Did this happen because I wished for rain?* And again, with humiliation: *Was I asking for it?*

The wild thoughts that come with guilt over wanting comfort in a cruel world and realizing the comfort you seek is really control, and you are not going to get it. The wild thoughts that come from living in America, where we are trained to internalize every crisis and blame ourselves for every systemic failure.

We walked around the park, surveying the damage. Ducks floated on a new pond that used to be the lawn. Pieces of pool chairs hung from trees with jagged shards of broken fence, glittering like a pantomime of Christmas. Behind them, the pool overflowed with toxic brown water. There was a swamp where I used to swim.

At night, the rain stopped, but the mystery of what had happened continued. On social media, I watched people from around the world comment on viral videos of my street that I had not posted. We were the daily climate disaster, and there would be a new one tomorrow. No one understood what had caused the rain—to this day, no one fully knows—or why a similar record rainfall devastated eastern Kentucky later that week, but we began to understand why our street had been hit so hard.

In the park is a river so shallow that the garbage strewn across it has nowhere to sink. Many mistake it for a creek, but it is the River Des Peres, named for French priests who explored it in the 1700s. Because the river is so pitiful and is thought of mostly as part of St. Louis's sewage infrastructure, many don't realize it intersects with the Mississippi River. But it was the propulsion of the Mississippi that caused the River Des Peres to overflow in the flood of 1993 and to devour my neighborhood in 2022.

I didn't need to seek it out anymore. The Mississippi River had come to me.

My memories of the rest of that summer are as hazy as heat rising from concrete. I remember we left for an abrupt vacation, handing over our house to my sister-in-law's family for ten days so they could have it to themselves. I remember our family park becoming a FEMA site. I remember a neighbor telling me that the FEMA site was a government plot and me arguing that this was impossible because the federal government didn't care enough about Missouri to bother declaring an emergency for weeks. He noted that our hard-hit neighborhood was primarily Black, and we pondered whether a place like this attracts more malice or neglect.

I remember standing in line at a polling site in the ruins of a bankrupt mall to vote for the politically inexperienced heiress to a beer dynasty fortune because she was superior to the other candidate, the insurrectionist attorney general who had taken my reproductive rights and had his mind set on taking more. The heiress lost the election, as I knew she would, and the man who had signed away my bodily autonomy became my senator.

I remember being afraid to go back to Creve Coeur Lake because I thought it would be destroyed like the park, but it had survived mostly intact and reopened in August. I remember anticipating deep waters and finding, for the first time, that my kayak kept getting stuck in the mud because the flash flood had done nothing to remedy the drought. The flash flood had been a fuck you, that's all, a flip rearrangement of a broken ecological order. Two climate disasters did not equal relief but repelled each other like matching sides of magnetic poles.

I remember feeling, as summer turned to fall, a secret satisfaction that the Mississippi River was still there, even though it had come to my neighborhood and attacked me. Mark Twain had warned of this behavior, after all, noting that this was part of its allure: it was so ferocious, so independent, that it offered respite from the predictable breakdowns of the man-made world. I would go back out on the river, I decided. I would get the kids and we would rent a canoe and we would explore islands and have adventures. We would sail to Mosenthein Island under the light of the moon.

Until one day, the impossible happened: the Mississippi River was gone. In patches and then in miles it dried up, causing a shipping crisis that extended to the Gulf of Mexico. Parched soil lay where water had once roared. The river became walkable in a way that made the grand bridges above it seem ridiculous, and that they were ridiculous seemed obscene.

Famous Missouri sites known for being surrounded by dangerous whirlpools, like Tower Rock, which I had also described as an unchanging monument in my cursed book *They Knew*, were suddenly sitting on sandbars, covered in people. A desert grew on the river grounds outside Memphis, reminding me of the evaporated Aral Sea in Uzbekistan, a sea destroyed by the Soviets, a sea that fewer and fewer people could recall existing at all because human memory is an endangered species.

In September, I left St. Louis to go on a book tour throughout the Midwest, crossing the Mississippi River repeatedly. I averted my eyes when it approached because I did not want to witness the disappearance of my old friend. The only reliable thing in my life had become the only disaster I had managed not to envision.

By fall, my neighborhood had recovered from the worst of the flood. The FEMA center down the block turned back into a park. Life went on, without rights and without the expectation of remedy or redress, as life here does. The River Des Peres shrank back into its usual meek form, and I eyed it with suspicion.

I avoided the Mississippi River until I was sure it had rained enough to recover. I drove to Chain of Rocks, a former Route 66 bridge between Missouri and Illinois that had been used as the set for the postapocalyptic movie *Escape from New York*. I walked to the center of the bridge and gazed out at the water, a view I had seen hundreds of times before, a view I knew like my own reflection.

The river looked the same, but I knew what it had done. I knew it had comforted me, and then hurt me, and then up and left. And I knew I loved it anyway because I'm an American woman, and we can't help ourselves.

It is impossible to be a twenty-first-century romantic about the Mississippi River, and I know because I tried.

2
The Twain Shall Meet

Get ready, kids, we're going to Florida!" I yelled. My children emerged from their *Minecraft*-induced stupor, lowering their gaming consoles and turning to me. A trip to Florida? In May 2020? *During the pandemic?*

"Are you serious?" my daughter asked.

"I'm completely serious," I said, stuffing a beach bag with towels. "We're going to Florida, and we're going to stop in Louisiana, and who knows, we may even hit Santa Fe on the way home."

"When are we coming home?"

"Around midnight."

"What?" My daughter's eyes narrowed. She had figured out a plot was at hand with only one question remaining: how big of a loser was her mother? "Where are you really taking us?"

"To Florida, I told you."

"No, we're not! Who goes to Florida and back in one day? And, um, Santa Fe is in New Mexico, Mommy."

"I'm one hundred percent serious. We are going to Florida. By tomorrow, you will be able to tell your friends, 'I have been to Florida.'"

"But I've already been to Florida," my daughter said softly, remembering our 2018 trip: the long drive south until she saw the highway end at an infinite blue horizon. The white sand of the panhandle; the way my son shrieked when he stepped on the beach, first in surprise and then joy. He had never walked on sand and didn't know he would sink, but then he realized he was supposed to, and he loved it. They both did. Dolphins in the water, oysters on the half shell, seagulls and sunsets. My children were ten and seven and had never seen the ocean. I wanted them to see it while they had the chance, in case something bad happened. We were supposed to return to Florida in March 2020, but something bad happened.

"This is a different side of Florida. You'll like it. It's less crowded."

"How crowded?"

"The population is zero."

"How can the population of Florida be zero?!"

"Because," I said, "I promised you a trip to Florida, and I promised I would try to keep you safe from covid, and I am a woman of my word."

"Oh Mommy," my daughter sighed. "You're always trying."

That afternoon, my husband and the kids and I set out for Florida, driving past waterways filled with birds and barges. We stopped, as promised, in Louisiana, and fishermen greeted the kids and told them they would share their best spots as long as they kept them a secret. In Louisiana, you could walk right up to the water, a deep blue surrounded by forest green trees, lush and vivid in that preternaturally beautiful spring when the weather was acting like an apology for what humanity had to endure. An American flag swayed in the gentle breeze, a conciliatory consolation, a wind whispering an explanation that I didn't understand.

We lingered at the shore and then drove back to town. At a traffic light we stopped in front of a nineteenth-century bank with a mural painted on the outer wall. In the center of the mural was a man who looked like he was wearing a covid mask. It turned out to be a portrait of John Brooks Henderson, whose white mustache and beard were so thick they covered the lower half of his face. The mural was a commemoration of the Thirteenth Amendment to the Constitution, which abolished slavery—an amendment that Henderson, a Missouri senator, had coauthored.

"I know he's not really wearing a mask, but I think it's creepy that he looks like he is and that we saw him, today of all days," said my daughter, averting her gaze.

"I think everything is creepy," my son announced and put his headphones on.

We turned west down an empty two-lane drive. The roads became flatter, as roads do when one is approaching Florida, and we passed stores selling fishing bait and tackle. The stores were closed, with handwritten notes on the windows explaining that people were sick. They would be back when they could. They asked us not to forget them.

After about half an hour, signs of water appeared. I told my kids to take off their headphones and pay attention. "These are the waters of Florida. You should bask in their beauty," I said, but by the end of my sentence we were back on dry land.

"Stop saying we're in Florida when we're not!" my daughter exclaimed.

"Oh really," I said. "*Really*. Then what's that?" At the intersection of state highway 107 and county road U was a hilltop dirt mound with the word FLORIDA in large white letters.

"We *are* in Florida," my son marveled. He was nine years old.

"Florida, Missouri!" I said. "See, I would never lie to you."

"Is the population really zero?" my daughter asked as we

turned off the highway and the landscape became thick with tall trees and the glimmer of a lake.

"Yes."

"Then why make a big sign?"

"Because before the population was zero, before everybody left, the most famous American writer was born here."

Mark Twain is from Missouri, and Missouri will never let you forget it. In the south, the Mark Twain National Forest sprawls for over three million acres, about half pure wilderness. This is not to be confused with Mark Twain State Park, which was where we were going, off of Tom Sawyer Road near Mark Twain Lake in north-central Missouri. There is also Mark Twain Cave in Hannibal, the town where Twain grew up and whose economy largely rests on his legacy. There is the Mark Twain Hotel and the Mark Twain Casino and the Mark Twain Dinette serving Mark Twain Fried Chicken and countless other attractions to remind you that this is the birthplace of American literature. Twain is not alone: many pop culture luminaries came from Missouri, the state where conceptions of America are created and contested. Scott Joplin conceived ragtime in Sedalia; Walt Disney dreamed up animation on a farm in Marceline; Chuck Berry invented rock 'n' roll in St. Louis.

But Twain is particularly revered because his American literature is about Missouri, and his Missouri literature is about America. However far he traveled, he never left his home behind.

"I was born on the 30th of November, 1835, in the almost invisible village of Florida, Missouri," Twain wrote in his autobiography. He added that his older siblings had been born in Tennessee but that he "was postponed—postponed to Missouri. Missouri was an unknown new state and needed attractions."[1]

Of all the Mark Twain sites in Missouri, Florida is the least visited. It is out of the way, and there is not much to see because there was not much there to begin with. This made it an ideal destination for May 2020, when covid had left many places closed and others laden with risk. My family spent a lot of time outdoors that spring, wandering through cemeteries when the parks closed down, then returning to the parks when they reopened only to find they resembled battle scenes from a surreal and quiet war: water fountains wrapped in crime scene tape, nature centers bolted shut, posters of birds spreading their wings six feet apart with advice for humans to emulate them. Human beings were an invasive species now, invading each other's trust and mourning each other's memories.

The past hurt too much to stay in the present, so we had to leave it for new terrain. You can't hike an uncanny valley. I wanted to go somewhere that did not remind me of anything. A town with a population of zero would do just fine.

Mark Twain's birthplace sits in the center of an empty field. It is a stone and log cabin reconstructed to look like one built in the 1830s, modest in a way that makes you think of big dreams. He did not live there long, departing when he was four years old for Hannibal, the river town that formed the basis for the adventures he made immortal. Near the cabin is a plaque the state of Missouri constructed in 1913: MARK TWAIN: HE CHEERED AND COMFORTED A TIRED WORLD. World War I would start the next year, and then the Spanish flu four years after that. The world did not know how tired it was going to get.

The Missourians who preserved the Twain home were grateful for small comforts, including the communal rite of mythmaking. I could relate. In 2020, exhaustion was the default mode. The covid pandemic had followed years of political chaos. Americans were trying to ride out the bad times in the belief that it would end, unaware that our worst-case scenarios were now simply scenarios. I wanted a demarcation, a definitive date when this darkness would recede and I would no longer be frantically conserving energy like a dying star.

With no relief in sight, I retreated into the Mark Twain past, that homespun patchwork quilt of tall tales and discarded dreams, and let it blanket the uncertain future.

When I was seven years old, my father took me to see Halley's Comet. At the top of our street in my hometown of Meriden, Connecticut, there was a hill with a water tower. In the summer, we would watch fireworks on the Fourth of July because you could see not just our city but the skylines of surrounding towns. In 1986, we returned in winter to watch the sky's latest show.

My father and I were alone—*it's too cold for this comet shit*, my mother had proclaimed before retreating to the warm glow of the TV. I was nervous what the night would bring because the most recent astronomical event had been the *Challenger*, which I had watched explode with my second-grade classmates the month before.

As we waited, my father pointed out constellations: the Big Dipper, Orion's Belt, Cassiopeia. I already knew them because I had a children's guide to the solar system that said humans would inhabit outer space by the year 2000, a book I regarded with suspicion as years passed with promises unfulfilled. *Space is full of explosions and lies*, I thought, but I kept this view to myself. I also did not tell my dad I already knew the constellations, because he is not a talkative man, and I liked that he was talking to me. It was a special night and not because of anything in the sky.

There were a few other families on the hill. I listened to them debate whether the flashes of light we saw in the sky were the comet. No one could tell, and I don't remember whether I actually saw Halley's Comet or imagined I did, but I do know this was the night I heard about Mark Twain.

"There's a famous writer," my dad said, "and he's from Connecticut, you know, you can go see his house. There's a writer named Mark Twain who was born when Halley's Comet appeared, and he predicted that he would die seventy-five years later when Halley's Comet returned. And then—he did."

"On purpose?"

"No. He died naturally, like he said he would. Like he had written a story inside his mind and it became real."

The cabin where Twain was born is near Mark Twain Lake, a reservoir that surrounds the ghost village of Florida. In the spring of 2020, the campgrounds by the lake were filled with people fleeing covid restrictions. They lit up the night with firepits and music and booze. We waved to our fellow travelers and left because this crowded scene wasn't the escape we were after. We walked to a lake lined with rocky bluffs and watched teenagers leap off the edge, screaming and laughing, basking in the novelty of holding their breath for a welcome reason. Then we were back in the car, zipping through the pines, until we arrived at a small pond without a soul in sight. I spread the beach towels on the grass.

"You know what looked fun? Diving off a cliff," my daughter said pointedly before exclaiming, "Oh! Fireflies! Look at all the fireflies!"

Tiny orbs blinked like Christmas lights, fluttering near our faces and dancing across the pond. My children examined their strange bodies as the dusk masked all but their flickering glow. With nightfall came a cacophonous chorus. Frogs croaked from the water like drunks in a tank; mosquitoes buzzed and cicadas droned and birds screeched that nighttime was here, nighttime was *theirs*. We were tourists on their terrain.

It was loud for a town with a population of zero. My son dared his sister to walk around the pond in the dark, and she dared him back to do it, and in the end they each held one of my hands and we walked around the pond together.

"Are you enjoying your trip to Florida?" I asked.

"It's not as good as the real Florida," my daughter said, then quickly, "but it's still nice."

"It'll get better," I said. "Wait for it."

We lay down on our towels and rolled up old clothes from past road trips, stuffing them under our heads like pillows.

"Why is this called Florida?" my daughter asked.

"I don't know. Why does Missouri have a Cuba, a Lebanon, a Brazil, a Louisiana, a Nevada, a Santa Fe—"

"So people can pretend they don't live in Missouri?"

"Maybe. People in Missouri like to pretend things."

"Hey Mommy," my son said, "that guy, that writer guy, we just saw his house—"

"Mark Twain? The most famous American writer?"

"Yeah, yeah, yeah, him. Mark Twain. Mommy," my son said, barely able to contain his laughter, "Mommy, since this is Florida, does that mean Mark Twain is a Florida Man?"

"Yes," I said. "Mark Twain is one hundred percent a Florida Man."

"Would he like that meme?"

"Of course. Mark Twain invented memes."

"No he didn't!" my son exclaimed, even though I was right. "You don't know what a meme is because you're old. I meant, would he like that joke?"

"I think he'd like that joke a lot."

"Did he make fun of being from Florida?"

"He made fun of everything. He made fun of Missouri. He made a whole living making fun of Missouri."

"You can make a living making fun of Missouri?" my son exclaimed.

"Back when people made livings, absolutely."

"When was he alive?" my son asked.

I told my son the story of Twain and Halley's Comet, the same one my dad had told me in 1986, the one that had left me wanting more.

"Twain said he and the comet were both unaccountable freaks of nature, and because they came in together, they should go out together."

"He called himself a freak?"

"He meant freak like a compliment. Freaks see everything, including all the people who call them freaks to try to shut them up. They see everything, and they see through everything, too."

"I want to see a comet," my son said dreamily. "That would be cool."

"Want to see something cool? Turn off your phones. And look up."

The night was black and the noise ceaseless. My son clutched my hand because he was a small boy in a strange land. My twelve-year-old daughter lay on my other side, stoic as usual, until she could see in the dark.

"This sky is so clear," she marveled under a ceiling of stars. The longer we looked, the more stars appeared. We didn't know if it was the dark of a new moon or our imaginations or our eyes, but the stars multiplied, hypnotizing us out of the moment and into a timeless place. The kids pointed in excitement at constellations that my husband and I had shown them on past trips. They remembered those nights, and the memories didn't hurt because stars don't quit on you like the world does.

"Let your eyes adjust," my husband said, "and look over that way."

"What way? We can't see what you're talking about. We can't see *anything*!"

"A valid point. Keep looking up. You'll know it when you see it."

The first time I saw the Milky Way, I was forty years old. One of my biggest regrets is that I did not see it sooner. The delay had been the result of being born in a time when, within half a century, the Milky Way changed from something most of the world could see to something visible only if you isolated yourself from the rest of humanity. The ability to see a universal wonder is now dependent on the severing of our human bond. This collective loss marks a rift in mankind's development that's more than a metaphor, a loss that can be understood only once you see firsthand what was stolen.

My children were with me when I first saw the Milky Way— North Dakota, August 2019—and they didn't understand why I started to cry, and neither did I, if it was awe or sadness that it had taken me so long to find something that had always been there. But now it greeted me like a trusted friend. I lay on my back and held my children's hands because the Earth feels like it's spinning when you stare into a galaxy. It is a pleasant sort of dizziness.

"How did you know we would see it?"

"New moon, old town, population zero."

"Population us," my daughter corrected, "for now."

"Population us and the ghost of Mark Twain," my son said. "Did he see the Milky Way?"

"He saw it. And it looked the same as now."

We left soon after, retracing our route home, through Florida and Louisiana, the river town to which Twain had floated from Hannibal when he was seven years old. We drove down the Great

River Road, the clusters of stars fading town by town until we approached St. Louis and could barely see any at all.

Samuel Clemens—the man who would become Mark Twain—was born in 1835. At the time of his birth, Missouri was fourteen years old and considered the western frontier. By the time Clemens turned fourteen in 1849, Missouri was the center of the United States, and the United States was headed to war with itself.

Missouri, the bellwether state, had already seen wars at every border—wars not usually described as wars because they were acts of ethnic cleansing. Most of Missouri's enslaved African Americans lived in the area where Clemens grew up: Little Dixie, so named because families like his had arrived from southern states with human bondage in tow. Southwest of Little Dixie were the starting points of famous routes: the Santa Fe Trail, the Oregon Trail, the Trail of Tears. Missouri is a state famous for all the ways to leave it.

When Clemens was ten years old, he saw a white slave owner beat a Black man to death with a piece of iron and face no consequences. This was one of many acts of violence he would witness in his childhood: stabbings and drownings and shootings that shattered the myth of his idyllic young town in his idyllic young country. When Clemens was eleven years old, new congressman Abraham Lincoln gained prominence for demanding "spot resolutions" that would force the US government to specify where American blood was spilled on American soil. These resolutions were never honored because America was producing too much blood to keep track.

"After each tragedy I recognized the warning and repented; repented and begged; begged like a coward; begged like a dog; and not in the interest of those poor people who had been extinguished for my sake but only in my own interest. It seems selfish, when I look back at it now," Clemens wrote in his autobiography of the violence he had witnessed in his teenage years. He recalled how when day would break, the tragedies "faded out and shredded away and disappeared in the glad splendor of the sun. They were the creatures of fear and darkness and they could not live out of their own place. The day gave me cheer and peace, and at night I repented again."[2]

Lincoln's call for spot resolutions was prompted by the US war with Mexico. But the most dangerous war was the one brewing within America's borders: a moral war whose immoral architects needed neat geographic boundaries and found them in new states like Missouri. This was a war that Clemens, as a teenager, absorbed and ignored at once.

Clemens did not need to leave Hannibal to see what lay beyond it, though that was his goal. The world arrived at his doorstep daily through steamboats that went up and down the Mississippi River, stopping at midway port towns like Hannibal, where he would hitch rides and dream of being a river pilot. For nearly half the population of Hannibal, those same ships were symbols of African American bondage, the threat of being "sold down the river" forever looming. Clemens did not recognize or condemn this casual tyranny until he was older. The character of Huckleberry Finn was modeled after a childhood friend, Tom Blankenship. But Huck's proclamation that he was willing to go to hell for protesting slavery—a moral triumph, a social disgrace—was all Twain.

In 1848, Clemens's father, a lawyer, died, plunging the family into an uncertain financial future and forcing teenage Clemens to seek paid work. He spent over a decade as a typesetter and steamboat pilot until 1861, when he was drafted. Missouri had declared itself "armed neutral" in the Civil War: a declaration to stay out of the war that ensured it would be dragged into it. In Missouri, neutrality meant you could fight for any cause, regardless how extreme. The state government spent 1861 issuing alternating resolutions to remain and secede while citizens joined both sides and battled each other: brother against brother, neighbor against neighbor.

In June 1861, Clemens joined the Marion Rangers, a pro-Confederate Missouri militia. He lasted two weeks before running away to Nevada. Two months later, the first Civil War battle west of the Mississippi River broke out in Wilson's Creek in the western Ozarks. Missouri was in play; Missouri would suffer; Missouri would burn. Twain spent the Civil War years in the West as a prospector, vowing to make his fortune in the gold rush.

But he was a writer, and with the publication of his first story under a pen name in 1863, a new man was born. He entered the Civil War as Samuel Clemens and emerged from it as Mark Twain.

It is 2023, and every day I wake to a pundit or member of Congress calling for civil war—or its euphemistic parlance, a "national divorce." They cloak their ambition as civic concern, but I know the real plot. They want to strip the United States down and sell it for parts, partitioning it into oligarch and plutocrat fiefdoms that will war with each other for profit, and they want ordinary Americans to think it was their own idea.

I know this is the plot because the plotters have told us and because I have spent years detailing their agenda in books and articles. I am not alone: hundreds have written books and documents revealing other facets of coordinated malign intent. Despite the undisputed veracity of the threat, no officials have acted to stop it, and the media will rarely spell out their vision of the Divided States of America.

I do not think we, the American people, want another civil war. But I know we are being pushed there, and I refuse to go.

To be an American in the twenty-first century is to be viewed by officials as disposable. This is not a new feeling for the majority of Americans who have lived under various forms of subjugation—racial, ethnic, class—but what is new is how wide the net has been cast and how overt the agenda is.

Our current era—when American institutions greet their own dissolution with a shrug, when rights and resources are tossed away as if the collapse of the country is not only inevitable but desirable—has no precedent. Throw in digital surveillance and climate change and there is no clear road map out of an old war fought with new technology under a relentlessly ticking clock. Lincoln warned in 1838 that if the United States of America died, it would be by its own hand. But what we have is more like assisted suicide.

It is easy to love your homeland and hate your government. I have done it all my life and consider myself in the company of patriots. But there is a pain in loving a place that is so terrible and wonderful at once. You love it like a child and you love it like a parent, with an irrational depth and the fiercest desire to protect it from harm. You mourn the lost leverage of the ordinary American—of elections, of courts, of protest, of documentation. You remember when those things seemed to matter, or at least when the powerful felt obligated to pretend they did.

When a calamity hits, I research what past writers were doing when they faced the same hardships. What I find is that they spent most of their time surviving—thus the dearth of literature about the Spanish flu—but the pain haunts their subsequent work. This is most obvious in books written after a war, even when they do not cover the war itself. *The Great Gatsby* is just as much a World War I novel as *A Farewell to Arms*. In art a person can process the dark emotions society forbids them to express. This is why power brokers want to replace artists with artificial intelligence. There must be no lingering memory of what was because that might remind us of what we thought we would be. There can be no intrinsic humanity in art because then you start seeing people instead of mythic red and blue lines. You start tracking the blood, like Lincoln wanted. You start feeling for the people who bleed.

The Civil War haunts Mark Twain's work even though he rarely addressed it outright. Twain grew up in an America of rapid growth and political instability. He entered early adulthood when America was at war and spent the rest of his life watching an American aristocracy sell the public an illusion as they undid the progress toward equality made in the war's aftermath. Twain was born in a state that was neither north nor south, a state everyone wanted so badly they kept assaulting it. His solution in 1861 was to flee the fire and immortalize the flames. Tom Sawyer, Huck Finn. Sam Clemens, Mark Twain.

Dreams by day, repentance by night. You preemptively tear yourself apart so that the people who want to do that to you and to your country cannot do it first.

And then you piece yourself back together in prose because there is nothing left to be but an American. There is nowhere else to belong than to a colossal contradictory land whose sins persist to the present, whose potential is unlimited, whose threatened dissolution taunts you. A land built on principles never fully practiced, a land whose new tenets—the mainstreaming of elite criminal impunity, the contrived and bloodthirsty "national divorce"—build off the worst of this country's history to create a future of unprecedented danger. You reject it and also know that abandoning America is the most self-destructive move of all. Where would you be without each other, you and this terrible, wonderful country?

"You cannot lay bare your private soul and look at it," Clemens wrote in 1899, discussing why he would not publish his autobiography. "You are much too ashamed of yourself. It's too disgusting. For that reason I confine myself to drawing the portraits of others."[3]

So you write about America, you write about history, you write in the second person, you write for a second chance. You wander America like an open wound that past and future conspire to never let heal. There is some consolation that others wandered the same roads and shouldered the same weight.

When Twain went out with the comet, it was not with the silent satisfaction of a life well lived but with fear that he would become the icon of a country besieged by newly empowered predatory forces: mercenary capitalists and scheming imperialists. People who were as good at understanding human nature as he was and who used that knowledge to inflict pain. People who were as good at inventing America as he was and could undo that creation with a pen and a sword and an offshore account.

The people who want to destroy my country are banking on us not missing America. To miss America is to remember America. To remember America is to explore America. To explore America is to see the best and worst in everything—to reconcile, to repent.

"There's a famous writer," I told my daughter when she was seven years old. "And he's from Missouri, you know, you can go see his house."

Mark Twain's boyhood home is in the center of Hannibal, on a cobblestoned square where significant buildings from his early life were preserved. You know you are getting close to it when you begin to encounter the total commercialization of Twain, whose face is slapped onto anything a person can sell. There is no object too banal for a portrait. Twain's arch condemnations of human gullibility line signposts on town streets as tourists embody the very idiocy he mocks. This is more fun than it sounds because it is refreshing to see an irreverent man with horrible business sense flourish after he's dead. You get the sense he would laugh—and approve—if he saw Hannibal now.

The knockabout nature of Hannibal is not new: the town was built on legends and lies. At the southern approach to Hannibal is Lovers' Leap, a fenced-in cliff over the river marked with a plaque honoring two doomed Native Americans who allegedly plummeted to a watery grave. This tale is so ubiquitous in America that Twain noted in 1883, "There are fifty Lovers' Leaps along the Mississippi from whose summit disappointed Indian girls have jumped."[4] The origin of the Lovers' Leap myth, in which either a Native American couple from feuding tribes or a Native American and their forbidden white lover die in a suicide pact, is likely a manifestation of nineteenth-century white guilt. Natives were being massacred and romanticized and commercialized all at once. Ellis Parker Butler, a brochure writer for Midwestern towns, remarked in 1919 that Lovers' Leap was such a popular concept that a backstory would be invented when none existed: "There was always an Indian legend, and always the same one. If there was no legend, we wrote one, and it was again always the same one."[5]

In 2006, my husband and I drove past Lovers' Leap and entered Twain's hometown for the first time. I was twenty-eight and pregnant with my daughter. I did not know I would never move and that she and my son would be Missourians. I had grown up in the postindustrial region of central Connecticut between Hartford and New Haven, an area that made national news in the 1990s for its gang and crack epidemics. Like Twain, I spent my childhood wondering what was beyond my hometown and longing to break free.

When I was ten and visited the Mark Twain House in Hartford, I saw for the first time a life I wanted: to write, to travel, to have a family, to live in a creepy old house filled with objects from around the world. I spent fifth grade writing extra-credit reports on Twain for my teacher while getting my ass kicked by classmates for my meticulous nerd treatises. I didn't care: I had a local to emulate, and he had pissed off everyone too. I drew cartoons of Twain being condemned by society for upsetting their delicate sensibilities. I drew him enjoying the chaos he wrought because it did not matter so long as he had what he needed: his family, his writing, and America.

In my twenties, I moved around an America of diminishing opportunity, settling in Missouri not out of intent but inertia. As I've said, people of my generation don't have dreams, we have circumstances. But even if I'd had enough money to move, I would have stayed. My unluckiest and luckiest circumstance is the same as Twain's: I live in Missouri and I write everything down.

The weirdness of America permeated Twain's stories as it did everyday life, and Twain stood out for his willingness to record it. He refused to give greater weight to the highbrow over the lowbrow, enjoying the way they feed off each other and make everyone nervous. Folklore and vernacular and hypocrisies and politics merged in books where the most damning views come through the eyes of a child. *Huckleberry Finn* is one of the most banned books in American history, first receiving the designation in 1885, one year after publication. It remains contested in our era of rampant school censorship. Detractors of Twain often hate each other, with one group finding offense in the pages the other admires and the other admiring the pages that offended their foes. You know you have written the great American novel when each detractor has a different reason for banning it.

Hannibal's central attractions capitalize on the characters of Twain's books. There is a white picket fence where the fence that inspired *Tom Sawyer* once stood and a brush so you can pretend to paint it like a sucker. The house of Twain's childhood crush, who inspired Becky Thatcher, is on the same block as his father's law office. Next door is the pharmacy of Ulysses S. Grant's cousin, with whom the Clemens family lived after his father's death. Later, Twain would go on to commission Ulysses S. Grant's bestselling autobiography, rescuing the Grant family from financial and reputational ruin.

A small house belonging to Tom Blankenship, the good-hearted vagrant who inspired the character of Huckleberry Finn, is a block away. When we visited it in 2023, it was closed because a drunk driver had smashed their car through the fence outside. This seemed like the kind of thing that would happen to the actual Huckleberry Finn, so we considered it part of the Hannibal experience.

I have immersed my children in history since they were small because history buffs know their audience is limited and therefore usually don't charge admission. This is how my kids wound up doing things like watching a reenactment of the 1872 election between Ulysses S. Grant and Horace Greeley on a summer afternoon in 2016. (My nine-year-old daughter and I voted for Grant only to have volunteers tear up our ballots because women couldn't vote; Greeley was the choice of my five-year-old son, a member of the "fans of flamboyant neckbeards" voter bloc.) During their elementary school years, when their leisure time was at my mercy, my children saw every museum and historical site in St. Louis. When I ran out of free attractions in town, I took them to nearby sites in Missouri and Illinois.

I like traveling with children because they notice things that adults don't, and they haven't learned enough manners to not point them out.

My children have been to Hannibal a half dozen times. But until recently, they did not consider Twain an important part of the town. They saw him as a kind of mustachioed mascot who kept popping up on strange objects, like the giant rotating mug of root beer at the Mark Twain Dinette.

But they knew Hannibal. They knew that was where we went to watch a murmuration of migrating geese from Lovers' Leap in winter, to spot islands from the deck of the Mark Twain Riverboat in summer, to explore caves and pull pranks and have sword battles with driftwood on the Mississippi shoreline all year long. My children were unwittingly living the twenty-first-century version of an idyllic Twain childhood as the same malevolent forces that threatened to destroy Twain's America threatened theirs.

Above all, they knew Hannibal for the feature that defined it in Twain's time: it's a river town. A twenty-first-century Missouri river town is a living ruin premised on phantoms and fantasy. Hannibal has the requisite river town setup: floodwalls, railroad tracks, old-timey ice cream parlor, shops selling dubious "antiques," a ghost hunter, a psychic, a thriving historical reenactment theater industry, a sign proclaiming it Mural City (every Missouri small town is Mural City unless it is Fireworks City, and sometimes it's both), and ubiquitous historical markers commemorating when the whole country agreed Hannibal was someplace special.

When my kids were young, they could not grasp why one man had birthed an industry, but they went to the Twain museums to humor me. As they grew up, they found his quotes funnier and then more poignant. The Civil War–era chronology of his life became familiar in an awful way: an omen and a prelude. A history that never rested or repented but reaches from the grave to grab the present—to shake it to its senses or to strangle it, we do not know.

I am waiting for my children to discover *Huckleberry Finn* on their own because there is no surer way to get a child to reject a book than to insist that they read it. But I do want them to understand Twain because then they will understand what happened to America—his, theirs, ours.

In 2023, the memories come and won't let go:

Hannibal, 2006, pregnant at the top of the Mark Twain Lighthouse, wondering if my baby would someday see this view, my husband holding a mug that says "It is better to remain silent and be thought a fool than to open one's mouth and remove all doubt," which he bought from a tourist trap; the two of us in the Becky Thatcher Ice Cream Parlor listening to veterans bemoan the Iraq War as we look at each other and wonder what world our child will inherit;

Hannibal, 2010, a living museum to a dead town devastated by the Great Recession and a 2008 flood, tourist traffic reduced to me and my husband and our stroller-bound daughter who points at a man with a "Don't Tread on Me" T-shirt and waves at its funny coiled snake as he vanishes into an alley between vacant stores bolted shut;

Hannibal, 2016, on a ferry ride to see Jackson's Island alongside international tourists and Missourians wearing MAGA hats and Missourians wearing Black Lives Matter shirts who all bask in the same summer-boat breeze and marvel over the same island birds before remembering to eye each other warily;

Hannibal, 2018, stopping at the gas station on the way to find geodes in Keokuk, Iowa, because I want to prove to my children that something that seems ugly and unremarkable has a magical secret inside;

Hannibal, 2020, turning the car around because everything is closed and everything is ending and the only place open is the cliff with the curse;

Hannibal, 2023, recovered economically but broken psychologically, or maybe that's just me, not sure whether to wear or remove a mask, not sure how much of a person should be revealed, but there is still Hannibal with its literature, Hannibal with its history, Hannibal that never had the answers but wrote down the questions, Hannibal where you can literally read the writing on the wall and it says, "If you tell the truth, you don't have to remember anything."

Twain is not buried in Missouri or Connecticut. Twain's wife, Olivia, was from Elmira, New York. Her sudden death in 1904 devastated Twain. She had requested to be buried in her hometown. This is where Mark Twain's grave is found, resting beside his wife and four children, three of whom died before him. Twain wrote parts of *Huckleberry Finn* in Elmira while visiting his in-laws, contemplating the America of his childhood that lingered like a ghost, weaving the past and present together in a way his soul could bear.

In March 2019, my family and I drove east toward Elmira, a new direction for the kids. It was spring break and we were low on money and lower on time, though we did not yet know it. We were headed to Connecticut and it was a sixteen-hour haul, so we split the drive to see Pittsburgh on the way in and Cleveland on the way back. I love these two cities: they remind me of St. Louis with their grand, free museums and cheap food and their sense that a longer stay is necessary to learn their secrets. They were stopover cities that I left wanting to make destinations.

But I was on a pilgrimage of obligation. I was taking the kids to see their grandparents and give them a taste of where I had grown up. Meriden, the city where my parents lived their entire lives. Meriden, the city I last called home in a different century. I was anxious to leave when I visited that spring, to get back on the road and see something new. But now I would walk all the way from St. Louis to Meriden if I could have one more day with my parents in 2019.

When you have a normal visit at your parents' home for the last time, all you remember later is that it was the last time. I have hazy memories of family activities—steamed cheeseburgers in Meriden and clam pizza in New Haven, finding a nature trail at a Connecticut beach and asking my parents if they had walked it and discovering they had no idea it existed despite living forty minutes away their entire lives. My parents had met when they were twelve and wed at twenty-one and stayed married for more than fifty years. When I asked the secret to their marriage, my mother replied, "Inertia and propinquity." She was an English teacher and a wiseass; my father, a quiet man who liked routine. They never understood my ceaseless need to move around, but maybe that's because they found what they needed most in life at home with each other.

On the drive from Meriden to Cleveland, we got caught in a snowstorm in Bethel, New York. When my parents were teenagers, my mom's cousin invited her and my father to the Woodstock music festival, but my dad thought it was too long a drive and "wouldn't be a big deal," a take my mom gave him shit over for the next half century. I took note of this cautionary tale when I was young, vowing to see anything and everything. Now, fifty years later, I made the trip to Woodstock my parents never had. There was nothing there but fields covered in the softest white, a snow-globe land of endless quiet with only a plaque to make you believe the concert happened. Woodstock felt like repose.

The snow slowed and then cleared as we drove through Binghamton, New York, the home of *Twilight Zone* creator Rod Serling, and down Highway 17, which I recognized from the fictional terrain of Peter Straub's *Ghost Story*. This was haunted land, and I thought of all the invented Americas I got to visit, how the Twain and Serling visions fit together, the horror and humor they found in everyday American moral rot.

By midday we reached Elmira. We pulled into Woodlawn Cemetery and walked down a path to a well-attended family plot. There are two graves in Elmira: one for Samuel Clemens and one for Mark Twain. The Clemens grave has a small headstone bearing his original name, his pseudonym, and his dates of birth and death. The Twain grave is an obelisk bearing his portrait along with that of his son-in-law, the Russian pianist Ossip Gabrilowitsch. His daughter Clara, the sole child to outlive her parents, had commissioned it.

"Death is the starlit strip between the companionship of yesterday and the reunion of tomorrow," it says.

I don't know who came up with this quote, but I think about it when I gaze at the Milky Way, searching the sky for something that won't leave me. Death is the memory of the future that never was.

In June 2023, we drove sixteen hours from St. Louis to Meriden again. My sister flew in from Dallas with her two children. There was an occasion, and it was unspoken. My job was to not ask questions and pretend everything was normal, that my father had not just been diagnosed with terminal stage four lung cancer. Pretending nothing is wrong goes against every instinct I have. I forced myself to envision our time together in a different way. My job was to create new, good memories. To be part of a story still unfinished but ending far too soon.

We stayed at my parents' house. At dawn my father woke, like me, with the sun. Every morning, he would make me scrambled eggs for breakfast because he did not know how to talk to me, but he knows that I think he makes the best scrambled eggs in the world. Every day I would play Chopin nocturnes on the piano because I did not know how to talk to him, but I wanted him to know how I felt. Sometimes he would make an offhand comment that broke me—"I never saw the Pacific Ocean, I always wanted to"—and I would go to another room to cry. He did not want a scene. He never asked for much, but he asked for that. And I swallowed my instincts, swallowed my pride and my pain, and faded into the background as the children played.

"We made that," my mother said to him, pointing at the six of us, my sister and our children, and he smiled.

The kids had been to Meriden but had never seen the street where I'd grown up. My parents had moved out of that neighborhood long before my children were born. My sister and I and our kids walked from our parents' new house five miles to our childhood home. We stopped and stared at it, reliving decades in a glance. We walked to the water tower where my father and I had watched Halley's Comet, a hill that seemed impossibly small compared to the summit I remembered. We doubled back and turned onto a busy street, passing burned-down buildings and gritty strip malls until we reached our favorite ice cream stand, like we had when we were little. A gang of girls roaming the road, dodging traffic and expectations.

It was surreal to watch my own children re-create my childhood adventures. I remembered Twain writing in *Life on the Mississippi* of his shock at returning to Hannibal and finding the little girls he had played with were, somehow, grandmothers. And that he was old, and that home had not been home in a long, long time.

The next day, I decided to take the kids to the Mark Twain House in Hartford. I had not been there since 1989. I wanted to see if it had changed or if I had. I had accomplished many of the things I had dreamed of there when I was ten: I wrote books and lived with my children in a creepy old house filled with objects from trips around the world. I had gotten some Twain-style gains, and I was headed for some Twain-style losses. Now I would learn how those felt, too.

The Mark Twain House was as remarkable as I remembered, full of bizarre, intricate furniture and funny, sad stories. I answered the tour guide's trivia too readily, and he asked where I was from.

"Missouri," I said. Then, changing my mind, "Connecticut. Except I haven't lived in Connecticut this millennium. Missouri!"

"She pulled a reverse Mark Twain," my husband explained. "She grew up in Connecticut and moved to Missouri."

"Not a lot of people do that," the tour guide said politely.

As a child, I had wandered through the Mark Twain House, dreaming of writing books and seeing America. As an adult, I listened to the guide reciting his familiar biography, knowing it culminated in the death of Twain's family. How those losses broke him, and how his pain was exacerbated by the feeling that America was breaking at the same time. Twain left the Hartford house in 1891 and sold it in 1903. It was too lonely to live in without the people he loved.

What remained was his ability to write everything down, even if it were purely for himself. He made his publishers promise not to print his autobiography until he had been dead for one hundred years, a promise they kept. There were things Twain could not bear to let the people closest to him know, parts of himself he could not surrender to the public eye.

We drove back to Meriden, stopping at a seafood shack for lunch. I texted my dad to see if he wanted us to bring him anything, and my mom responded that he was too tired to eat. When we got home, he was feeling better and sweeping the kitchen floor. My father loved to clean. It was one more thing I had not inherited.

"How was the Mark Twain House?" he asked in the baffled tone reserved for inquiries into my behavior. He knew I was writing a book involving the house, but that was a strange thing to do. Then again, writing a book at all is a strange thing to do.

"I loved it," I said. "It's fun to show the kids that there's a famous writer from Missouri and Connecticut, and that you can go see his house." He nodded, and I held his gaze.

"I remember the day I heard about Mark Twain. It was a long time ago. I doubt the person who told me even remembers doing it. But it meant more to me than I can say."

3
Route 66

Setting Out

It is the Fourth of July in 2017, and I am in a parking lot in Branson, Missouri, looking at the abandoned head of Ronald Reagan. It weighs ten thousand pounds. Behind him stand two American flags, drooping like afterthoughts.

Reagan is wearing a concrete shirt and a concrete tie and a concrete smile. His form is not so much white as colorless. He is staring at Heavy Metal Highrise, a go-kart track, and he will do so for eternity, for he cannot be moved. His eighteen-foot cranium rests between an overflowing dumpster and a store called the T-Shirt Shack offering custom airbrush and replica guns. On the side of the T-Shirt Shack someone painted a friendly scene—cows and tractors and a big red barn—but it is blocked by Reagan's gigantic head. There is nothing explaining why the head is there. The easiest explanation is that once it arrived, it was hard to get rid of, much like Reagan himself.

What does one do with the five-ton head of Ronald Reagan? Take it to Missouri because no one will think it unusual, much less object to it. Drop it near Route 66, where it will join its spiritual brethren: the World's Largest Rocking Chair, the World's Largest Catsup Bottle, the Museum of the Vacuum Cleaner ("And *this* vacuum cleaner belonged to the grandmother of James Earl Jones!"), the World's Largest Roll of Toilet Paper. Drop it in Branson, the bedazzled buckle of Missouri's Bible Belt, a place where I took my children for fun before they got old enough to question the virtue of Evangelical Vegas. Dump it near the five-ton concrete head of John F. Kennedy, which sits in an RV lot seven miles from Reagan, cultivating its own mystique.

There is no reason to it, just rhyme, and that's the appeal. The heads are big because they're big, and they're there because they're there. We went to Branson because it's a short drive from Route 66 in Springfield, where we had watched the sun rise over the World's Largest Fork, hailing the dawn's early light gleaming from its tines like lasers.

There is nothing that does not belong on Route 66 because there is nowhere Route 66 belongs—not anymore. Route 66 beckons you to the freedom of the open road, but the open road keeps terminating without warning.

Route 66 displays the World's Biggest Objects and invites you to solve the World's Greatest Mysteries from faded billboards on dead-end streets. Route 66 is neon lights that burned out before your grandma was born and motels boasting signed photos of celebrities your children can't name. Route 66 makes you nostalgic for experiences you never had in places you never saw with people you never met. Route 66 is America's mental breakdown lane, a postcard from your subconscious marked return to sender.

Route 66 is America, and America is falling apart.

When it was completed in 1926, Route 66 was to roads what the Mississippi is to rivers: the big one, the highway of the American Dream. Constructed when cars were new, it symbolized an

American longing for freedom modeled as a roadway to escape. Escape was the fantasy of the postwar 1920s like impunity is the fantasy of the permanent-crisis 2020s. In the twenty-first century, a fragile ideal of freedom based on hope became a cruel vision of freedom based on power. Freedom based on hope lets you coast on illusion. But impunity, the sadist's view of freedom, gets off on stealing even that.

The impunity crowd avoids Route 66: it's in flyover country, and we are specks to sneer at from the sky. Everyday Americans seeking escape also avoid Route 66 because it's too slow. Nowadays Route 66 is a road to take to get lost instead of to find your way, but that wasn't always the case. In the first half of the twentieth century, the two-lane, newly paved highway stretching from Chicago to Los Angeles was the fastest and sometimes only route west. Route 66 provided escape, in a grim way, for the refugees of the Dust Bowl and the Black exiles of the Great Migration. Route 66 was escape, in a frivolous way, for the mid-century Americans whose most treasured inalienable right was the pursuit of happiness.

Americans drove Route 66 believing you could reinvent yourself at the other side: escape the law, escape society, escape yourself.

Route 66 will turn one hundred years old in 2026. I am afraid it is going to die, much like the dream of escape is dying in an era of digital surveillance and climate catastrophe. But I keep chasing it, the road and the dream, because I am its target audience, the American fool.

Route 66 is the mother road because it makes you feel like a child. It was designed to make you that way: impressed by giant things, magical things, idiotic things. Feats of dubious merit, awards of dubious veracity, signs beckoning you to drop your standards to a bar so low only a simple mind could clear it. The spirit of Route 66 lives on in Branson or any nostalgia trip town with a Ripley's Believe It or Not Museum and an excess of shame-lessness and fried pie. Any place that takes your money but not a lot of it, because if you had real money you would not be driving on Route 66.

Route 66 is the origin of the American Road Trip: the notion that the highway should be entertaining in and of itself. That early twentieth-century Americans decided to make Route 66 interest-ing even though they knew people would *have* to drive it seems considerate in an opportunistic way. The desire to win Americans over with weirdness has been supplanted by bland buildings and billboards slapped with QR codes designed to destroy the offhand, offbeat view.

Today Route 66 belongs in spirit to the freaks and in practice to American regions that peaked around 1950 and depopulated soon after. Those who remain tend the road like grave keepers, beck-oning you with stories and shrines. In big cities, Route 66 blends into the landscape to the point that it needs to be announced to be noticed. The road snakes through St. Louis, and I often find myself on it by accident, jolted from a steady stream of strip malls by signs proclaiming I am on Historic Route 66. I am not running errands, I tell myself; I am *being historic*.

Route 66 had a thirty-year mythic run before President Dwight Eisenhower knocked it out in 1956 with the creation of the Federal Highway Act, which commissioned a "national system of interstate and defense highways" to allow Americans to flee nuclear war at a brisker pace.[1] Its efficacy destroyed by Cold War fearmongering, Route 66 gradually faded and frayed. In 1985, President Ronald Reagan officially decommissioned its remains. Parts of it were absorbed into new highways, parts of it became frontage roads, and parts remain intact in small towns and rural regions with no alternative paths. As a St. Louisan, I live five hours from its Chicago starting point, marked by a

Route 66 sign so covered in stickers and graffiti you can barely make out the numbers.

Over the course of my life, I have driven all of Route 66 except for the final stretch in California. There needs to be something left to imagine. A little piece of past in the future, waiting for me.

The first time I drove Route 66 I was nineteen and had never driven west of New Jersey. My boyfriend, whom I had met in 1997 on an *X Files* online fan forum, lived in Lubbock, Texas, and we dreamed of visiting Roswell, New Mexico, to be abducted by aliens. I had saved up enough money working as a Record Town cashier in the Meriden mall to buy a plane ticket and fly alone for the first time. In the Dallas International Airport, I transferred to a rickety plane that took me over a series of large brown squares until landing in Lubbock, where I looked out the window and saw my boyfriend waving from the airport gate.

I remember this arrival with surreal sentimentality, like air travel couldn't have possibly been that simple and trusting. But it was, and so was I. The only surveillance on my mind was the prospect of men in black deterring our paranormal quest. This was low-stakes late-1990s living, the final freedom before the fall.

My boyfriend had grown up in Lubbock and hated it with a pathological intensity. He would quote country singer Mac Davis's line that "happiness was Lubbock, Texas, in the rearview mirror," reminiscing about the times he'd gotten out and cursing the bad luck that had brought him back in. He expected me to echo his revulsion, but to his horror, I thought Lubbock was great. I asked if we could move there after I graduated from college, and he shrieked like I had stabbed him. He would never understand: he was a native, and I was a drifter. In Lubbock, strangers greeted me with a smile. The men said "howdy" and the women called me "hon" and I was not savvy enough to crack southern codes, so I assumed I was unusually well liked. Lubbock was where I discovered the culinary marvels of Vietnamese food and guacamole and Whataburger. Lubbock was so cheap that the money from my minimum wage job took me far, and I liked that too.

But what I loved most about Lubbock was the sky. The Texas sky that stretched like an endless horizon of blazing possibility, back when Texas felt like that. The Texas that still lives in the rearview mirror of my mind.

One night my boyfriend and I were at Kmart buying ice cream and I said to him, "This parking lot has sunsets so beautiful, I could stay here forever," and he asked if I had noticed that the whole town smelled like cow shit. I said yes but that was just one more thing that made Lubbock exciting.

"Man, you are one cheap date," he said, shaking his head as I sat on the curb eating ice cream, eyes on the sky.

The next day we set out for New Mexico. I was excited not only to visit Roswell, the site of the legendary 1947 UFO crash, but to see mountains and desert. I had spent most of my life in a landscape limited to a twenty-mile radius of my childhood home: not out of choice but because I was a teenager with no money and no means. Now I was a semi-adult, free to explore America on my own terms, with a list of destinations so long I wondered how I would get to them all. I was racing against time, and my homebody parents had left me behind the starting line. Texas seemed a good point of departure, especially with a Lubbock native who knew all the best ways to leave.

This was my first road trip. I don't remember much about the car except that it had manual transmission, so I did not know how to drive it. This suited me fine, as it left me free to gaze out the window. I was put in charge of maps, which were bound in a battered atlas kept in the trunk. I flipped through them, noting with envy past trips marked with a highlighter, cross-country drives taken so casually. Our route to New Mexico was laid out in high-lighter, a future only we could see.

Like pre-9/11 air travel, road trips without GPS or cell phones are something I only vaguely remember. They feel improbable, like something I did in a dream, with dream logic I can no longer decode. I was twenty-one at the dawn of the twenty-first century, too young to grasp what I was about to lose. I have spent my adult life watching my countrymen trade freedom for security, at first on command from the government after 9/11 and then through semi-voluntary submission, as smartphones evolved from a luxury to a convenience to an invasive requirement.

In 1998, it was easy to disappear, a prospect that then seemed scary but now seems both liberating and impossible. You can no longer get off the grid. The grid is a Google Map attached to your phone and tracking your life. If we had been told in 1998 that we would be stalked by digital devices and photographed by strang-ers, we would have protested in indignation. If we had been told we would announce our locations and real names and plans to the world of our own volition, we would assume future overlords had brainwashed us. We did not know that the surveillance lore of our beloved *X Files* would become the guiding precepts of the twenty-first century. Now everyone works for the men in black, even if they don't know it.

My boyfriend had devised a route that took us northwest through New Mexico and then south, saving Roswell for last. I agreed it was a good idea to work in some tourism before our extraterrestrial abduction. He and I broke up not long after this road trip, but I appreciate that he shared my inane goals because they were what led me to Route 66.

He told me we would drive north through the panhandle. I asked what a panhandle was and he explained it was a land mass of oil fields and dirt farms strung together by telephone wire. He said that there are two types of Texas small-town names: obvious truths (Plainview) and obvious lies (Happy). We passed them both before arriving two hours later in Amarillo, the first Route 66 city I visited, one I would revisit for decades to come.

Amarillo looked like a strip mall and smelled like a rendering plant. But I was promised wonder around the bend. He turned right and pulled over on a frontage road near an open field.

We had reached arguably the most legendary site of Route 66: Cadillac Ranch. Though technically not on Route 66, Cadillac Ranch checks all the boxes: tacky and poignant, ridiculous and gigantic, beautiful thanks to the eyes—and spray paint—of its beholders. The site consists of ten Cadillacs partially submerged nose-first in the ground at the same angle of the pyramids of Giza. The Cadillacs were placed there in 1974 as a public art installation by a hippie collective called Ant Farm, making them buried longer than they had been driven. The year 1974 was when American wages had begun to fall and American auto manufacturing had begun to decline, never to recover, though the creators could not have known that then.[2] They were just making art, an American Stonehenge on the Texas plains, funded by an eccentric oil baron and a band of beautiful freaks.

It is easy to write pretentious ruminations on Cadillac Ranch— that it symbolizes a half-dead American dream or the peril of fossil fuels or the expendability of luxury objects, all of which I just made up—but it is more fun to color giant cars with spray paint, which is what I actually did.

The glory of Cadillac Ranch is that it is a participatory project. It stays the same by always changing. There are free cans of spray paint at the site, and visitors are encouraged to leave their marks on the cars, knowing they will soon be painted over by others lured by rainbow tailfins from the road. I have visited Cadillac Ranch every decade of my adulthood: as a nineteen-year-old far from home for the first time, as a married woman in my twenties, as the mother of two young children in my thirties, as the mother of two teenagers in my forties. I changed, and Cadillac Ranch changed too, but in a way that feels comforting, different on the surface but recognizable at the roots.

"The cars look like a family," my son said when I took him there when he was six, and though his rumination was inspired by a Pixar cartoon, I could not help but agree. Cars from different generations lined up like a family photo, decades of decay offset by layers of color and words. Everything changed around them, but they stayed together because that's what families do.

I don't remember what I wrote on Cadillac Ranch in 1998. I don't remember much about the drive that night into New Mexico other than how astonishing everything my Texan boyfriend took for granted was—the emptiness of the open road, the shocking visibility of the stars, how the desert brush lay so low you could see the plains give way to hills and the hills to mesas and mesas to mountains, the distance never leaving you, the sunset receiving you, the possibilities never-ending.

I still do not take these sights for granted. I keep waiting for a moment when the landscape of America will seem less remarkable, but it has not come. Maybe it is because I travel with children, and when you have children, you view the world through fresh eyes. Maybe it's because over my adult life America changed from a land of mystery into one where you can see everything with ease, but through a screen, images decontextualized until they are devoid of meaning.

Every subject I wondered about as a teenager has been investigated but in a way that makes the questions seem pointless and the answers cheap. Maybe it's because when reality is under assault, the firsthand view matters more—a reprieve from the automated and algorithmic, the letdowns and lies. Or maybe it's because over twenty-five years, so much was stolen so fast that taking even one thing for granted feels like a luxury we cannot afford.

It is March 2007, and I am driving down Route 66, six months pregnant with my first child. My husband and I want one last trip before our independence ends. We have been warned that the good times are over, but we do not know yet that we will treat parenting like we treat marriage: with irreverence and an endless quest for small good things. We spent our childless years traveling around the United States and the world, breaking backpacks and stretching dollars. Now we are traveling alone together for the final time, with fifteen hundred miles to go until we hit the Grand Canyon. We know the best way to get to Arizona from St. Louis is Route 66. We know this because the song told us so.

The song, "(Get Your Kicks on) Route 66," was popularized by Chuck Berry, a St. Louis native who was one of the few singers to have stayed in the city after getting rich enough to get out. A mile from my home, there is a statue of a young Berry grinning and playing guitar. The statue is on the Walk of Fame, a sidewalk covered in brass stars honoring famous St. Louisans, most of whom left and did not look back: T. S. Eliot, Tina Turner, Tennessee Williams. But Chuck Berry remained, and St. Louis made the most of him. His statue sits across the street from a rock 'n' roll–themed restaurant, Blueberry Hill, where he popped in to play shows well into his eighties. Berry died in a mansion in the suburbs, miles away from his childhood home in an impoverished part of the city.

Berry's 1961 version of "Route 66" was a cover of a 1946 hit by Nat King Cole. The song celebrates the highway by listing the towns you would drive through, some of which were famous, some of which were obscure but completed the rhyme, all of which became legendary in verse. I am a sucker for any song that name-checks American towns regardless of whether it is logical or good. It is debatable whether "Route 66" is either, but we belt it out every time.

Even as they lauded Route 66, neither Cole nor Berry could drive the celebrated road with ease. During its peak, Route 66 was filled with sundown towns and motels announcing that they served only white people. Route 66 passed through cities with histories of mob attacks on Black Americans, like Tulsa, Oklahoma, and Ku Klux Klan strongholds like Springfield, Missouri.[3] Route 66 sites that did not discriminate were listed in the Green Book, a compilation of safe harbors for Black Americans traveling in the Jim Crow era.

Route 66 was no more racist than other highways. But like everything else in America, its pretense of freedom for all was a myth.

At the height of Berry's popularity in 1959, a time when he was gaining a large audience of white fans, he was arrested for allegedly transporting an Apache teenager across state lines "for immoral purposes."[4] After a two-week trial with an all-white jury, Berry was sentenced to five years in prison. This was reduced to three years and then to a year and a half as his lawyers continued to appeal due to racist comments from the judge.[5] In 1961, as he received his three-year sentence, "Route 66" became a radio hit. Berry was singing about the freedom of the open road in a country whose power brokers found his popularity so threatening they sought to physically constrain him.

Everyone who drove Route 66 in its heyday is now dead: rich white people driving it in freedom, poor Black people driving it in fear, Black singers who turned a highway into a dreamland for middle-class white families seeking road trip adventure. Those drivers are gone: Route 66's glory days were so long ago that collective memory of them is based on myth and marketing, not direct experience.

The road's ghosts of memory also include the white people who drove it in misery—like the climate refugees of the Oklahoma Dust Bowl—and the Native Americans trapped on reservations over which Route 66 was built. Route 66 overlaps parts of the Trail of Tears, the path of forced exile that resulted in the deaths of thousands of Indigenous Americans and the expulsion of tens of thousands more. In a perverse inversion, a mythical ideal of the American Indian became part of Route 66 iconography, with white-owned concrete teepees dotting a road built on stolen land.

We remember Route 66 like we remember the American Dream: a passageway of promise for prior generations. Promises that some insist were real and others condemn as traps meant to keep free thinkers on the straight and narrow, never to truly arrive. Like the American Dream, Route 66 marketed the notion that you could come from anywhere and make yourself anyone, that if you keep going the journey pays off. That the past is something you escape instead of relentlessly reencounter. By the 1990s, an era when 1950s icons like Elvis and Marilyn Monroe were revived in commercial nostalgia, Route 66 had transcended the mythology around it, becoming as contradictory and self-aggrandizing as America itself.

It is a strange thing to wander the faulty memory of a faded dream, but that is what it feels like to drive Route 66. The road is lined with rotting monuments and broken into detours—but what's still there is so revealing, you hope it remains. You need it to stay because America likes to pave over its lies, and you want proof of what happened. To show your children the roots of the fables spun to cover the damage done, to see that alongside the huckster totems there are relics of sincere belief—from people who had faith in America whether they should have or not.

If Route 66 in the twentieth century was the American Dream, Route 66 in the twenty-first is the American Reality. One century into its existence, it has become an honest road. It is full of bombast and tragedy, but its sin and joys have been laid plain. You can't be a mean liar in a place that is equal parts bravado and ruin. You can only be a funny one or a sad one, desperate for a friend. Route 66 invites you to join in, to leave your mark, to be a fellow traveler. It is a strange thing in America to feel wanted like that.

We set out in 2007 in what my husband called "the rolling couch": my grandfather's 1997 gray Buick LeSabre that was given to me after he died. It was what a seventy-five-year-old man would find desirable in an automobile: large, reliable, and made in the USA. This was an old man car for an old man road.

My paternal grandfather had died of cancer in April 2006. My maternal grandmother had died of Parkinson's disease in January 2007. When I'd seen my grandma for the final time, in December 2006, I'd told her she was about to become a great-grandmother. She touched my pregnant belly, her shaking hands struggling to hold steady as she looked at me, her face frozen from Parkinson's but tears of joy shining in her eyes. I like to think that she and my daughter connected in that moment, that they met each other after all.

I named my daughter after her and after my paternal grandmother, who had died suddenly in 2003, a month before my wedding. We had been very close, and I had never faced such deep and personal loss. On my honeymoon, I was still overwhelmed with grief but found relief came with ceaseless motion: *as long as I keep moving, I can bear the pain*.

It wasn't that I didn't want to think about it. I went to Często-chowa, Poland, to light a candle for her at the pilgrimage site for which her Connecticut church was named, a gesture my sensible grandma, who never left the United States, would have found silly had she lived to see it. I could hear her in my head, admonishing me to not make a fuss, to be practical about money and time, but it was too late: I was on the run.

My husband and I kept moving and moving, finding the cheapest places in the cheapest countries, exploring Eastern Europe from Lithuania all the way down to Turkey, where our money ran out and we took jobs teaching English in Istanbul. We did not want to go back to the United States. We were fleeing the horror of 9/11, which we had both covered for two years at our jobs at the *New York Daily News*, and I was fleeing the pain of a loss I did not know how to process. I was dodging death and looking for ghosts because I did not know another way to survive.

In March 2007, I was mourning a grandmother yet again, but now I was mourning while pregnant. Along with the grief came joy that my life would soon change forever, that a new life would fill the void in my family and in my heart. The first trimester of pregnancy had been fascinating in a sci-fi sort of way, like I had finally lived my dream of being abducted by an alien, only it was growing inside of me. When I wasn't vomiting, I was craving, and when I wasn't craving, I was asleep. The second trimester came with the added intrigue of tiny hands and feet pounding on my internal organs. My ob-gyn told me my daughter was the most active baby he had ever encountered—until I got pregnant with my son, who was so wild in the womb he made my daughter seem staid.

I was in pain but I couldn't blame them. They needed to keep moving, just like me.

In March 2007, my husband and I had lived in Missouri for less than a year and hadn't yet driven southwest through the state.

Everything was new, and I was paying attention because when you travel while pregnant you constantly evaluate the conditions of the country your child will inhabit.

In 2007, this was a futile endeavor: our region would soon be decimated by the Great Recession. We were driving economically battered terrain—the Missouri Ozarks, Oklahoma, the Texas panhandle, rural New Mexico—headed for a lethal blow. We got one last glimpse of the Before Times, when there was still hope things could get better, before "I'm a bitter gun owner clinging to my religion" became the most popular bumper sticker on the road and empty office buildings and malls joined the old-time ruins of Route 66.

We planned the trip with a combination of printouts from Google Maps and library books. There were no smartphones and we did not check email on the road. We could have been found—we had flip phones—but what kind of jerk would call a couple on vacation? We were not expected to do work or to share our journey with strangers. We took photos with a digital camera, over one hundred of them, which seemed an incredible and indulgent amount, and never showed them to anyone. We were approaching the end of the analog age and the mindset that went with it. We were still the observers instead of the watched.

In 2007, my husband and I considered ourselves to be living in grim times—the Iraq War lies, the color-charted pseudo-terror—but we never questioned whether America would survive. If anything, America seemed too strong, too powerful: cruelly protective of itself at the expense of the world. We did not know we lived in a bubble country set to pop. We did not know that the abuses our government levied against other countries would soon be aimed at all Americans but for a minuscule elite. We did not know what methods they would use to market the controlled demolition of our homeland as normal and even desirable.

We knew it would involve weaponizing religion for social control: the signs were all around us. But we could no longer decipher what signs to take seriously because "holy shit" had long been the motto of our slice of America. The religious right had converted heartland anxiety into an end-times marketing scheme. After too many public proclamations of salvation and doom, a motorist starts to lose discernment about whether true danger lurks round the bend. Sometimes a sign of the apocalypse is just a sign of the apocalypse, and sometimes it means something bad.

My husband and I were used to evangelical monuments as a pervasive presence. Before Missouri but after New York, we lived in southern Indiana, where the warnings of the religious right faded into the landscape with passive ubiquity, like corn.

During the Bush years, roadside warnings of our hell-bound future grew larger and longer, much like American debt and American wars. Driving west, we would pass the giant cross of Effingham, Illinois, made of steel and cement but resembling 198 feet of aluminum siding, like someone went to Home Depot and got a little too excited. For seventeen years, Effingham had the largest cross in the United States, until it was outdone by a cross near Branson built in 2018, a 220-foot white behemoth studded with blue tears signifying grace and beacon lights signifying compliance with Federal Aviation Administration regulations.

If you pass Branson from Highway 55 in the south, you will see the giant cross on the left and an exit sign on the right, aligned in perfect parallel.

Route 66 is the land of the World's Largest Objects, and religion is no exception. They go hand in hand, literally, which is how in 2007 we ended up seeing competing versions of the World's Largest Praying Hands.

The first was in Webb City, a small town in southwest Missouri nicknamed Flag City for its Old Glory enthusiasm. Its World's Largest Praying Hands are thirty-two feet tall and weigh more than twenty-two thousand pounds and are surrounded by American flags. Like Cadillac Ranch, the hands were created in 1974—a big year for big art on Route 66—by a twenty-one-year-old Webb City artist named Jack Dawson, who loaded his titanic creation on a flatbed truck and deposited it on a hilltop that overlooks the town. Dawson said that he made the sculpture in response to the turmoil of the 1960s and as "an everlasting reminder to the passing public to stop and pray."

There is a photo of me in 2007 in front of Webb City's giant praying hands, visibly pregnant, imitating the pose and grinning at the camera. I am smiling because I am happy: I am on the road with the man I love, and I have no idea that fifteen years later, pregnant women making the same trip will live in fear of facing complications in Missouri because the *Roe* repeal has made doctors afraid to treat them.[6] I am smiling because the symbolic merger of church and state feels like a curiosity instead of an omen. I am smiling because I like giant objects and I do not oppose the idea of the sculpture, since prayer is personal, and I am naive enough to believe it will stay that way. I am smiling because I assume my body could not become state property and that if a court were to proclaim it so, people would protest and protect me. I am smiling because I cannot see what is before my own eyes.

From Webb City we left Missouri and crossed into Oklahoma. We stopped in Vinita and ate at the World's Largest McDonald's— my preferred shrine—then went to Tulsa to see the other pair of the World's Largest Praying Hands and decide which was better. We found the rival hands at the Christian fundamentalist Oral Roberts University: thirty feet of thirty tons of bronze so huge it can be spotted from a plane.

The hands were originally laid in front of a faith-healing hospital, towering 640 feet tall. That's about 300 feet shorter than Jesus, according to televangelist Oral Roberts. In 1977, Roberts claimed that a 900-foot Jesus appeared to him in a dream and told him to build the center, though Jesus apparently did not tell him how to avoid getting sued for using that center to commit $15 million of fraud. After Roberts lost the fraud lawsuit in 1988, the giant praying hands were moved to the university entrance, and the City of Faith tower became a debt collection agency.

We decided Webb City had the superior World's Largest Praying Hands and gave them a high five on the way home. We may have been sinners, but we picked ourselves a winner: Oral Roberts University was sued for fraud again a few months after our visit.[7]

I have lived in or near the Bible Belt for twenty years, and I have yet to be converted by a highway monument, but I get the appeal. There is something touching about the ones that are not overly proselytizing or riddled with crime, that are simply super-sized pillars of devotion—that is, until you remember you are under attack by fanatics by virtue of your gender or your sexuality or your refusal to submit to the government's pretend piety. As one of the targeted, I understand the danger, but I can still divorce myself from their intent and let the spirit fill me, the same way I do in respected American shrines, the ones I never get questioned for visiting, like the churches of New Orleans or Santa Fe built by bloodthirsty colonizers and conquistadors. I know what's up when people frown on my roadside reliquaries because it's the same look I get when I return from a monster truck rally. My real sin, for which there can be no absolution, is having bad taste.

Hate the sin, love the sinner, treasure the World's Largest Objects. I love seeing a stoned-looking Wheatfield Jesus peep out from a highway billboard in Colby, Kansas. I enjoy waving at the colossal Christ of the Ozarks lit up in the mountains across from a haunted hotel in Eureka Springs, Arkansas. I like that I was tricked into reading Bible verses in Casey, Illinois, a cheat town of custom-made World's Largest Objects (pencil, wind chimes, birdcage, golf tee, pitchfork) displayed on one street. It was a thrill to walk inside the World's Largest Mailbox and be informed by a sign on the wall that I was not a mere tourist but a "letter from Christ (2 Corinthians 3:2–3)" marked for priority delivery. Who knew?!

I should not like these hallowed and hollow roads, but I do. That these sights gave solace to generations of strangers, for whatever reason, is worth something. But my real source of comfort is not that of a convert or a cleric: it's instinct. It's the logical conclusion that enormous problems require enormous symbolic displays, because that is American logic, the logic that raised me, the logic that trades facts for feelings, the logic that fills arenas, the logic that blinds us to crimes, the logic that grins before it bites you, the logic of the World's Greatest Salvation and the World's Worst Sinner and the World's Biggest American Dream and the World's Best American Bullshit and of the pilgrims who prostrate themselves on highway rest stops because they are so *tired*, so tired that they yearn for giant hands to hold them and a gleaming cross to guide them and a sign that they still have a home in the broken-promise land, and what is more American than an oversize object looming lonesome by the road, held together by money and faith?

We spent the rest of the 2007 trip following the Chuck Berry road map—going through St. Louie; Joplin, Missouri; Oklahoma City looking oh so pretty (*as long as I stopped thinking about the bomb*); Amarillo, where I spray-painted Cadillac Ranch again and my husband tried to eat a seventy-two-ounce steak so it would be free; Gallup, New Mexico, where Ronald Reagan smirked at me from a line of autographed portraits of long-dead Western stars in the El Rancho Hotel; the rhyme-scheme tagalong town of Winona; and Flagstaff, Arizona, from where we departed for the Grand Canyon. We also drove the 1920s stretch of Route 66 to Santa Fe, where I surrendered my fear that buying anything for a baby jinxes a pregnancy.

Santa Fe is so stunning that it replaces scary old superstitions with soothing new ones, smothering your psyche with a haze of incense and piñon smoke. In a back-alley toy store, I bought a mobile and let myself imagine my daughter lying in her crib, gazing up and smiling. The mourning cleared: I let myself imagine my daughter as real. My dream of her as a future person no longer felt like hubris but faith.

My 2007 trip down the Mother Road was overwhelmed by my status as a mother-to-be. The future seemed as overwhelming as the Grand Canyon that I gazed upon rapturously before seeking out a place to vomit. Just like Jack Kerouac did, when he was on the road.

Icons of the American road trip are almost always men: the Kerouacs and Steinbecks and Ken Keseys and Hunter S. Thompsons and others who took wild rides down new avenues of American pseudo-liberation once the Mother Road had broken down. There are exceptions—photographer Dorothea Lange, who drove Route 66 to document the Great Depression, for example—but the female American road trip is usually a tragedy and usually fiction. Thelma and Louise plunging into a canyon, Janet Leigh heading for the Bates Motel. The consummate depiction, the 1960 *Twilight Zone* episode "The Hitchhiker," is about a woman who drives a Route 66–style highway cross-country by herself without realizing she had died at the start. Some of the most famous road trip anthems are written by women: Merle Haggard's "I'm a Lonesome Fugitive"— *I'm on the run, the highway is my home*—was written by country songwriter Liz Anderson, who never could have driven that high-way alone in peace.

I have driven Route 66 alone many times, but close to St. Louis. The long journey has always been a family affair. The long journey has always felt like a dark reunion, with old bridges and monuments greeting me in altered states, warning of impending collapse, edifices inseparable from the psychic toll of bringing new life into a dying land. The Mother Road is scarred like a C-section no one bothered to stitch up right.

That is why, despite all the men, I feel like the road is mine.

Motherhood was supposed to end my freedom, but it never felt like that. This is in part because the older I got, the more I realized I had never been that free in the first place and was likely to become less so in the future. But it was mostly because once my children were older, I decided to take them along. I wanted them to see America before it ended, and I wanted them to see it through their own eyes, not my recollections.

I was worried that America's national parks and monuments would be destroyed before they had the chance to visit them. This was not a new worry, but it was accelerated by Trump, who kicked off his presidency by eliminating federal protection for the Bears Ears and Grand Escalante monuments in Utah, the largest reduction of national landmarks in American history, and an attack on treasured Native American sites. (President Biden restored the protections in 2021.)

By 2017, I was wondering if the government would annihilate America's natural beauty before climate change took its final shot. I was in mourning, not for my family as before but for my country. When I worked at the *New York Daily News*, I learned that newspapers write the obituaries of ailing celebrities in advance. I wondered if they should start doing that for nations.

The biggest obstacle to traveling with kids was money. We

barely left Missouri between 2007 and 2017. But in fall 2016, my kids started kindergarten and fourth grade. With both of them in school, I started working full time, and we became a two-income family, achieving fiscal stability just in time for the political apocalypse. I had spent my career studying authoritarian kleptocracies in the former Soviet Union. In 2016 I continued that work, documenting the networks of corruption and organized crime that sustain dictatorships. But now I was documenting it in my own country and getting death threats for my efforts. By spring 2017 I was exhausted.

"I need a break," I told my husband, and he nodded. "I need a break from the mafia," I clarified, and his eyes turned that numb, futureless color a man gets when his wife becomes a target for a living.

I told him I wanted to go where nobody could find me. A place where I could mourn America while standing in awe of it, and no one could see my face. I wanted a road that was not inviting or cell-phone friendly: a hokum terrain that nobody with access to an oligarch yacht would deign to visit. It also had to be child-friendly and cheap and drivable from Missouri.

"Route 66?" he said, and I said of course.

We decided to retrace the road trip we had made a decade before, in abbreviated form, following Route 66 to New Mexico and back. This was in part to cut costs and in part to provide clarity to questions my six-year-old was asking like "Did Blay Jobert Boppendeimer feel bad when he created Godzilla?"—but most of all because New Mexico had never let me down.

New Mexico is a state I save for when things are very awful or very anxious, which means I should have moved there permanently around 2001, but that would have ruined the appeal. Missouri has my heart, but New Mexico has a piece of my soul. I worry that if I visit too much it will betray me, so I take no chances. Reprieve is a luminously temporary condition, one that dissolves if you experience it too long.

We set out for Route 66 on the first day of the kids' spring break, establishing a trail of sights marking our progress through the Ozarks: the giant water tower labeled BOURBON in the town of Bourbon; the rival American flag stores trying to out-jingo each other in the town of St. James; the hairpin bridge off Teardrop Road in the town of Devil's Elbow; and the Uranus Fudge Factory, where we browsed rows of penny candy and deadly weapons and old-school novelties and modern-day moonshine before purchasing a magnet supporting the Uranus #2 Fudge Packer's Union. Uranus is a fake town whose economy rests entirely on scatological jokes. Its "mayor," Louie Keen, owns all the attractions as well as the local newspaper, the *Uranus Examiner*, in which he publishes campaign missives while posed in an American flag jacket waving a banner that says MUGA.

"Thank you for picking Uranus!" the storekeepers said cheerfully as we left. We shouted back that we loved Uranus but didn't want to get stuck there. We headed for our car, which was parked equidistant from a neon sign of a dinosaur eating a UFO and a large antipornography billboard erected by the Pulaski County Christian Ministerial Alliance. Behind us, the World's Largest Belt Buckle glistened in the sun.

"This trip is working. I am off the grid," I told my husband as we hit the road. "Because no one can find me in Uranus!" He rolled his eyes as the kids howled in the back seat.

We continued on Route 66 until we reached the state line, where it was time to get lunch. Having accidentally bypassed the only Steak 'n Shake on the national historic registry in Springfield, we stopped in Joplin for barbecue and pie. Our meal came with sweet tea as the default beverage—the surest sign a person has entered the South.

The restaurant was near the apartment of Bonnie Parker and Clyde Barrow, the outlaw couple who terrorized and transfixed America in the 1930s. After lunch, we drove to their hideout.

"Why are we at this boring place?" asked my daughter. It was a two-story beige home, contemporary and bland.

"Because famous people lived here."

"What'd they do?"

"They rob banks!" my husband said, and the movie quote hung in the air, over their heads.

"What, you like robbers now?"

"This is a historic house," I explained. "In the 1920s and 1930s, when alcohol was illegal and people were poor and crime was every-where, gangsters ran from the police on Route 66. Bonnie and Clyde, John Dillinger—they all came through here. They were all over the news; during the Great Depression, everyone wanted to read about them. It's how regular people stayed entertained."

My children stared at me.

"Entertained," said my daughter slowly, reading the plaque in front of the house. "This sign says they killed people."

"Yes. . . ."

"Why didn't anyone stop them?" asked my son.

"They didn't get away with it in the end," I said, deciding to omit the grisly details of that ending. "They got caught because they couldn't stop taking pictures of themselves. They left crime spree selfies in this house, and that's how the police identified them."

The crime scene selfie explanation made innate sense to my children in a way that chilled me to the bone. The house seemed ominous—too modern, too familiar. We found out later that the murder lair was a part-time Airbnb. When my daughter pressed me on why Americans made folk heroes out of Bonnie and Clyde, who had killed two men on the spot where we stood, I had a hard time explaining—not because I didn't know but because I did not want to tell. I was a voyeur, guilty as the rest.

Bonnie and Clyde are a classic American example of criminal culture marketed as counterculture, of equal interest to Hollywood and the heartland. The pop version of Bonnie and Clyde is what most folks imagine when they hear the names, revived in the 1960s in everything from country music ballads to the glamorous 1967 *Bonnie and Clyde* movie. But the real Parker was a poet, and I was standing in front of the house where her most famous poem was found. It was called "Suicide Sal," and it is a parable of life on the run in a country that hangs you out to dry.

> The "gang" hired a couple of lawyers,
> The best "fixers" in any man's town,
> But it takes more than lawyers and money
> When Uncle Sam starts "shaking you down."[8]

"Suicide Sal" is the kind of poem that drains your morality line by line: the musings of a real-life murderess with a talent for martyrdom. Police who found the poem gave it to the press, who published it, to the thrill of Great Depression readers hungry for an antihero. The poem is a reminder that criminal impunity was always an American dream and the media its faithful partner. Parker, a twenty-three-year-old Texan, would never get impunity in life: she had been born too poor for that. But she won it in death, shot by police with Barrow in their getaway car. She had the posthumous impunity of blood and romance that elevates a woman when it is too late to matter. She is an icon of the doomed female road trip, a roadside attraction I failed to resist.

I had turned my phone off, seeking a break from the news, but I needed it to map the route to Oklahoma. It lurched to life with headline alerts about the president's latest threats and bribes and

bouts of self-pity. One of the tamer stories alleged that the home
of Trump's national security advisor Steve Bannon had a hot tub
full of acid, the kind that dissolves bodies, but no one was going to
do anything about it but savor the tabloid tale.[9]

  The 1930s had never left: criminals posing as aggrieved patriots, Uncle Sam high-fiving fixers and thieves, crime spree selfies
all around. It is easier to pretend that the all-American celebrity
criminal is a modern icon, a monster you dodge when you detour
into the past. But escape is a promise no road can keep. There's a
hitchhiker on the highway of the mind, and it is your conscience
flagging you down.

  I watched the scenery fly by, the same scenery Parker had seen
from her car as she'd fled Joplin. My husband was behind the
wheel, my kids were buckled in the back, and I was a woman on
the road in a sick country, trying to keep my distance. That's what
these trips boil down to sometimes, a desire to keep my distance:
I want to grab a distance and make it mine, reserve it for me and
me alone. I want to delineate its terms and narrow its byroads, as if
the logic of my heart were any less wild than the logic of my land,
as if the two had not fused long ago.

  I wanted to keep my distance and disappear inside. But my
children were here, and I could not take them with me, and I
could never leave them behind. We crossed the border together,
their company a redemption I treasured but felt I did not deserve.

We drove on through Oklahoma, a state of crystal-clear streams
and rocks shaped like roses that most people never see because
they stay trapped on the interstate and its flat succession of truck
stops and casinos. There were places I wanted to see on Oklahoma's Route 66, but we skipped them to make it to Amarillo by
night, deciding to show the kids a good time after our Bonnie and

Clyde debacle. In Shamrock, Texas, a town just past the Oklahoma border, we visited the old-fashioned gas station that was an
inspiration for the movie *Cars*. The kids were overjoyed: here was
an American fantasy they recognized. Now they, too, could bask
in a memory of a Route 66 no one alive could remember.

Wind turbines spun like pinwheels of pink dust as we drove
through panhandle pastures under the setting sun. Upon entering
Amarillo, a BIG TEXAN COWBOY sign announced we were approaching the Big Texan Steak Ranch, the Route 66 tourist trap where
my husband had failed to eat a seventy-two-ounce steak a decade
before and therefore lived to tell the tale. My kids were ushered to
their seats by a waiter dressed like a ranch hand and served tiny
steaks with tiny Texas flags affixed to them inside straw cowboy
hat bowls, which they flipped over and wore on their heads when
they were done.

The Big Texan is a supersized version of my favorite thing
about restaurants in Texas, which is their ceaseless need to remind
you that you are in Texas. Walls adorned with maps and longhorn
skulls and cowhide place mats and Texas-shaped everything because there is no object that cannot or should not be molded into
the glorious shape of Texas.

This was my children's first trip to Texas. They would return
many times after my sister moved to Dallas, and we would stay at
her house, where she made the kids waffles with her Texas-shaped
waffle iron and served them on Texas-shaped plates, because she
had grown a Texas-shaped brain. But in 2017, Texas was new
territory.

Since my children grew up in Missouri, Texas was their first
encounter with state pride. Since they were excited to be there,
we did not explain the dark side of Texas pride—the militias, the
secessionists, the things people would rather you not remember
about the Alamo—and let them revel in Good Texas, because

Good Texas is real too. The Texas of strange places and friendly strangers and boundless dreams and skies, the Texas of Texans who deserve better than the vicious laws of soulless politicians encircling them like barbed wire. The diverse and complicated Texas I would call a microcosm of America except everyone knows Texas is bigger than all the United States combined, come on now.

In the morning, we spray-painted Cadillac Ranch under the rising sun. We were almost done with Texas save one more stop: a brief trip to Palo Duro Canyon, the second largest canyon in the United States, a canyon we would visit four years later under very different circumstances.

But it was still 2017, a year that felt apocalyptic at the time and now seems innocent by comparison. Palo Duro loomed before us, wild and free. My daughter scrambled up the canyon ledge and grinned at us from inside a red rock cave. My son leaped across orange boulders, his *Minecraft* jacket zipped over his face like a ninja. The Texas wind whipped us on that frigid plain, but we didn't mind.

We had descended into a beautiful hell, a hell of our choosing. If the world was going to end, make it end like this, in crags we could climb and cling to. If the earth was to swallow us, let it swallow us like this, in a fire and brimstone playground, in the straightforward mercilessness and merciful straightforwardness of a land that does not lie.

We wanted more time, but we had to go. I promised the kids we would come back someday. We crawled out of the canyon and into the car, covered in red dust. We drove back to Route 66 and passed through Glenrio, a border town that belongs to both Texas and New Mexico and to neither because it is a ghost town. Graffiti covered its few remaining buildings, telling us in English and Spanish ominous tales of its demise.

Route 66 is full of ghost towns or ghost towns in progress—

particularly in New Mexico, the long and bloody history of which
sent a diverse array of folks to flight. We ate breakfast in Tucumcari, a legendary Route 66 town where the billboards are blanker
and the neon dimmer every time I go. But I love it because there
are no replications, and I mourn it for the same reason. I dread the
day I drive through Tucumcari and see only ghosts.

The landscape became lusher and rockier as we went west. My
children gasped when snowcapped mountains appeared on the
desert horizon. They had never seen a mountain, or a desert, or a
canyon. They were seeing everything for the first time all at once,
as I had in 1998. I told them, as we departed Route 66, that the best
was yet to come.

In 2017, I toured the Manhattan Project site in Los Alamos with
a nine-year-old and a six-year-old in tow. Technically, it took us
three days to get there, but the real journey took thirty years.

When I was a child, my family would take one week of vacation. It was always the same place: a rented cottage we shared
with another family near a Massachusetts beach, where my parents would spend every day lounging in the sun. My memories
are mostly of restless misadventures, of being eight and seeing if
I could float on a tube to another town (I could, to everyone's dismay); of being ten and begging my mother to get me a library
card so I could have a more exciting vacation inside my mind. But
my fondest memory is the year my father decided to play twenty
questions with us in the car. He had never participated because
he rarely spoke, which is an impediment to playing games with
small children.

"I've got a good one," my dad said, "probably too easy, though."
I was seven years old; my sister was six.

"I know I'll get it," I announced. I had an advantage, I figured, because I had paid attention the few other times my father had spoken at length, which tended to involve tales of random historical trivia: Lincoln and Kennedy both being elected president in a year ending in '60 with a southern vice president named Johnson; Calvin "Silent Cal" Coolidge being challenged to say more than two words and responding, "You lose." I used to pretend the Coolidge story was my father making an autobiographical analogy, explaining his reluctance to converse. Family life often felt like a guessing game, and I welcomed a real one.

We cataloged the clues: male, dead, white, scientist, famous in the midtwentieth century, but not Albert Einstein. We were at an impasse.

"Just tell them," my mom said. "This is getting boring." She didn't know either.

"It's easy," my dad repeated, "they'll get it. They can have extra questions, but they won't need them."

We kept trying, throwing out the names of every famous person we knew, figuring someone was freelancing some science on the side. We kept going for an hour, our curiosity at a fever pitch, until my mother declared the game over.

"Well, that's too bad," said my dad. "I think you would have gotten it with a few more tries. It's J. Robert Oppenheimer."

"Who?!" my sister and I yelled as my mother said, "They're in first and third grade!"

"You don't know who J. Robert Oppenheimer is?" said my dad, genuinely incredulous.

"No!"

"How can you not know who J. Robert Oppenheimer is?"

"Because they're busy learning how to read cursive and add!" shouted my mom.

I asked who J. Robert Oppenheimer was, and my father proceeded to tell an unusually long story incorporating World War II,

Japan's military strategy, moral debates over nuclear power, and the Manhattan Project laboratories.

"Six," my mom said, pointing at my sister, whose eyes had glazed over around the first mention of Trinity, "and seven!" She pointed at me, but I was interested. This was the most horrifying story I had ever heard.

For decades, "J. Robert Oppenheimer" became an inside joke in my family for my dad's inability to come up with appropriate conversation. ("I still don't understand why you didn't get it," my dad would reply, still not getting it.) The details of the Manhattan Project became garbled in my third-grade mind, but what I had learned for sure is that real history is far more interesting than the watered-down version we got in school. This basic truth is now a matter of contentious debate for my children's generation, who grew up watching a widespread push for historical accuracy followed by a backlash codified in law. They live in an America of legislators telling them that discussing abuse is worse than experiencing it.

Neither of my parents had any sense of what constituted a normal topic for children. My mother's love of celebrity scandals and her *SPY* magazine subscription were why I knew Donald Trump's criminal history by the age of ten. She was my gossip buddy while my dad hardly spoke. But when I asked them about history or current events, they did not sugarcoat anything. They never would have dreamed of keeping me away from books. We had few rules in our house, but one was that I could stay up as late as I wanted—as long as I was reading. I am grateful for their willingness to let me explore my interests—or their Boomer indifference to my Gen X self-reliance. It's a fine line.

I have never blown off a question from my children because talking things through—not proselytizing but talking and encouraging them to ask questions and keep investigating even after I have given my views—is the only way around the modern informational quagmire. The internet, with its decontextualized clickbait and algorithmically determined narratives, is one hellscape. Political attacks on intellectual freedom are another. It is getting harder to teach children about the historical antecedents of the very campaigns designed to constrain their knowledge.

Despite these challenges, helping them learn about the world has never felt like a burden. I love talking to kids about history because they ask more imaginative and honest questions than adults, and their innate morality has not yet been compromised by life.

And that is how we ended up road-tripping to Los Alamos. Both kids were interested in nuclear war because Trump was constantly threatening it. But my son had an alternate fascination, which derived from his obsession with Godzilla.

When my son was home sick from kindergarten, I felt so bad for him, I told him he could watch any movie he wanted. He chose a Japanese-language Godzilla flick, and I agreed, only to realize he couldn't read the English subtitles. He cuddled next to me as I acted out every line, wearing myself out creating different voices for different panicked Japanese scientists. These are the parenting moments that drag on when they are happening but you would give anything to relive when they are gone.

"How did Godzilla become Godzilla?" he asked when the movie was over, and I said, "Well, that's a long story, and to really understand it, you need to know about J. Robert Oppenheimer. . . ."

My son listened to a history of atomic warfare that my husband and I would repeat for years to come, trying to answer his questions accurately but in a way that was not too terrifying and that also established, somewhat to my son's dismay, that Godzilla was not real. He was fascinated but appalled. My son had been to Harry Truman's house in Independence, Missouri, and he had trouble squaring the museum's image of Truman as a nice old man with the president who allowed over one hundred thousand innocent Japanese people to be incinerated. We all did.

"Do you think Harry Truman is bad?" he asked.

"I think what he did is very bad. How he ended up in a position to do it, and how much control he had over his actions, is complicated."

"Mommy," he started, then laughed, then stopped.

"What? You can tell me."

"That's the same thing you said about Godzilla."

We drove west along Route 66 toward Los Alamos, getting lost due to my refusal to enter the surveillance world of cell phones, detouring into the ghost town of Duran, where we wandered into an abandoned century-old general store covered in graffiti saying HELL WILL SAVE US and NIETZSCHE LIVES and GO HUG SOMEONE. We worked our way back to Clines Corners, where we stopped for gas at a Route 66 travel megaplaza and had our fortunes told by the Amazing Zoltar, a robot genie who lived inside a plastic box and told you your fate for a dollar.

Then we drove north, past Santa Fe, until we landed at the front door of J. Robert Oppenheimer.

The Manhattan Project was developed in one of New Mexico's most serene landscapes, a mesa of aspen and pine trees with air so fresh and cool it's like inhaling life itself. The government campus where scientists devised the capacity to annihilate the earth resembles a poet's retreat: quaint log cabins, gardens in the clouds. In the 1940s, the existence of the site was unknown even to neighboring locals, revealed only after its monsters were unleashed.

In front of the campus stands a statue of J. Robert Oppenheimer, clad in a fedora, hand on his chin, permanently frozen in thought. My son examined the statue as if looking for clues. My husband, who is a few years older than me, told the kids how he had spent elementary school waiting for nuclear war, unnerved by Ronald Reagan and the TV movie *The Day After*. I told them that unlike my husband or my parents, I had never worried about the bomb. The Cold War ended before I was a teenager. It was only in 2017 that I felt the threat of nuclear annihilation for the first time.

"So you had no nuclear war threats," noted my daughter, "and no intruder drills." *Intruder* was her school's euphemism for *shooter*.

"And we have *everything*!" said my son. He told me I was lucky. I hadn't felt lucky growing up—in the 1990s we had AIDS, crack, gangs—but I realized I was rare, that my microgeneration had an anomalous youth. My high school and college years were between the fall of the Soviet Union and 9/11, a period so calm it feels in retrospect like a contemptuous ruse, a mocking preparation for a peaceful future no power broker intended to give.

But the world my children had inherited was worse than anything I could have imagined. I look to history for perspective on how past generations handled obstacles and overcame them, but I cannot find a model for any generation being handed all the obstacles of the past at once.

"What's the opposite of *unprecedented*?" my son asked me in 2021, after hearing that word used in discussion of the global pandemic and the attempted coup and "worst ever" weather disasters and record mass shootings. "Because that's what I want. Is it *precedented*? Is *precedented* a real thing?"

Inside the Los Alamos History Museum, we saw exhibits about the history of the region and the nuclear scientists that covertly inhabited it, creating Fat Man and Little Boy, the nicknames for the bombs dropped on Nagasaki and Hiroshima. My daughter was surprised by the childish names for deadly weapons and shocked when I told her that the nickname for the suitcase carrying the nuclear codes is *the football*. She did not believe me when I said the current president had showed off the football (a satchel containing the nuclear codes) to rich guests in his Florida golf resort and that a guest posted selfies with the aide who carries the football on Facebook—state crime selfies, a presidential variation on Bonnie and Clyde.[10] But it was true.

"Is that normal?" she asked. I gave my standard response to that question, which is that we should ask less whether it is normal than whether it is right. There are too many things in US history that are both normal and wrong for normal to offer any reassurance.

My son asked me to show him more Oppenheimer stuff. We wandered the museum until I found a draft of Oppenheimer's October 1945 speech warning of apocalyptic horror if humanity did not learn from his actions. I told my son this speech was important and began to read it. Oppenheimer proclaimed that the people of the world must "unite, or they will perish." He noted that a "false sense of human history" could give baseless assurance to future generations that they were no longer in danger. But my son was distracted by a different quote.

"I am," he read slowly, sounding it out, "beco . . . what does this say?"

"'I am become Death, the destroyer of worlds,'" his sister read. They turned to me.

"In answer to your earlier question," I said to my son, "yes, Blay Jobert Boppendeimer felt bad for creating Godzilla." I took each of their hands and we walked out the museum door together, the mountain air hitting my lungs like a last gasp.

Santa Fe enveloped us like a dream. This is the trip I think about when I'm so sad I want to quit: my daughter at the Georgia O'Keeffe

Museum sitting cross-legged on the floor with a pad of paper and crayons, carefully copying the paintings hanging on the wall; my son climbing a ladder into an ancient Native American shelter in Bandelier National Monument and waving from a window; both kids thrilled by tableside guacamole and street art and ubiquitous Spanish and the sights and smells of a place both foreign and familiar. By chance we walked into the same toy store where I had bought my unborn daughter a mobile a decade before, and upon realizing it, I was overcome with relief that she was *real*, that we had survived, that I was lucky enough to have two children and to live in America, in *this* America, the good America. I let them each choose a toy, and we emerged from the alley into a plaza of adobe lit up by the bright cloudless blue of the sky, a dark, vivid blue that defied description, an abyss that stared back like heaven.

On the last day of the trip, we drove to Alamogordo. The kids had learned at the museum that this was the location of Trinity, the first nuclear test, but we had told them nothing more. We entered the White Sands Missile Range and watched the earth disappear into a sea of blankness, waves of white stretching for miles at each turn. We drove until we reached White Sands National Monument and found we were the first people to arrive. At the visitors' center, we rented four round sleds and navigated the infinite white until a field of towering dunes emerged. We climbed to the top and slid fast to the bottom, surrendering to the sway of the sand, tumbling into gypsum, laughing as we spit out the grains that fell into our mouths. My children grabbed their sleds and ran back up to do it again, and again, and again. We raced together and apart, and when I was done, I watched them for a while because they were happy, and it was a perfect day.

Then I turned and walked into the desert alone. I knew my husband could see me because I was dressed all in black, and I hoped in his heart he believed I would return. But I needed to be alone, I needed to feel it: that nothingness, that all-encompassing void, that wanted wasteland, that final freedom I had been seeking for so long. I walked until I could see nothing and nothing could see me, and I lifted my head to the sun, a sun I wanted to blind me so that I would see nothing forever. I turned as blank as the sand as I walked, and the color returned to me only when I came back to them, to the song of my daughter's laughter, to the echo of my son's call, to the quiet understanding in my husband's eyes, to the realization that the sand was not white at all but held all the colors of the world at once.

4
Arkansas Crime Scene

We did not intend to go to Arkansas. We were trying to escape Missouri. This is a tale as old as time, or at least as old as the creation of the Arkansas state line and literature from *Huckleberry Finn* to *Gone Girl*. Arkansas is a wrong turn you make when you are running from a situation you think is as bad as it gets, only to realize it can get worse.

You are not supposed to go to Arkansas on purpose. You are supposed to flee it and, in doing so, prove that you are the right kind of American. That is how Arkansas has been presented my whole life, ever since Bill Clinton ran for president as "the man from Hope" and was rebranded as a New Yorker after leaving office. He did it for his wife, the New York Senate candidate. It stood out from all the things he did not do for his wife back in Arkansas.

Everyone forgets Arkansas, but Arkansas remembers everyone. "Power is impenetrable," wrote social scientist Elias Canetti. "The man who has it sees through other men but does not allow them to see through him." By this standard, Arkansas should have more leverage than any state in America. Arkansas is watching you from the hills and hollers, watching you not give a shit, watching money-drenched bravado slip through your hands like opportunities. Arkansas is the slow roll to the big con, the launchpad of political implosions. Arkansas is nicknamed the Natural State because organized crime is the natural state of America.

The scenery is the official reason for the motto, and it is a worthy cover. Arkansas has a rare, rueful beauty that prompts you to pull off to the side of the road and stare into the distance and say things like "this is God's country." That transcendent allure is another thing you are not supposed to know about Arkansas. I'd ask you not to tell, for fear people will show up and ruin the view. But it's okay. No one will believe you.

We ended up in Arkansas after fleeing Kansas City in 2022 with a blizzard at our back, part of an ongoing weather curse. On our last Kansas City trip, in 2018, we left in a hurry to outrun a "snownado" (half blizzard, half tornado) as traffic lurched to a stop on I-70 due to a stolen 18-wheeler exploding after a hundred-mile police chase. My children shrieked as we veered off the exit to dodge the flames, driving the backroads blind until the storm tapered to a state of manageable peril.

We should have rejected the interstate and retraced the lonely road we'd taken in, the one Missouri's tourism bureau calls the Way of the American Genius in a vain attempt to get people to drive it. Highway 36 features American Geniuses like Walt Disney of Marceline; J.C. Penney of Hamilton; and the town of Chillicothe, which claims to have invented sliced bread. Distracted as I was by all the genius on display, in Chillicothe I took a wrong turn and wound up in Mormon heaven.

Adam-ondi-Ahman is land left over from when the Mormons decreed that they had found Paradise on Earth—and that it was in Missouri. According to the legend, in 1838, God told Mormon leader Joseph Smith that after Adam and Eve were expelled from the Garden of Eden, they decided to live out their golden years near Kansas City. God told Smith that Missouri should have a spectacular Mormon temple and that Smith should have lots of money to build it. Smith agreed, christened the land Adam-ondi-Ahman, or "Valley of God, where Adam dwelt," and set out on a crusade for cash. The Missouri government responded by imprisoning Smith in a town called Liberty and killing or exiling his followers. Smith broke out of the Liberty jail only to end up murdered by a mob in Illinois.

Today, Adam-ondi-Ahman looks like a gospel-themed golf course, with long stretches of manicured lawn between stations showcasing Mormon theology. The Latter-day Saints repurchased the site in the 1940s, including three thousand acres of farmland. It's a nice place to wander, full of heavenly tractors and holy corn. You can imagine Adam driving, Eve shucking, retirees enjoying life in runner-up Eden.

What you rarely see are people. This is because after Smith's violent death, God told his successor, Brigham Young, that he didn't mean to say Missouri after all. What he had meant to say was Utah. Everybody makes mistakes.

After our inadvertent detour, we returned to the highway and entered Kansas City, only to be chased out by the snownado. If it had occurred to me in 2018, I would have driven south to Arkansas, that reliable avenue of escape, just to see what was going on. When another storm hit in December 2022 during an aborted attempt to do some Kansas City sightseeing, that's what we decided to do.

We began driving south to our fallback town, the artsy village of Eureka Springs, and my fallback hotel, the Crescent: a seedily stylish century-old hotel haunted by the victims of its former proprietor, Norman Baker, a 1930s con man who ran a fake hospital for cancer patients and buried their remains on the hotel grounds. I had written about the Crescent in my 2022 book *They Knew*, drawing parallels between Baker's scams and con artists of the present, and I was not ready to return. We had planned to skip our usual stopover in Eureka Springs before heading to my sister's house in Texas, bypassing Arkansas entirely.

But Arkansas was calling me away from the storm, into the safety of familiar ghosts.

It is four hours to Eureka Springs from Kansas City, but like the gangsters and outlaws and runaways that long preceded us on this route, we kept getting sidetracked. Distractions beckoned, both sacred and profane.

Every time I am south of Kansas City, particularly when I hit Jasper County, I am aware I am in the fictional terrain of *Road House*—one of few movies set in Missouri and the best one. It tells the tale of Dalton, a "cooler" (overseer of bouncers) recruited from New York City to small-town Jasper to clean up a raucous bar called the Double Deuce so that a Kansas City businessman can fulfill his dream of building a JCPenney. At least five men die in pursuit of this goal. When the movie premiered in St. Louis, the producers invited the Chamber of Commerce of Jasper County, a nod to the fictional Jasper, to attend.[1]

Despite the occasional palm tree peeking out in the background, *Road House* captures the essence of Missouri. It is the best bad movie ever in the way that Missouri is the best bad state ever. It is overwhelmingly violent and full of surprises: Zen wisdom from unexpected sources, one-man political corruption so strong it keeps a whole town in line before blowing it to pieces. Everything explodes in *Road House*, including your expectations.

After traversing *Road House* territory, we hit the town of Nevada, which, like Eureka Springs, is home to an early twentieth-century fake medical facility run by con men to steal the money of the dying. The Weltmer Institute of Suggestive Therapeutics was shut down in 1933, and its proprietor, Sidney Abram Weltmer, was described by the British Medical Association as "one of the innumerable freaks of the charlatan fancy which flourished only on American soil."[2] The town also boasted several asylums, one of which held the mother of Carrie Nation,[3] the prohibitionist who would go on to smash unruly bars with a hatchet, the Dalton of her time.

Today, the biggest attraction in Nevada is the World's Largest Morel. This fiberglass sculpture towers over the highway, a tribute to Missouri's most elusive mushroom. We pulled over to admire it, for I am an avid participant in the spring hunt. I have my hot spots and honey holes, and I am not sharing them. A proper morel hunt requires that you walk the woods eyes to the ground for hours, the outside world irrelevant. You stagger like a zombie until a morel emerges like a brain, and then you leap to life and snatch it. The morel is a symbol of freedom: nothing is more immune from corporate power. They grow for only a few weeks each year and are not sold in stores. You cannot fake them, you cannot mass-market them, and you can never replicate the serendipity of the search.

The World's Largest Morel is weathered like a broken umbrella, but that's okay. A morel that easy to find shouldn't look great anyway.

Our next stop was Lamar, the birthplace of Harry S. Truman. We did not know this until we pulled into town looking for snacks and stopped at a place called Beef Jerky Experience across from a sign that said CRAP GALORE. Crap Galore turned out to be a glorious name for a cash-only auction the residents of Lamar hold on weekends. The man behind the counter sweet-talked us into buying an excess of beef jerky ("no such thing," said my son) and told us Harry Truman's house was down the road.

"Harry Truman? The president? The bomb dropper?" said my son. He remembered from his J. Robert Oppenheimer obsession days.

I wanted to get to Eureka Springs by night, in case the storm moved south, so we vowed to make it a quick stop. We walked to a small white wooden house with a plaque declaring it Truman's childhood home. We wandered into the backyard, which had an outhouse with vintage Sears, Roebuck and Co. catalogs to approximate what the Trumans read on the shitter and a shed where the Trumans stored their smoked meats. I wondered what the Trumans would think of Beef Jerky Experience, whether they would be proud America had come so far.

A white-haired man approached us and asked whether we would like to go inside. It was closing time, but he was enthusiastic, so I was too. I never turn down tours in small towns because they tell you things you won't hear elsewhere, and sometimes those things are even true.

The tour guide told us that the family of Wyatt Earp, the notorious outlaw and sheriff, had sold this home to Harry Truman's parents in the early 1880s. Wyatt Earp's father, Nicholas, was Lamar's first constable. Wyatt became the second in 1870 but quit after calamities ranging from the death of his wife to an arrest for being a horse thief. He fled to manage a brothel in Peoria, as one does, before moving on to gunslinging in Dodge City and Deadwood and Tombstone, vacillating between being an arbiter or a violator of the law as he saw fit.

Inside the Truman home, we entered a modest bedroom with a tiny bassinet. This is where baby Harry Truman slept, oblivious to the chaos outside. When Truman was born in 1884, southwest Missouri, still devastated by the aftermath of the Civil War, became overrun by a masked gang called the Bald Knobbers. Depending on whom you ask, the Bald Knobbers plunged the region into carnage or saved its soul. (After the bloodbath ended, the Bald Knobbers also inspired carnival attractions in nearby Branson, including a Vigilante Zipline.)

Seeking stability, the Trumans relocated to the Kansas City region, and Harry grew up embroiled in the Kansas City political machine until its leader, Thomas Pendergast, went to prison for tax fraud in 1939. By this time, the Lamar property had been purchased by Wyatt Earp's second cousin, Everett, who became known for tall tales about the two families—but nothing as wild as the tall tale I hear on the regular, which is that "America is a nation of laws." The history of Lamar alone debunks that delusion.

We thanked the tour guide and hit the road. Near the Arkansas border, I told my husband to make one final stop. We were in Diamond, the home of George Washington Carver.

"George Washington Carver, the father of the peanut," my children dutifully intoned. Like all Missouri children in a majority Black school, my kids had spent a lot of time learning about Carver, the botanist born into slavery who transformed global agriculture.

George Washington Carver is one of those historical figures who seems corny when you are little but becomes intriguing as you grow old and the things you took for granted seem miraculous and fragile. When I wander the southern Missouri woods and see an unfamiliar plant, I think about Carver beholding the same land with the same reverence. He understood the majesty of its mystery even as a child.

"Anything will give up its secrets if you love it enough," Carver wrote. "Not only have I found that when I talk to the little flower or the little peanut they will give up their secrets, but I have found that when I silently commune with people, they give up their secrets also—if you love them enough."[4]

Carver was born in 1864. After his mother was kidnapped, he was raised by her former enslaver, Moses Carver, whose farm eventually became the George Washington Carver National Monument. Moses treated him as a son, but that did not protect him from discrimination. It was the land of Missouri, and *only* its land, that gave Carver comfort and inspiration. The land loved him when the white world refused him; the land could never let him down. After fleeing Missouri as a teenager, Carver searched for a university that would accept a Black scientist. He moved to Kansas, only to witness a lynching, and crossed the country until he could enroll in the Tuskegee Institute in Alabama, newly opened by Booker T. Washington.

The museum at the George Washington Carver National Monument was closing when we arrived. But the land surrounding it was open, and since the land was what had mattered to Carver, that was what we explored. We walked in a prairie turned gold and rust by the setting sun, with a trail decorated with stone-carved quotes from Carver. "The further anyone gets away from themselves, the greater will be their success in life," read one. "You can't get very far in life if you don't get away from self and see a richer and broader horizon."

It was December 21, the darkest day of the year. The branches of barren trees stretched out like hands trying to catch the ball of sun sinking to the soil. I wanted to examine everything. Every broken bough, every faded flower: both in their own right and because this land had been loved by someone who loved nature, survived great suffering, and found peace in a world outside himself.

I do believe that if you love something enough, it will give up its secrets. But the other kind of secrets, the cruel kind—those need to be forced out, or they devour everything. We crossed the border and headed to Eureka Springs.

The blizzard arrived in Arkansas at midnight. I woke to sunlight blazing through the ice of the window bars, lighting them up like a crucifix. We were trapped in the Crescent Hotel, but it was haunted, which meant we would not be lonely. My daughter and I decided to climb the crooked stairwell to the fourth floor, where we'd had a paranormal encounter five years before. Even my sensible daughter admits this happened.

There is a split in our household. My husband and daughter are the rational ones, while my son devours books on history's mysteries, many of which he borrows from me. If he ages out of his credulous curiosity, I will become the most willfully gullible person in the family. The nice thing about little kids is that for a few years you seem reputable by default.

The first time we visited the Crescent Hotel, in 2017, my daughter was ten, and she did not know its horrific backstory. She did not know that Norman Baker was a xenophobic demagogue and career criminal who amassed a massive following through radio broadcasts proclaiming that vaccines were tools of a demonic government. She didn't know that next to the basement spa there was a morgue where he stashed his victims. She knew the hotel was haunted—the Crescent plays this up—but thought it was cursed by magic, not man.

The halls of the Crescent are lit by ceiling fan lights with cords dangling beneath. We noticed that the cord on one light was swaying wildly, even though the fan barely moved. As we approached, the cord stopped.

"Are you a ghost?" my daughter asked. "Go this way for yes"—she moved her hands vertically, away from her chest—"and stop moving for no." The cord began swinging toward us. I gasped and got out my cell phone and started filming.

"Calm down, Mommy," said my daughter. "Ghost, don't worry. We come in peace. Did you die here?"

The cord swayed toward us again, then stopped.

"Are you a grown-up?" she asked. The cord stayed still.

"Are you a kid?" she asked, and the cord swayed a definitive "yes." I gripped my daughter's hand.

"Ghost, I would like to be your friend," my daughter said. "Will you show us your true form?"

"Noooo!" I protested. "Bad idea! New question!"

My daughter rolled her eyes but indulged me. She asked if the ghost was a girl. The cord swayed affirmatively.

"Ghost, can you tell us your story? Can you tell us what happened to you?" The cord moved back and forth, then in wild circles, like it was angry. The ceiling fan began to spin like blades about to be unleashed.

"Let's go!" I said at the same time my daughter yelled "Mommy!" and we ran down four flights of stairs until we reached our own room, wide-eyed and out of breath.

"Do I even want to ask what you were doing?" my husband said as I collapsed on the bed, and my daughter began bouncing around, reciting our tale. I half listened while searching the internet until I found something that made me reel in shock.

"Oh my God!" I started, then shut up.

"You looking up ghosts, Mommy?" my daughter asked. Nothing gets by her.

"No, I'm looking up breakfast! The hotel has a buffet. Unlimited biscuits!" I said brightly. She side-eyed me and continued her story. What I had discovered was that in the very spot where we had stood, a child had plummeted off the balcony to her death in the 1930s.[5] I decided not to tell her because I was scared for real, and sad.

Years later, when my daughter was a teenager, I told her what I had learned. Every time we have stayed at the Crescent since, we have returned to that hallway to find the ghost, without success. Every year, my daughter is more poised and less inclined to believe in the supernatural, and I stand behind her, torn between a morbid desire to see if it would happen again and the sorrow of the dead girl's tale. I have our encounter on video, so I know we did not imagine it. But I don't have a rational explanation. Maybe it was an extremely coincidental trick of the ventilation. Or maybe the ghost talked to my daughter because she was a child then too and could be trusted.

The day after our encounter, I asked my daughter why she thought it would help the ghost if we learned her story and shared it.

"Because that's what frees ghosts," she answered, as if this were obvious. "Then they can go to the Other Side."

"Oh," I said, and she looked at me curiously.

"Isn't this what you're always talking about? How we need to find the truth?"

"Yeah," I said. "But I don't know if the truth makes you free. It makes you free of other people's lies, but what comes after that? What you do with the truth when it's ugly and sad and no one wants to hear it, that's the part I don't know how to handle."

"Do you think that the ghost is lonely?" she asked.

"Not anymore," I said. "Because you said you would be her friend. And that was very nice of you."

"Do you think that's why she talked to me?"

"I think it's exactly why she talked to you." My daughter seemed satisfied with this answer.

As a teenager, my daughter doesn't believe in ghosts anymore, but she doesn't disbelieve in them either. She is a musician who disappears into another reality when she plays. She knows there is a secret place both beyond this world and of it, a sacred space where time stretches or stands still, and you emerge from it altered. I know this place. I enter it involuntarily when I'm lost in my own creative pursuits, and I'm grateful every time it happens because it's the only way to survive the real world. A real world that leaves real people feeling like ghosts with untold stories, trapped in limbo, looking for a friend to free them.

The next day we left Eureka Springs and headed for Texas. We drove through the town of Fayetteville, home of the University of Arkansas, where Bill and Hillary Clinton had lived in the 1970s before he became governor. The house was now a museum, closed due to the snowstorm. We had trouble finding it because the city had plowed all the streets except the one on which the Clintons once resided. I don't know if this was intentional. But I do know Arkansas holds a grudge.

Arkansas was the last southern state to turn Republican, remaining a Democratic stronghold until 2010[6] in part due to loyalty to Clinton, its native son. It is now one of the states mostly likely to elect Republicans, and I suspect it will stay that way for a while.

I would not, however, call Arkansas a Republican state because nearly half of those eligible to vote do not. In 2020, Arkansas ranked last in both voter turnout and voter registration[7] while its population, in particular Latinos, faced voter suppression.[8] Arkansas is a state whose most conservative residents are both active and actively recruited by the national GOP while other Arkansans, reluctant to define themselves, have tuned out of politics and been abandoned by politicians who buy into "red state" clichés. Their situation is similar to Missouri's except that Arkansas is a more rural state, which affects how citizens receive and remember information. Arkansas was one of the last states to get cable news or household Wi-Fi. Many areas lack modern technological infrastructure—or shun it. Your GPS is of no use here; Arkansas does not want you to follow the plot.

Arkansas is a land of scandals that only Arkansans seem to

remember in detail. Even then, the details are hazy, especially for those too young to remember the 1980s. Conspiracy aficionados know the buzzwords—Mena Airport, Fort Smith, Whitewater—and their status as the roots of a bitter national bloom. A disproportionate number of major events—Iran-Contra, the Oklahoma City bombing, the 2000 presidential election, the evolution of organized crime—have an Arkansas connection, and this long precedes the Clintons' rise to power.

Arkansans live surrounded by unfinished business. Going to Arkansas is like finding buried treasure and then digging for the map.

For centuries, dating to when it was primarily inhabited by Native Americans, Arkansas was famous for steaming hot mineral waters believed to have magical healing powers. These springs are what enabled the medical fraud schemes of con men like Norman Baker. They are also what sent Meyer Lansky's national crime syndicate south for spa days and lured national politicians for gambling getaways served up with a dash of moonshine. As lawmakers became compromised at illegal bars and brothels, the mafia began to recognize the appeal of Arkansas, where grass is green as dollars and steam is blurry as truth.

By the midtwentieth century, New York gangsters had put down roots in Arkansas, to the public dismay and private pleasure of many local officials.[9] "The people of Arkansas will not tolerate the establishment of an underworld stronghold in this state," Governor Sid McMath said in 1951 when mob boss Frank Costello announced he was now an Arkansan. Costello protested that he did not have "the remotest idea of engaging in or being connected with the gambling business" and was there only for the "incomparable mineral baths and hospitable people."[10] Arkansas law enforcement developed an eye twitch from simultaneously winking and looking the other way.

Arkansas was where America's legalized crime spree began. Before there was Las Vegas, there was Hot Springs.

Hot Springs is the real hometown of Bill Clinton, where he lived from age seven until he left for college. Clinton was marketed as "the Man from Hope"—how could any politician resist that hook?—but Hope, Arkansas, was his grandmother's town, where he would visit summer friends like his childhood neighbor Vince Foster, later known for his tragic and politicized suicide. I took my kids to visit Bill Clinton's childhood home, now a museum, in 2016. They called it "Hillary Clinton's Husband's House" because that was their only point of reference. Bill Clinton had spent his earliest years in a white-wood home of flowered wallpaper and cheerful photos, including one of Miss Marie Purkins' School for Little Folks, showing a tiny Clinton and a tiny Foster smiling side by side.

"Why did Hillary's husband and him stop being friends?" asked my daughter, then eight years old. I did not tell her about Foster's suicide or the theories about it, because the sight of those little boys hurt my heart. They looked like my son, who was only five. I told her that sometimes people grow apart.

Hope, Arkansas, was pain marketed as triumph. But Hot Springs is where Clinton learned about the slippery lure of law. Hot Springs is where he spent his teen years watching mobsters and politicians pass through until gambling was outlawed in the late 1960s and the action—and the money—moved away. Clinton left too, for Yale, following the well-worn path of American southerners who learn new ways to be slick from the Ivy League, knowing that being dismissed as a yokel can be a boon if you play it right.

The seedy southern glamour of Hot Springs, with its run-down art deco spas and sizzling waters, feels like Bill Clinton. It's bright and sleazy and full of historical insight and disturbing facts. The town makes for a memorable family outing: you can take your kids to a diner for biscuits with chocolate gravy, hike the colorful rock trails of Hot Springs National Park, and finish the day with a trip to the Gangster Museum of America, where you can learn about the most terrible criminals in the United States.

The ones they show in museums, anyway. The rest you have to drive to. And you have to make sure not to stop and stay too long.

The drive from Eureka Springs to Dallas is a slow loss of beauty as the secluded slopes of the Ozark Mountains turn into the trafficked plains of suburban Texas. Halfway along this route, at the border of Arkansas and Oklahoma, lies Fort Smith, the largest city in the region. Fort Smith has long been known as a rough borderland, immortalized in the classic Western *True Grit*. But its recent history is the most disturbing and rarely recalled.

In 1988, fourteen white supremacists were acquitted in Fort Smith for sedition after a two-month trial. They were part of a group called the Covenant, the Sword, and the Arm of the Lord, which had been started on a militia compound in the now defunct town of Elijah, Missouri, in the 1970s. The leader of the terrorist group, Jim Ellison, was a polygamist who crowned himself King James of the Ozarks.[11]

The CSA sought—among other things—to overthrow the federal government, create a separatist white supremacist country in the Pacific Northwest, poison the water of New York City with cyanide, and blow up the Alfred P. Murrah Federal Building in Oklahoma City.[12] One member, Richard Snell, murdered a Black Arkansas police officer in 1983 and a shopkeeper he mistakenly thought was Jewish in 1984. The CSA rose in tandem with another white supremacist group, the Order, who assassinated Jewish radio host Alan Berg in 1984.[13] Snell, like other militia members, rarely stayed in one place, roaming the Ozarks borderlands of Arkansas, Missouri, and Oklahoma.

On April 19, 1985, the Elijah compound was raided by the Bureau of Alcohol, Tobacco, Firearms and Explosives, a siege that ended peacefully with the arrest of Ellison. This siege was in stark contrast to the deadly ATF raid in Waco eight years later on April 19, 1993, though few reporters noted the date or other parallels. After Elijah was raided, Snell and his partners began frequenting Elohim City, a private white supremacist militia compound on the Oklahoma border thirty miles from Fort Smith. While the rest of the defendants in the 1988 Fort Smith sedition trial went free, Snell was indicted for murder and sentenced to death.

His execution date was set for April 19, 1995. This is the exact same day that Timothy McVeigh, who had frequented Elohim City in the early 1990s, carried out the Oklahoma City bombing. Prior to his execution that evening, Snell remarked to guards that he was satisfied with the terrorist act and claimed that he'd known in advance that it was coming.[14] McVeigh had fulfilled his dream: Snell and Ellison had first cased the Murrah building in 1983. Now 168 people were dead, and Snell had been executed before anyone could interview him about his foreknowledge. Fort Smith federal prosecutor Steven Snyder went to the FBI about Snell and Ellison following McVeigh's arrest, but the FBI did not want to hear about it or investigate the broader white supremacist movement in the region.[15]

Bill Clinton was the governor of Arkansas during the Fort Smith sedition trial. He had no influence on the verdict, but the release of fourteen violent white supremacists was humiliating for the Arkansas justice system and dangerous for Americans, particularly for the minority groups the terrorists despised. Many of the freed terrorists remained involved in white supremacist activity. Some committed more anti-Semitic murders, including slayings at a Jewish community center in suburban Kansas City.[16] By the time of the Oklahoma City bombing in 1995, Clinton was president. His DOJ went to great pains to limit the scope of the investigation to McVeigh and Nichols, ignoring ties that traced back to Fort Smith and Elohim City.

On April 20, 1995, Clinton's deputy assistant attorney general, Merrick Garland, was sent to Oklahoma City at the behest of his boss, Deputy Attorney General Jamie Gorelick. After a press conference, Garland flew back to DC, and the case was turned over to US attorney Joseph Hartzler.[17] This has not deterred Garland and Gorelick from portraying Garland as someone who played a seminal role in catching and prosecuting McVeigh, even though he did no such thing.[18] His involvement, like that of most DOJ underlings, was limited to burying evidence from public view.[19]

Garland left the DOJ in 1997 to become a DC circuit judge. Gorelick, Garland's best friend and mentor, departed the same year and went on to play a role in most major controversies of the twenty-first century.[20] These include 9/11, where she was accused of creating a "wall" between the FBI and CIA that made the attacks possible and then refused to resign as a member of the 9/11 Commission; profiteering over student loan crimes; representing opioid peddlers,[21] corporate oil spillers, police who kill Black men, and big tech corps who spy on citizens; and serving as the "ethics lawyer" for Jared Kushner and Ivanka Trump,[22] ensuring they got into the White House despite their security clearance violations. Gorelick is a Democrat. She was trained at Harvard Law School by Trump lawyer Alan Dershowitz, who is also a Democrat. Garland and Gorelick both serve in the Biden administration, where Garland, as attorney general, has been criticized for his refusal to hold the wealthy Republican organizers of the January 6 attacks accountable.

"It's one big club, and you ain't in it," George Carlin famously said. The revolving door cover-up club of the DOJ speaks to his observation. America's worst crises are not born of partisan rancor but of bipartisan collusion. They are crises of blood and money, obfuscation and betrayal. In Washington, DC, the deals are struck, the past buried. But the roads of the twenty-first century lead back to Fort Smith, back to the sedition trial, back to Arkansas, back to the down and dirty places they want America to forget.

Every time we drive through Fort Smith, I remember.

Before Richard Snell was executed, he claimed to know a secret about Bill Clinton. Any secret told by an imprisoned neo-Nazi terrorist should be considered unreliable until proven otherwise; he does not deserve the benefit of the doubt. But Snell was far from the only person to raise the issue: what did Governor Bill Clinton know about the Iran-Contra affair? Specifically, what did he know about drug smuggling by the CIA at the airport in Mena, Arkansas, where Snell would film planes coming and going, hoping to use his footage as leverage against the government?[23]

On December 26, 2022, my family left my sister's house in Dallas to return to Missouri, with a few stops in Arkansas along the way. We decided to drive the fifty-four-mile Talimena National Scenic Byway, which stretches through the Ouachita National Forest from Talihina, Oklahoma, to Mena, Arkansas. There was a lot to take in: no state combines scenery with sin quite like Arkansas.

Arkansas is a generous state that lets you take treasures where you find them. One state park, Crater of Diamonds, is the only place in America where you can show up with a shovel and pocket down-home bling. The buried diamonds are the result of southern Arkansas being formed over a ninety-five-million-year-old dormant volcano. Every year someone gets lucky, and every year that someone is not us. We had visited the park several times, armed with a bucket and a dream. We dug for diamonds, and all we found was useless dirt, much like Republicans in the 1990s.

In 2022, we were on a quest for quartz. Earlier in the year, on a weekend trip to Hot Springs, we had driven the eastern half of the Ouachita National Forest to Crystal Mountain, the quartz capital of the world. The colors of the Ouachita region are a child's crayon version of nature: its forests are forest green, its waters the brightest blues, and its soil a deep ruddy brown. On a trail near a rest stop, we found quartz crystals lying on the ground like they had been sprinkled by a fairy. They were so clear and fine you could see through them without polishing. We took only a few, in case other families were on the way. We did not want other children to miss out on the magic. But there was no one coming. Every time we drove the Ouachita, we drove it alone.

In December, the Talimena National Scenic Byway veered from evergreen pines to utter desolation. We wandered a forest trail and found a nineteenth-century pioneer cemetery with unmarked graves and a sign saying a teenage girl had frozen to death on a tree limb here after being chased by wolves. We kept walking, past large stones in such precise cubes they seemed handmade, but they were not, just extensions of Arkansas's all-too-perfect geology, another drawing from a child's page. At the end of the route, we passed a rock wall covered in graffiti, nearly all of it profane save a painting of the American flag and the word HONESTY inside a blue oval.

The scenic drive ended in the infamous town of Mena.[24] Mena, the hub of Iran-Contra; Mena, where pilot Barry Seal flew weapons and drugs between Arkansas and Nicaragua as part of a CIA plot to support the Contras before being murdered by the Medellín Cartel.[25] Bill Clinton was the governor, Ronald Reagan was the president, and Bill Barr was the attorney general Iran-Contra cover-up guy installed in 1991 by George H. W. Bush.[26] The Reagan, Bush, and Clinton presidencies all sought to bury the details of the conflict, as did the media. Early coverage of Iran-Contra was frequently dismissed as wild "conspiracy theories."[27] Journalists reporting on Oliver North and the other Iran-Contra players found themselves censored or unemployed.[28]

Even after the crimes were confirmed, leading to a series of hearings and lengthy government reports, how exactly Mena factored into the operation remained unclear. Clinton's Arkansas aides were alleged to have participated in a long-running cover-up of Mena's criminal activity.[29] The institutions that knew best—the FBI, the CIA, and the IRS—stayed silent. No one was meaningfully punished for Iran-Contra crimes thanks to blanket pardons by George H. W. Bush, and every administration from Reagan's onward, including Biden's, hired prominent Iran-Contra participants. The players who did not get a policy position had to settle for jobs like cable news host or head of the NRA.

In 2020, the FBI finally admitted the Mena airport drug smuggling allegations were true.[30] But the human cost of the crimes and the cover-up remained as underexamined as it had been decades earlier. In an article commissioned for the *Washington Post* titled "The Crimes of Mena," journalists Sally Denton and Roger Morris noted, "The tons of drugs that Seal and his associates brought into the country, officials agree, affected tens of thousands of lives at the least, and exacted an incalculable toll on American society. And for the three presidents, the enduring questions of political scandal are once again apt: What did they know about Mena? When did they know it? Why didn't they do anything to stop it?"[31]

The *Washington Post* censored the exposé, set to run in January 1995. The article ended up in *Penthouse* instead, buried in pornography, away from mainstream view. The tentacles of Iran-Contra reach out from the past to strangle the present and the future.

When faced with current state crimes, people invoke Watergate because it was solved. They forget Iran-Contra because it was streamlined.

It was around noon when we exited the Talimena National Scenic Byway. We rolled past a "Welcome to Mena" sign declaring the town a "basecamp for mountain adventures," a claim beyond contention.

"I want to see the airport," I told my husband. He sighed and told me he'd figured as much.

"Why are we going to an airport?" my son asked, excited. "Are we flying somewhere?"

"It's the Iran-Contra airport. The one where the US government trafficked drugs to fund right-wing death squads in Nicaragua."

"Oh yeah, you told me about that," my son said. I would say my husband and I had stopped hiding history from our children, but we never started.

"Since you're making me go the Iran-Contra airport," my son continued, "can we have McDonald's?"

"Yes."

We got lunch at the Mena McDonald's and headed for the Mena Intermountain Municipal Airport. My children were eating McNuggets as we entered the 1980s nexus of transnational state crime.

"This is boring," said my daughter as we passed a bland blue building. "It's just a little airport."

"A little airport for *1980s government drug runners*!"

"It's still boring. Criminal boomers on a plane, big deal."

"Does this place do Iran-Contra tours?" asked my son.

"No, I checked."

"Are we, uh, supposed to be here?" We had looped around the airport road, passing a fenced-off lot, the Ouachita Mountains looming in the distance.

"No one is supposed to be at Mena Airport. That's the main thing you would learn if they did have Iran-Contra tours."

"They should do the tours," my son said. "They'd make lots of money."

"The other thing you'd learn on an Iran-Contra tour is that there are much quicker ways of making lots of money than by doing Iran-Contra tours."

My husband drove through the airport exit and headed north. It was time to bid Mena goodbye. We had one more Arkansas crime scene left to go and a long road ahead.

The backroads of Arkansas wind like a riddle, traversing around churches and cemeteries punctuated by the occasional Walmart. Walmart originated in Arkansas, bursting on the national scene in the 1990s with the Clintons, their combined force shifting the country into a neoliberal transformation. What does it say about America when Booger Hollow—a once thriving hillbilly spoof town famous for its two-story outhouse—can't stay in business in the twenty-first century? Probably nothing, possibly that Arkansas has become enough of an American afterthought that there are no longer enough tourists for the old-timey tourist traps. We drove through the ghost town of a self-effacing joke: Booger Hollow had been picked clean.

We were headed back to the Ozarks, away from anything resembling a highway. The only large city in Arkansas is Little Rock, and it still has only around two hundred thousand people. We had visited Little Rock briefly in December 2019, stopping at the William J. Clinton Library and Museum as part of our quest to see every presidential museum in America. The Clinton museum remains my children's favorite due to its collection of objects from 1990s TV shows: Mulder and Scully's FBI badges from *The X*

Files, Kramer's ASSMAN license plate from *Seinfeld*, the couch from *Friends*.

While the kids explored the iconography of my youth, I spent my time examining old newspapers, drawn to a 1973 article called "Attorney Rodham to Investigate Impeachment." It described how "a 26-year-old Park Ridge woman" named Hillary Rodham had been selected by the House Judiciary Committee to inspect the crimes of Richard Nixon. We were visiting the Clinton museum during the first impeachment of Hillary Clinton's presidential rival Donald Trump, whose campaign advisor Roger Stone had worked for Nixon as Nixon's impeachment loomed.

Hillary Clinton and Roger Stone had faced off in the 1970s and were still at it half a century later. In between Nixon's and Trump's impeachments was Bill Clinton's impeachment, which featured many of the same players from Trump's world, politicos Hillary correctly accused of being involved in a "vast right-wing conspiracy." Hillary Clinton had featured in every impeachment of the modern era, her life unfolding like a sleazy American version of *The Crown*. The players never changed. The political story of my generation is bookended by Boomer feuds.

Little Rock was the only place we ever encountered traffic in Arkansas, and as we left the city, Arkansas again felt like a reprieve, a place where you could breathe in America without inhaling bullshit. I remembered this feeling from 2019 and planned our drive accordingly. Now it was December 2022. In the intervening three years, Trump had been impeached a second time, for fomenting a coup, and was running for president again because the Biden administration countenanced sedition.

It was one big club, the passing of a baton they use to beat us, and I wanted out. I needed a retreat from the world and knew where I might find one. You don't study the worst people in America for a living without learning how to hide.

We ascended Highway 7, singing to Chris Stapleton's "Arkansas"—*"Gotta get down to Arkansas / Havin' so much fun that it's probably a little bit against the law"*—and stopping at an old rest stop as the sun began to set. There's a line in Stapleton's song where he describes a place on Highway 7 in the Ozark Mountains that feels like sitting on top of the world, and I am convinced it is a rest stop set up by Rotary Ann—two wives of Rotary Club members both named Ann—in the 1930s. I have been up much higher mountains in the West, but no place *feels* higher than this overlook when the sun is bathing the twisted landscape below in gold. Eureka Springs has a colossal Christ of the Ozarks statue that towers over the hills, but the *feeling* of that statue is at the Rotary Ann rest stop: like something truly wondrous was created beneath you, and you are seeing it through God's eyes. You get why people build such statues here, and also why they are superfluous.

After the sun set, we had a perilous drive through the cliffs until we turned onto a barely paved backroad that I cannot describe, for we drove it in the dark and could see nothing at all. At one point, a Tyson chicken factory lit up like a beacon, and then it was gone, and we turned onto gravel paths, struggling to find our way. By the time we arrived, we could see nothing but stars. I fell asleep in a strange bed to the sound of rushing water.

I woke at dawn and stood on the back porch. The White River stretched out before me amid acres of untouched forest: oak and sycamore trees nested among moss-covered boulders, hawks diving into water flush with fish, songbirds greeting the morning as sunlight burned away the fog.

We had found paradise. We had found Whitewater.

The area of Arkansas where we stayed has no official name. The closest town is Flippin, population 1,345, home of the Flippin

Church of God and the Flippin Christian Church and the Flippin District Court watched over by the Flippin police. Next to Flippin is Yellville, home of Yellville City Hall. Across the state line, in Missouri, is the area where militias had compounds in the 1980s. In the midst of it all is an unincorporated rural expanse broken up by cabins like our rental. Back when this area was known, it was known as Whitewater.

Whitewater is the scandal that begat all other Clinton scandals and, in turn, possibly brought down America. The downfall was a controlled demolition—if it was not Whitewater, it would have been something else—but Whitewater is what led to the appointment of Kenneth Starr as special counsel, which led to Clinton's impeachment for lying under oath about getting a blow job, which led to the close 2000 election abetted by Republican dirty tricks, which led to the post-9/11 wars and the 2008 economic collapse and President Trump and his attempted coup and the general hellscape of the twenty-first century. It all began here, on 230 acres of remote land in northern Arkansas.

I was on vacation inside a twentieth-century scandal, and I liked it.

Whitewater is shorthand for the Whitewater Development Corporation, a small real estate company cofounded by Bill and Hillary Clinton and their partners, Jim and Susan McDougal— the former of whom went to prison for his role in a savings and loan bank fraud scheme, and the latter of whom went to prison for refusing to answer three grand jury questions, back when friends of presidents faced consequences for not cooperating in federal probes. The Clintons had purchased the land in the 1980s, hoping to develop it into a vacation property and failing. The Republicans claimed the Clintons had made an illegal deal, and after this claim proved boring, they added allegations of murder and general intrigue.

The Whitewater hearings lasted thirteen months and produced ten thousand pages of testimony. In the end, the Clintons
were cleared of all wrongdoing. Whitewater became eclipsed by
broader political chaos, and the land was largely tied up in legal
wrangling until the twenty-first century, when enterprising Arkansans built cabins for fishing retreats, as the Clintons had intended. Turned out Whitewater was a great idea after all.

On the first morning in Whitewater, I walked down a dirt path
in my bathrobe like Tony Soprano, to honor the fake crime scene
and because there was no one around to see me. Whitewater was a
blue and gold paradise where sunlit trees met clear-sky waters and
the air was pure enough to cleanse my aching soul.

Sometimes you do not know how much you are hurting until
you have the chance to heal. I was recovering from knee surgery
and had been afraid to walk far, but I felt like here I could try. I
had needed surgery because my knee snapped after I had ignored
an injury for years, suffering in silence because the cost of health
care scared me more than the pain. This is the most American way
to land in the hospital. I thought about how, in 1994, after Hillary
Clinton called for universal health care, she had to wear a bullet-
proof vest to rallies because militants were threatening to kill her.[32]
I thought about how both Clintons reneged on universal health
care not long after, as did every president who followed them.

Now I hobbled through her bygone real estate fiasco in a region still favored by militias, nursing the wounds of America's
bad bargains and discarded dreams. Somewhere beyond this land
a pandemic raged, one whose victims were unknown because the
Centers for Disease Control and Prevention had stopped collect-
ing data. If you don't count the bodies, then you can't get blamed
for the deaths, the thinking went. Genocidal thinking, distilled
until it was commonplace and cavalier, expressed by every administration. This was one reason my soul ached more than my body.

I kept walking, passing hills dotted with small caves near the top. I wondered where they led, but I was too injured to climb. Later in the day, my daughter scampered up the hill and crawled inside them, and I felt a wave of pride that I had raised her right. She was looking for adventure, and I had found a new place for her to be free. My son followed her but got distracted by oddities he found in the earth: frozen tree bark that looked like it had eyes, half-cracked geodes promising crystals, stones unturned until we arrived. They were American children, raised on lies, and I wanted to show them promises.

Arkansas buries everything: America's secrets, America's treasures. But I felt safe in this rugged land where my phone was as dead as the future. Here I could forget the facts, like that American life expectancy had plunged to the same level it was in 1996, the year I was seventeen, the year Hillary Clinton testified about Whitewater.[33] Sometime during the pandemic, I had gone straight from being a young woman to being an old one, skipping middle age because life expectancy had fallen so far so fast. I missed that midpoint marker with the rest of my generation, left behind by a Grim Reaper who shifted goalposts and then jumped them, sneering like a show-off as he galivanted along.

America was moving backward, knocking out progress and promises. It felt like the decades since 1996 had never happened, except the bad parts. And in the midst of that downfall, I had created life, two lives for whom I was responsible, two children I wanted to know freedom, so they would recognize it when it is taken away. America was moving backward, so I found a backward place to unwind.

I walked back to the cabin. My children were exploring the bank of the river, chasing each other like they had when they were little. My husband was on the porch, and I saw his shoulders relax as I came into view.

"I didn't know where you went," he said. "I tried calling and texting, but the phones don't work."

"I know," I said. "Isn't it wonderful?"

"You're walking pretty good," he said, gesturing at my knee, "considering it was too complicated for you to get out of your bathrobe."

"It's the magical waters of Arkansas," I said. "They have healing powers, don't you know."

He poured me coffee and we drank it on the porch, watching our children play. A flock of migrating geese flew overhead, and for once I did not envy them. I had everything I needed. I had found an escape from reality in the place that had birthed the very reality I sought to escape.

"When the end comes, I want to be in Arkansas. Because anything that happens in the world takes twenty years to reach it." This is a quote from either Mark Twain or the actor Hal Holbrook, known for playing Mark Twain onstage.[34] No one is sure who actually said it, but either way, it's true. Time moves slower in Arkansas, including the end times.

I watched my children run free and tried not to think about what awaited at home. That's the thing about Arkansas: when you live in the past, you still get a future.

5
The National Parks

American Daydreams

In 2016, I decided I needed to see all of America's national parks, and fast. I had to see them before they vanished, and I needed my kids to see them too. My husband felt the same urgency. The four of us began visiting the parks every chance we got: spring breaks, summer vacations, long weekends. We were low on money but lower on time, and time was the real problem. I envisioned future disasters of biblical proportions: fires, floods, madmen rejoicing at it all. Our landmarks would be disfigured, our people afraid, our air too untrustworthy to breathe.

This all came to pass.

There are three Americas that live in my mind: the America before 2020, the America after 2020, and the America pieced together from a lifetime of devouring magazines and movies and car commercials. It is that third America, the half made-up one, that lets me withstand the others.

I do not believe in the American Dream, but I believe in American Daydreams. The American Dream keeps you working for a future that never comes built upon a past that never happened. It is not so much a dream as a value judgment, a pretense of patriotism at a price few can pay and at a cost few can bear. But daydreams don't carry that burden. Daydreams are a protected realm, free from expectation. They soften things that are hard and bad, letting you imagine a past that went better than it did and a future that could go better than it will.

Daydreams are private and pointless. No one expects daydreams to come true—yet sometimes, to one's joy and surprise, they do. No one expects nightmares to come true either, which is why we need daydreams to compensate when they do too.

The national parks are America's daydream lands. They are where my mind goes when it wanders, and my feet feel compelled to follow. When foreigners fantasize about America, the scenery of the parks is often what comes to mind. They imagine our cities too, but cities are becoming more and more alike. You cannot replicate a national park. There is something monstrous about the idea of trying. The parks were built on the belief that America's landscapes are so unique and miraculous they must be preserved. There is a desperate sanctity to it, the postindustrial realization that you can lose everything and the world keeps turning as it burns.

The national park system was established in 1916, when Congress passed the Organic Act to "conserve the scenery and the natural and historic objects and the wild life therein and to provide for the enjoyment of the same in such manner and by such means as will leave them unimpaired for the enjoyment of future generations."[1]

I am a future generation. I was born in a futureless time, and my children are even more futureless than me. Our national parks tour, conceived at the centennial of the 1916 protection plan, was an end-times road trip. We were plutocrat prey seeking to assure ourselves that humans are a protected species. We wanted the country we love with our whole hearts to stop breaking them. I wanted my children to feel good about being American without feeling like liars, and there is no better place to do that than in the national parks.

National parks are one of few things all Americans support,[2] with the exception of corporate predators who want to drill and drain them. Due to their enduring popularity, the national park system is often called "America's best idea."[3]

But the parks are beyond an idea. An idea belongs to a person or an institution, but daydreams belong to everyone. Daydreams are intimate and endless. You revel in them; you wander in them. Sometimes you visit them in person, and they make your mind bloom.

The first time I visited a national park was in May 2002. My boyfriend—later husband—and I were living in New York City, working at the *New York Daily News* and covering the aftermath of the September 11 attacks. He wanted to take me to Acadia National Park in Maine. He had grown up in one of those families I envied as a kid, outdoorsy types who drove around the country camping like a less cursed version of *National Lampoon's Vacation*. I vowed that if I had children, I would take them everywhere and show them everything. He told me it was a drag, being on road trips with your parents, but I didn't believe him.

He had his own plans for Acadia. I knew them, and he knew I knew, but we both feigned ignorance. We drove up the Atlantic coast and checked into a cabin by Frenchman Bay. The next day we went hiking, and when we reached a summit, he proposed, and I said yes. Neither of us really gave a shit. He knew I thought the ritual was silly, which is why he picked a beautiful place in nature to do it, because a beautiful place in nature did mean something to me, and I would remember it forever. We knew we were going to get married and that it was our life together that mattered, not one moment or one day. Neither of us cared about the wedding, which happened a year later. We went through the motions: pick a dress, the first I found; pick a venue, the first I saw; hold a ceremony to make our families happy. We were told to put things we needed for married life on our wedding registry, but all we could come up with was a telescope.

We were bad at getting married but good at staying married. Twenty years later, we are still together, traveling around with teenagers in tow.

I don't recall much after the proposal, other than I was covered in dirt, and the diamond on my filthy hand made me laugh. But I remember the roar of waves against rocks, the way the Atlantic Ocean was bluer and lonelier in Maine than I'd known was possible, the way peace of mind came easily when we were away from New York. I knew we had to leave the city. Not because of the terrorism, but because it was expensive and boring—and boring because of the expense. We had navigated it on the cheap, but those avenues were closing to people like us, working people high on curiosity and low on cash. We quit our jobs a year later and never looked back. It would have happened anyway, but Acadia sealed more than one deal.

After Trump was inaugurated and began treating employees of the national parks as enemies of the state,[4] our family quest to see the parks began. We stayed local at first. In January, we revisited the Gateway Arch. I explained to the kids that this was technically a national park, and I am still not sure they believe me. We daydreamed of heading west but did not have enough money until the summer of 2018. Once we had it, we went all out, driving from Missouri to Utah to see five national parks in nine days. We never considered flying. As a family of four, it was beyond our financial means, and that wasn't how we rolled anyway.

"We're not the jet set," we sang along to Tammy Wynette and George Jones's 1974 hit as we cruised down the highway, Quik-Trip coffee sloshing in our cupholders, bags of junk food in the back seat. "We're the old Chevrolet set. And there's no Riviera in Festus, Missouri!"

That's a true song, you know. In October 2016, I covered a Tea Party rally in a Harley-Davidson parking lot in Festus at which a local right-wing blogger delivered a benediction for Donald Trump under a banner of Pepe the Frog while selling merchandise for Missouri Republican gubernatorial candidate Eric Greitens, who was later arrested for allegedly blackmailing a woman he had photographed while she was half naked and tied to exercise equipment in his basement. (The charges were later dismissed when the photos could not be found, but a report by the Missouri Special Counsel Committee deemed the woman's account to be credible.[5])

I did not need the Riviera. But I did need a break. We drove to the national parks like the good Americans we are, the type of trash that leaves no trace.

We began our journey down the highway at dawn, passing through Festus and turning onto Highway 21, a pastoral stretch of road known as Blood Alley due to its history of grisly car wrecks. We were heading to the Ozarks to pick up my ten-year-old daughter from wilderness camp. She had signed up for the most primitive camp, wanting to emulate her then-idol, Katniss Everdeen from

The Hunger Games, and learn to survive any situation. In 2018, this seemed like a wise move.

There is a myth that people in so-called red states are obsessed with strangers' politics, whereas in reality most don't care or don't want the hassle of confrontation. But as I looked around the camp, I was curious what the parents of girls from very conservative regions of Missouri wanted for our state. I wondered if they were glad their own daughters were learning survival skills—but for what future? I wondered whether our shared distaste for things everyone hated—corruption, greed, liars—outweighed our differences. Maybe we were more bound by the things we loved, like Missouri's natural beauty, than we were separated by the political manipulations of the wealthy. I liked that our daughters could live off the land together, free for one week from the adult world that failed them.

It felt good that day to be a Missourian, to make small talk and admire the view. We could pretend we weren't hostages of a state controlled by a vicious secret donor network. We were just regular folks enjoying a fun-filled day on Blood Alley.

My daughter emerged from her cabin filthy from camp, but we figured the goal of the week was to get filthy, so this was fine. She joined her brother in the back seat, and we took off for the West. We had five parks planned: the Great Sand Dunes, Mesa Verde, Arches, Canyonlands, and Rocky Mountain National Park. I had seen none of them, and Kansas, Colorado, and Utah were new states for the kids.

I still remember that week as one of the happiest of my life, which is odd because I remember 2018 as a year of mounting dread. That is the power of the national parks. They make you remember only the good things—for the most part. You remember the balm, and then you remember the wound.

We ate a lunch of gas station snacks and headed through a series of oddly named Missouri small towns—Peculiar, Tightwad (home of Tightwad Bank), Braggadocio, and my favorite, Climax Springs. We passed the Little Friendly Climax Market near Highway Double D and a large poster of Jesus proclaiming, "I'm coming!" It is impossible to tell whether Climax Springs is in on the joke—this is a real village of 124 people, not a Uranus-style fake out—or if I am very immature, but it provided enough stimulation for a day's drive through the monotony of Kansas.

Kansas is a state to which I am not going to do justice in this book because I have seen so little of it off the interstate. Kansas is the rectangular roadblock between Missouri and the West, and every time I drive through it, the trip feels too slow and too fast at once. I want to see the prairies and the parks and other places residents know and outsiders miss. When people dismiss Missouri based on a highway view, I feel a mix of annoyance and pity. So I do not judge Kansas by the interstate, even though its most famous son—Eisenhower—created it. In 2018, I knew there was more to see. I had read on a Kansas tourism board that there are Eight Wonders of Kansas, and they did not even include the World's Largest Ball of Twine in Cawker City on that list, so the rest must be truly astounding.

The first Wonder of Kansas we saw was Castle Rock. We knew if we planned it right, we would arrive there at golden hour, and the kids would remember Kansas for something awe-inspiring. I wanted the kids to appreciate all fifty states before propagandists tried to prejudice them. I wanted them to know that even in states notorious for political dysfunction, there are people and places to love. As Missourians, they needed that assurance, seeing that much of the country sees us as human garbage deserving of pain. But in 2018, they were still too young to know that. They were too young to keep having to explain themselves.

It was nearly sundown when we arrived in western Kansas. We turned south onto a flat, dark road with the same relentless blankness as the rest of the Great Plains, until in the distance, a mysterious shape emerged. It was Castle Rock: seventy feet of limestone turrets surrounded by rows of chalk badlands erupting from the earth. Circular swirls of dirt spun around it, as if the monument had landed from outer space and left tracks as it touched the ground.

The kids, delighted to be out of the car after a long drive, ran in circles around the mystery spire. I wandered into the distance to take in the sunset and the land and the way my children seemed to belong in this picture, in this America, this place that is ours to visit but not to keep. To share, even though that night we were alone. Kansas has a quietness that makes me uneasy but in an intrigued way, like anything is possible. A twister, a murder, a rock tower in a desolate plain. The children examined Castle Rock's ruts and crevices, perplexed by this ghostly pillar.

We wanted to see nearby Monument Rocks, Castle Rock's partner in Kansas Wonder, but by then it was too dark to see much of anything, so we headed to a hotel in the small town of Colby, where we would stay the night and then cross into Colorado the next morning. But even though we were headed to the most famous mountain range in the country, Castle Rock remains my favorite formation of that trip. It appeared like a roadside reward, a reminder of the secrets hidden off the highway. We would never be bored in America.

"This place doesn't look like Kansas," my daughter said, and I answered, "Yes it does."

The next day we woke early, exited Kansas under the watchful eye of Wheatfield Jesus, and set off for a five-hour drive to our first national park, the Great Sand Dunes National Park and Preserve. Despite being seven and ten, my children had more experience with sand than the average Missourian. By the summer of 2018, they had gone sledding in White Sands in New Mexico and played in Destin, Florida, the so-called redneck Riviera, renowned for its stunning beaches. The sand of Destin is pure white and super soft, like a blanket laid out by mermaids for drunks. There was no Riviera in Festus, Missouri, but there is one in a Florida panhandle party town where you can watch alligators wrestle before you eat them.

But now we had loftier goals, literally and figuratively. We were headed for the tallest sand dunes in America, the sand to beat all sand, a World's Largest Object cleverly disguised in national park form.

The Great Sand Dunes National Park is in southern Colorado, part of the same mountain range that we saw on our trip to New Mexico. As you drive there from the east, there is no dramatic surge in elevation but a gradual transformation from plains to hills dwarfed by distant dark-gray mountains. "Are those the Rockies?" my daughter asked, and I assured the kids we would visit later. As we approached Alamosa, the town where we were staying, the charcoal silhouettes were blocked by soaring beige dunes. These were the residue of dormant volcanos and dried-up ancient lakes, millennia of dueling winds sculpting grains of sediment into intimidating mounds.

The Great Sand Dunes were as freakish in Colorado as Castle Rock had been in Kansas, which is to say they fit in fine. Why not have a thirty-square-mile sand trap in a state famous for mountain resorts? Why not drop mystic hoodoos on the plains? Why not have landscapes that shock and subvert, rendering state borders and stereotypes irrelevant, the nation's imagination cracked open by geology? Geology doesn't care what you expect. It'll stick

around and surprise you until you learn its tricks, and then it rewards you with the wild and weird. Geology is the best friend
a girl can have when the apocalypse arrives, the only one who
won't bow down to the devil because it has already faced him
head-on and won. Geology is the devil's landlord, and its tenant
faces chronic eviction. That's why so many rock formations are
named for him.

At the Great Sand Dunes visitors' center, we rented sleds and
waxed them down, like we had at White Sands, feeling very much
like experts on dunes. There was only one problem: we were Missourians, adept in the sport of floating lazily on a river, transported
to Colorado, the land of skiing and rock climbing and other acts
of voluntary exertion. St. Louis boasts not one but two Taco Bell
Fitness Courses. We never stood a chance.

"The Colorado dunes are not light and airy like White Sands,"
I told my husband, "but hot and heavy, like White Castle."

"That's very poetic."

"Hey, they say to write what you know."

I told him I would take the kids down the dunes. They were
bouncing around, ready to roll, yammering like overcaffeinated
Frank Herberts, and I needed to make sure they didn't disappear.
Our greased-up sleds made for an exhilarating ride until the ride
ended and we realized effort would be required to repeat it. We
tried to drag the wooden sleds uphill, surrounded by hardier folks
who hid their pity with friendly waves as we collapsed in the sand.

"I want to go down, but I don't want to go up," my seven-year-
old explained, as if this insight had required great deliberation.

"Yes, that is a problem."

"Can you carry me?" he asked, giving me the sad eyes.

"Can you carry *me*?"

"Mommy! No."

"Then we're stuck here forever."

"Okay," he said with a shrug. "We can build a sandcastle and live inside."

My daughter, fresh from wilderness camp, was determined to sled the dunes and hike back up, and she did. Of the four of us, she is the one cut out for Colorado, and now I fear she will move there or to another more respectable state, leaving me and my low-down leisure behind. My husband had the good sense to not participate in this charade of athleticism at all but stayed at the top of the dunes "to keep an eye on things." I waved at him to let him know we were alive, sort of, and lay down on the sand and let my son build me a castle.

My son lived in his daydream and I lived in mine, fantasies where we could live in our beautiful wasteland forever. I listened to him babble about the magical fortress he was making in our new desert home—he was seven, an age I love because it is old enough to come up with deranged fantasies and young enough to have no qualms about sharing them—and I imagined how we looked from a distance. We were a dot in a landscape of patched-together pastels: strips of tan and green and gray so stark they looked almost fake. Around us, the dunes towered, layered in shadow, like the sky was unfolding a long swathe of cloth.

The dunes enveloped us, majestic and brutal. We had arrived at the height of the sun's power. The heat was relieved only by a whipping wind that spat sand in our eyes. I felt like I had died and God couldn't decide on heaven or hell for me so he picked a place that was both.

I told my son I would carry his sled and mine if he would climb back up himself, and somehow we managed it. I grabbed my husband's water and drank like a fiend and made my son do the same.

"Let's come back when it's dark," I told them, and everyone agreed.

The Great Sand Dunes is an international Dark Sky Place,

which my husband was excited to learn until he realized we would be there during a full moon that would render the Milky Way imperceptible. But I was happy. I could explore the dunes by moonlight. I told him we should get there early because everyone would have the same idea.

To my surprise, we had the dunes nearly to ourselves. By evening, the sand had cooled to the point that I could go barefoot, and I walked into the setting sun, following footprints that had accumulated during the day. We were at a section flat enough that I could walk far and still see my children jumping and doing cartwheels as they waited for darkness to fall. Red-tinged clouds hovered over the dunes, creating hulking shadows that chilled the ground as they passed. This earth gave way easily at night, I discovered. I was walking sands of surrender, luring me like an open invitation.

The dunes seemed as vast as an ocean, and I fought the urge to keep following them to see what would happen, to them and to me. I walked far enough so I could look in any direction and see no other soul, only waves of sand drenched in black and hills dotted with green in the area where the sun had not fully set. I wondered how many people had gotten lost out here and how many wanted to. Disoriented, I wandered back to the light, to my family. Darkness had settled in, and moonlight bathed distant dunes in a soft purple glow. Bats emerged from trees and flared in confusion over our heads.

We had brought along the telescope we'd gotten for our wedding. My husband set it up to view the moon, but it was so bright we could see the surface without it. The reflecting sun lit up every cloud and exposed every crater. The kids used the telescope to get a closer view, but I declined. I did not want to see the moon with anything but my own eyes. I wanted only its spectral presence above the soft, sweet earth, looking the same as it had for the travelers it had guided across these dunes for millennia.

My son said he was tired and curled up in my lap. We sat in the sand, and I sheltered him from the wind as he drifted off to sleep. We had only a few years before he would be too big to do that, and I treasured them. *This has to be heaven*, I thought. *It could not be hell*. I wondered if God wasn't still deciding on me, if maybe I was good enough after all. That's the power of the parks, that they make you believe in a delusion like that for one night, under the light of the moon. A place so powerful, you can daydream even the night away.

The next day we left Alamosa for Cortez, a town near Colorado's southwest border. The Colorado of national imagination began to emerge, a geology carved not of stone but of fear. The Colorado of perilous drives on curving cliffs, through tunnels of rock that let you out at indifferent drops, past landscapes so green and gorgeous they could distract you to your doom.

We stopped at Wolf Creek Pass to see the Continental Divide and stood ten thousand feet above a forest of trees so tall their tops were imperceptible from the ground. We were above them, and it felt like we shouldn't be. My husband launched into a scientific explanation of the divide, how it decides to which oceans American rivers flow, but the kids were too distracted by the freefall view to care. They had never been up so high, and it scared them. I told them to breathe deep, to taste the fresh mountain air, and they did, dizzy from the altitude and the dream.

We ate lunch in the Old West town of Durango in a restaurant with antlers and pelts on the walls and a menu declaring meat a condiment. After a lunch of meat sprinkled with meat, we got back on the road, driving until we hit Cortez, the city closest to Mesa Verde National Park.

We checked into the Retro Inn, where a bench with a plastic

statue of Elvis on it greeted us in the courtyard. My children recognized Elvis because I had dragged them to Graceland the year
before—"It's that man with the terrible house, that man who puts
rugs on his walls!"—and posed with his likeness. They liked the
Retro Inn. They were hypnotized by its ancient objects—a pay
phone!—and I told them even older wonders awaited. We drove a
winding road, stopping to let a baby bear pass into the arms of her
mother, a sight my children beheld with tender awe, and entered
the second national park of our trip.

Mesa Verde National Park was the home of the Ancestral
Pueblo people, who inhabited the southwest from roughly the
sixth to the thirteenth century. It maintains the largest intact cliff
dwelling in America, Cliff Palace. This sandstone and adobe do-
micile is preserved in intricate detail, with over 150 rooms and
kivas carved into the overhang of a mountain.

Ancestral Pueblo residents lived there at roughly the same time
that Cahokia, a city of Ancient Mississippians near St. Louis, was
a metropolis larger than London. Today Cahokia is notable for
featureless earthen mounds that need to be explained to be appreciated, but Mesa Verde is immediately impressive. It is the kind of
architectural triumph that forms an instant rebuke to Eurocentric
claims about the relative sophistication of Indigenous civilizations.
It's absurd that many US schools teach children that American
history began in 1492 when there was so much activity in those
two regions alone.

Today, Mesa Verde is in danger. It has been for centuries: first
by colonizers and conquistadors who plundered its treasure and
stole its past and then by fossil fuel industrialists who poisoned
its soil and stole its future. In 1906, Mesa Verde became the first
architectural site in the United States to receive protected status
from Congress. It is now an endangered UNESCO World Heritage Site.[6]

Between 1996 and 2003, over half of Mesa Verde National Park burned down. Too much acreage was destroyed to recover, and the landscape changed permanently. While wildfires are common in western Colorado, their frequency has increased in recent decades. Since our trip, Mesa Verde has been decimated by record droughts and other freak weather events. On our tour of Cliff Palace, the guide emphasized the interdependency of the Pueblo buildings and the wildlife around them. The loss of trees was not just a loss of trees but the loss of an irreplaceable environment that had birthed a civilization, one whose creations had lasted centuries—until now.

I had been in man-made structures like this all over America. Abandoned resorts, rotting cathedrals, houses with no windows or doors. But the decimation of the ancient dwellings felt crueler, since the threat was anticipated, and good people tried and failed to stop it. The first written proposal to protect Mesa Verde was in 1886. In 1889, one section of it became the first archaeological site in the United States to get federal protection. In 1906, Mesa Verde became one of America's first national parks. For centuries, scholars and activists and locals have tried to do right by Mesa Verde, only to lose to corporations doing the whole world wrong.

Brochures for the region advertise Mesa Verde as "a place that time has forgotten."[7] But time remembers, time keeps track. You are all too aware of time at Mesa Verde. You are wondering how much time we have left. When Mesa Verde became a UNESCO site in 1978, the fossil fuel corporations who would reshape the world's climate were already lying about the destruction they knew they had unleashed.[8]

My children were ten and seven when they toured Mesa Verde. When I asked them about it as teenagers, they struggled to remember the specifics. My heart broke a little, even though this was inevitable. They have been to so many places, including an

inordinate number of thirteenth-century Native American do-
miciles. I suppose there are worse parenting failures than your
children's inability to keep track of all the ancient dwellings you
have shown them, so I tried not to feel bad. But the same dread hit
me—the feeling that this childhood visit might be their only one.
The thought that they may have children of their own, and bring
them here, and find ruins of ruins, ashes of a place their mother
claimed they once saw. The fear that Mesa Verde would remain
only in memories, and that their memories were already fading.

I tried to revive them.

"Mesa Verde was the park in southwest Colorado that had
burned down, the one in danger of burning more," I explained.
"Don't you remember?"

My daughter looked at me helplessly and said, "But that's every
park. We're always outrunning fire."

Looking back, I realized she was right.

The fire never hit us directly. We would see it in the distance, devouring scenery like a dragon of smoke. In Missouri, state parks do
controlled burns, and we know their cycles. But we were strangers
in Colorado and did not know what we were witnessing, whether
this was forest restoration or something worse. We did not know
how to evaluate its danger or abnormality.

But we knew how to fall in love, and we knew how to grieve.

In 2018, we drove a scorched-earth route from Kansas to Utah,
making a series of narrow misses to which we were oblivious at
the time. Roads burned soon after we crossed them. This was true
of the Spring Creek Fire, which was started by an arsonist in Fort
Garland, a town twenty-five miles from Alamosa, three days after our stay. The Spring Creek Fire grew to be the third-largest
wildfire in Colorado history.[9] It happened again with the 416 Fire,
which started in the San Juan Mountains and moved north, trailing us to the Rockies.[10] We did not realize how close we had come

until weeks later, when we saw photos of blackened land, and I realized that this was the forest where I'd told my children to inhale the fresh mountain air.

On the final day of our trip, I stood in front of our hotel watching wildfires approach as my husband hurriedly packed the car. I was mourning Colorado. I felt most for residents suffering through the decimation of their state but also for my children, who were young and may or may not remember seeing the region intact. If they did, they would catalog it as a capsule from the Before Times, the way I remember life before 9/11 and other disasters. Colorado would become a daydream land: not the real-life refuge I envisioned but another memory they could not revisit.

At the first sign of fire, I began taking too many photos of my children in front of natural wonders, demanding their compliance in ways I rarely do. Usually, I want them to play, not pose. But I needed proof that they had been there, that these lands were their lands once upon a time. A piece of my heart was burning with my country, and I wanted its ashes preserved.

By the time we crossed from Colorado into Utah, it was 105 degrees. We arrived in Moab on the hottest day of the year in what was then the fourth-hottest summer in US history. (This record would be beaten in 2020 and 2021 and 2022 and 2023 and likely again by the time you read this.)[11]

Moab lies at the edge of Arches and Canyonlands National Parks. It is a tourist town of hippies and mountain bikers and nerds who sell rocks and hucksters who try to convince you their rocks are dinosaur eggs. I liked Moab, much as I liked Utah in general. I had been to Utah twice, both times to Salt Lake City: once for a conference on authoritarian regimes, before the United States became an aspiring one; and once for my uncle-in-law's funeral. My husband's uncle had been a jocular, hard-drinking sportswriter who boasted he was the only Utahan the Mormons did not want to recruit. His memorial service was packed with jokes and heartfelt tributes from the Utah Jazz. I wish I had gotten to know him better. He made me recognize Utah as a refuge for the restless, a state whose uptight image is misleading.

I had been to Utah's mountains but never the desert. I was shocked first by the heat, then shocked that Utah natives were shocked. The drought was far beyond the dry heat to which residents were accustomed. This heat grabbed at your throat and stripped it dry, making your tongue feel like a lizard hiding in the shadow cave of your mouth. In this kind of heat, you stop feeling like a person and more like a collection of malfunctioning parts. As a result, my memories of Arches and Canyonlands are hazy, and I struggle to remember what we did and when. I turned off my phone because I feared it would melt.

I also turned off my phone because it had become a doomsday device, its news alerts ringing like the singsong of an apocalypse prophet. The last time I turned it on, we were in a diner for air-conditioning and lunch. The kids and I grabbed a booth while my husband ordered at the counter. I decided I should check the weather but was stopped in my search by breaking news.

"No," I said. "Oh no. . . ."

"What?" asked my daughter.

"Anthony Kennedy is quitting the Supreme Court."

"Who's Anthony Kennedy?"

"He's an asshole."

"Isn't it good he's leaving then?" asked my son. "Because it's bad to be an asshole?"

"Don't say *asshole*. Yes, in life it is bad to be an asshole. But in government, it's like a job requirement. I'm worried they'll replace him with a worse asshole, and that this was planned. Kennedy is connected to a place called Deutsche Bank, and his son has been managing Trump's loans and the bank handles the money of criminals. It's too long a story to tell in a book, much less over lunch, much less to you two. I'll just say Kennedy is tied to Trump in ways he shouldn't be, and it's all bad."

"Like Dark Helmet and President Skroob," my son said, thinking of *Spaceballs*, his primary source on government and assholes.

"Yes. As Dark Helmet said, we are surrounded by assholes. But this is serious. I knew this would happen. I just didn't know when. And it turned out to be today. So I will always remember this day, sitting here, on vacation, telling you two about the end. The end of civil rights, the end of a chance at a different future. Once they have the Supreme Court, there is nothing we can do. The story of your generation will begin at the end. You will flip through life like a backward book. Your prologue will be an epitaph. . . ."

I could see it unfold so clearly, and when that happens the words pour out like a drink no one ordered, and I put my head in my hands to stop myself from talking. When I looked up, the kids were eyeing me expectantly.

"Are we still having hot dogs?" my son asked.

"Yes."

"It's good that there are hot dogs on bad days."

"This is true, and thank you for reminding me."

"Are women still going to be allowed to vote when I'm eighteen?" asked my daughter.

"I don't know. I hope so."

"Oh right, voting," my son remembered. "Hey, can't you vote the assholes out?"

"Stop saying *asshole*! That's a Mommy-only word. No, we can't. No one gets to vote for the Supreme Court. They decide the laws, and there's nothing we can do. They stay on the court until they die."

"I see," said my daughter. "So I won't lose my right to vote. Because I never actually had one."

My husband arrived with a tray of hot dogs and a smile, which faded.

"What now?" he said. I regretted telling the kids, even though what I'd said was true. It's one thing to study past horrors, another to see a grim preordained future. Especially for my daughter, who lost her right to bodily autonomy four years after this conversation.

"I was checking the forecast on my phone," I told him. "We're burning alive. America is on fire, and they're going to burn us all alive."

It was too hot to hike Arches and Canyonlands during the day, so we took scenic drives, gazing at the landscape from the air-conditioned car. The kids had never seen a sun-colored land like Utah—red dust and orange spires and stacked stone hoodoos, unearthly yet natural, because nothing felt normal anyway. The landscape suited the mood. We belonged in this slice of America, where the ground was too hot to touch and the rock was too strong to break, a fearsome land of beautiful doom.

We drove to Dead Horse Point State Park, stopping at the cliff where Thelma and Louise had plunged to their suicidal death. I'd grown up watching that movie, relating to it even as a twelve-year-old, and that day it felt prophetic. My husband took a photo of me at the canyon edge, hand on my hip, flashing a futureless smile. Below me snaked the green Colorado River, which would evaporate a few years later, plunging the southwest into an ongoing water crisis. We were in a canyon of corpses with more to come. Dead Horse Point State Park is named after wild horses that cowboys rounded up in the nineteenth century. The men decided some of the mares were not up to par and rejected them, letting them die of thirst and throwing them over the rim before riding away on more submissive steeds.[12]

"How could such a pretty place have such bad people in it?" asked my daughter when she learned the story of the name. It was a rhetorical question, one that applies to anywhere in America. I always remind them that the flip side is how so many run-down places have so many good people. This is why I raise my children in St. Louis and why I take them everywhere—because you never know what good deeds your fellow Americans are doing without credit or praise.

It is always worth committing a small act of kindness because you never know how large it is to the recipient. I remember when we had little money and I took the kids for a rare meal out in St. Louis. They wanted dessert, and I did not have five dollars to buy it. I explained we were on a budget and they would have to wait another day. They nodded and said they understood. I felt a wave of shame that has never left me, no matter how much more secure my situation has become. Anyone who has struggled to provide for their children knows this particular horror, the way it digs its roots in you and blooms a bitter perennial. I told the kids it was time to go home, and suddenly three pieces of pie appeared before us. An old man had watched me, a young mother with two kids and no money, and decided to give us a treat. He left before we could thank him.

We all remember that pie. My children may forget entire national monuments, but they remember the kind stranger who bought them pie.

From Dead Horse Point State Park, we headed back to Moab and drove down Highway 191, stopping like good St. Louisans at every Arch we encountered. The roads outside the parks are marked with geological curiosities. They are not clustered together as they are inside, but they are not unexpected either. They are the natural proprietors of the scorched earth that birthed them, stone guide-posts that kept us from getting lost. Our GPS and cell phones had stopped working, and we had only a paper map to keep us on course.

At a fork in the road, a massive bulbous gumdrop emerged. There was nothing else of note, only sun-scorched plains, and we got out to examine the rock oddity, hoping to get our bearings. It gave off a creepy vibe, maybe because its desolation echoed our own. We had water in the car, but the record heat was dangerous. This was not the kind of place you wanted to get stranded. The map said if we turned onto Highway 221, we would head back toward Canyonlands.

We decided to give it a try. Immediately we found ourselves at the abandoned compound of a psychotic cult.

We did not know about the cult at the time. We stopped at a sign saying "Marie's Place," carved into a piece of wood swing-ing from two poles. I looked behind the sign for people but saw only ramshackle buildings of rotting wood and brick. Who was Marie? Maybe a rancher, I thought. Maybe she could give us di-rections. Highway 221 was a desolate road, and I was nervous that we would not make it back before dark. A dirt path behind the sign led up to a dwelling that seemed inhabited. I was curious, but curious in the Missouri way, which meant envisioning someone greeting you with a gun, so I retreated. We huddled behind the fence, my husband surreptitiously taking photos of what seemed to be a compound.

We learned later that Marie was Marie Ogden, a rich widow from New Jersey. She believed that southwestern Utah had a mag-ical portal at the center of the earth, and in 1933 she moved there with the aim of raising the dead. She found over twenty people to join her and made these acolytes surrender all their possessions and work the land while promising them eternal life. She named her compound the House of Truth and divided it into three portals: the Outer Portal, where the cult's dormitory was stationed; the Middle Portal, where a chapel was planned but never built; and the Inner Portal, where she lived and claimed to receive divine revelations. Ogden proclaimed that only residents of the Inner Portal would be spared the agonies of the apocalypse. Members of her cult made pilgrimages to the gumdrop mound, which they christened Church Rock. Ogden briefly decided Church Rock was the spiritual axis of the universe, before changing her mind.

The cult lasted until 1937, when a member, Edith Peshak, died of cancer. Peshak had joined the House of Truth because Ogden had promised to cure her using the power of the portals. Her death made Ogden's acolytes suspicious of her credibility, but Ogden had a solution: she would raise Peshak from the dead. Ogden documented her efforts in the local newspaper, which she had purchased in order to control narratives about the cult, proving in the process that self-awareness was not a quality the magic portals imparted.

Ogden described force-feeding Peshak's corpse and washing it in a salt solution, insisting that Peshak was not dead but in a "state of purification."[13] Her articles alarmed local authorities, who began to investigate the compound, but Ogden had already ordered an acolyte to destroy the body. The incident terrified the remaining members, who fled the House of Truth. Ogden was never punished and lived out her golden years in a nursing home in San Juan County.

When I looked up "Marie's Place" later and told the kids the story of the compound, they recognized the parallels with the Crescent Hotel in Eureka Springs, where Norman Baker had run a fake cancer retreat, assembled a cult following, and remained largely unpunished. The 1930s were the darkest of times, and the architectural ruins of their con artists dot America like a flip side to the WPA buildings built on promises of hope. Hucksters, criminals, mafiosos—recurring characters in the American story, rarely acknowledged but not at all rare.

We drove on to Canyonlands, leaving the compound behind. We had seen too much reality, and now it was time to dream.

By the time we reached the section of Canyonlands called Needles, it was evening and the temperature was dropping. Needles is a cluster of red-and-white-striped spired formations that provide narrow shaded pathways of cool sand. This area became one of our favorite places, and we returned to it the next night as well. I don't remember much of our Utah evenings other than a sense of calm despite the heat and turmoil. The relief my husband and I felt that we were able to give our children a real vacation, to show them a land that defied time, that scorned its threats—that, unlike everything else, seemed poised to stand its test.

It felt good to be a family, having the sort of family adventures I had dreamed of as a child. It felt good to be with people who wanted me around, and I have never stopped being surprised by it. The national parks remind me of the limitations of my view—not only of my country but in how much more of life you see when you look at the world through four sets of eyes. How gratifying it is to explore new lands with your husband and children, to have people who help you over boulders and streams, who extend a hand without being asked. How incredible it is to be a mom, a source of comfort, a role you grow into until it is no longer a role but the essence of who you are. The feeling when your children thank you for bringing them to a special place, the way their eyes light up with excitement when they imagine what will happen next, a light so bright that it blocks out dread like an eclipse. The shock when your heart defies logic and envisions a future, a future that involves no canyon plunge or doomsday grind, a daydream future that you know is real because it is happening right before you. Here, in this beautiful hellscape, is everything you want.

For a moment, for a night, I felt safe—in this land, in this family, in this country. I could take that feeling home with me because it came from somewhere true. In the national parks, you are supposed to leave no trace. But they left their mark on me.

The next morning, we left early for the final stretch, an eight-hour drive to Estes Park, a town at the edge of Rocky Mountain National Park. We wanted to avoid the interstate so we drove a winding detour north, past abandoned mines and snowcapped peaks. At a cliff, we stopped to let mountain goats pass, and the kids were so charmed by seeing animals in the wild that they did not notice the death drop to our left. We passed few cars, and fewer places to stop, and when we finally found a restaurant, no one spoke English. We pointed at the menu—at this point, no one in the family spoke Spanish; we've all studied it now—and I got a fish with its head still attached and the kids screamed and laughed and I ate it and it was delicious. There was a whole world to explore here, but we needed to keep moving, and so we climbed the mountains again, my husband's knuckles white on the wheel. We entered the park from the west on the way to the place we would stay: the Stanley, the hotel that inspired Stephen King to write *The Shining*.

We had been staying in cheap hotels in order to afford two nights at the Stanley, which, in addition to being a Stephen King pilgrimage site, is supposed to be haunted. If a town has a haunted hotel, I always splurge, though the Crescent in Eureka Springs is the only one that has delivered a legit scare. (The Skirvin Hotel in Oklahoma

City, where NBA players claim sexpot ghosts have tried to seduce them, is my second favorite.) Upon arrival, however, the paranormal component barely registered. The setting was so luminous that I could not fathom leaving even if I was chased by an ax-wielding maniac through a hedge maze. Estes Park is a tourist town, but it lies in a tranquil valley of wild beasts. I could have stayed forever, until the fire burned forever down.

We had two days in the Rockies, and we cherished every moment. The kids begged me to watch *The Shining*—I had talked too much about it in the car—and I relented, not wanting them to miss out on my idea of a cultural milestone. They watched it on my iPad, which I would flip over when something gory happened, which meant that their version of *The Shining* was about twenty minutes long. But they got the gist, and we explored the hotel, which was not scary but still impressive. We fell asleep early, exhausted from the drive, excited for the morning.

We spent the next two days catching our breath, floored by the elevation and the scenery. My children had never hiked in the mountains, and I was glad to cross it off the pre-apocalypse bucket list. Oceans, mountains, canyons, deserts: places everyone should visit because no photo can replicate reality. I had not seen a mountain until I was twenty and studying in Austria, which meant the first mountains I saw were the Alps, and the first time I went hiking was also in the Alps. I could not believe the option of roaming through open land had been available my whole life and I had never done it.

I also wondered, in an amused way, if every future hike would be a disappointment with the Alps as my baseline. This was not the case. If anything, I like the smaller hikes better, the also-rans and little-knowns, the places that offer solitude and take time to reveal their charms. But there is nothing like an alpine view, and I am glad my children saw the Rockies firsthand.

We hiked trails that took us over twelve thousand feet above sea level, past wildflowers with fairy-tale names like Sky Pilot and Greenleaf Chiming Bells. We climbed to the crags, and I gasped for breath and watched my children bask in the joy of pelting each other with snowballs in June. Exhausted, we spent the rest of the day on a quiet forest trail with some of the same wildlife we see in Missouri—blackbirds, chipmunks, bluebells—but everything felt more vivid. We were close to the sun, but it did not burn our faces. It was the sun of clarity, a cool luminescence on a lapis lazuli lake.

A stranger offered to take a photo of the four of us. I usually say no—my husband and I hate getting our picture taken—but I said yes on a whim, and I am glad I did, because we look so happy. We are standing together smiling, our shadows in front of us merged into one dark mass. I keep this photo on my dresser. It is the first thing I see when I wake up and the last thing I look at before I go to bed. A family are the people who will share your shadow while you seek the sun.

In the summer of 2019, we did the unthinkable: we took a two-week vacation. This is a rarity in America, where businesses often grant one week or less off, and a luxury for us.

The westward trip of 2019 was the longest and most expensive vacation I ever took, and I do not regret it. I knew that it was now or never, and never was stalking my nightmares like a clock winding in reverse. Never was the future I could not avoid but could—for a little while—outrun. Never taunted and now beckoned, the open road luring me like a last-chance ride, and I took it as far as I could go. I documented my country like I was visiting a relative diagnosed with a terminal disease, trying to capture them before the cancer set in and became all anyone could remember.

In 2019, we drove through an America that, one year later, ceased to exist: an America that mutated like a virus, one that is still finding its final form. This was the last year both of my children were technically children, since my daughter turned thirteen in the summer of 2020. There was an innocence to this trip that I took pains to document, because I could feel it slipping away.

I have lived too much of my life in anticipatory retrospect. I don't know if that is a gift or a curse. But I am glad, at least, that it gives me time to collect evidence: a bulwark against my own mind.

Some daydreams you need to document because the impulse to forget them overwhelms you when things get bad. You want to pretend past joys were never possible so you can recuse yourself from expecting future ones. You don't want to admit defeat in a game you denied you were playing. You don't want to confess that all along, a little hope burned in you despite your best effort, a fragile ember you secretly stoked, a flicker you wished would become a flame. That hope was snuffed out like you knew it would be. That this outcome was predictable does not matter in the end because it is still loss, still grief, still pain.

And so you cherish the memories of the good times, even if the joy of them hurts. You catalog and keep them. You owe that to the people and places who made them good in the first place.

We were going farther west than ever before. We were visiting four national parks—Theodore Roosevelt, Glacier, Grand Teton, and Yellowstone—and landmarks along the way. We would drive through Iowa, Minnesota, North Dakota, Montana, Idaho, Wyoming, and Nebraska. By the time we returned to Missouri, I would have seen all forty-eight contiguous states, something I felt was important to do before 2020, though I couldn't articulate why. I was developing a fear of crowds and strangers. I was becoming more well known due to appearances on television and a bestselling book, and being recognized made me uncomfortable. I didn't know why the fear was so overwhelming, but at the time, I chalked it up to fame.

"I feel exposed," I told my husband. "I'm scared of being in public. I don't know how to handle the exposure." But that phrase—*I feel exposed*—taunted me like a monkey's paw as 2019 turned into 2020 and my home became a sealed sanctuary. I longed for the West and its limitless, liminal space. I wanted to disappear into a vast and open terrain where I could avoid all the terrible things to which a person can be exposed.

It had been a rough year, and the daydream lands of the national parks helped keep me going. My children were eight and twelve, perfect ages for an American adventure. There is a joke that Missourians are the descendants of the pioneers who set out for the West, got tired, said "close enough," and stayed put, thus birthing the stubborn shrug of Missouri life. We vowed to defy the trend. We would blaze a trail west on a highway, in a Honda. Willa Cather wrote in *O Pioneers* that a true pioneer enjoys the idea of things more than the things themselves. By that standard, I was a master explorer.

"Capture as much of this trip as you can," I begged my husband before we left St. Louis. He more than complied. For my birthday, he gave me a photo album he made of our journey. He titled it "We Did Not Die of Dysentery" in honor of the *Oregon Trail* computer game, in which you pretended to be a pioneer heading west, passing real-life landmarks along the way. Like many in my generation, I grew up obsessed with this game. We had traced much of the Oregon Trail, and I had spent two weeks gushing like a groupie.

"It's like meeting a rock star in real life!" I exclaimed when we arrived in western Nebraska at Chimney Rock National Monument, no longer reduced to a pixelated spire I approached with invisible wagon mates but the real deal. I gripped my husband's hand and dragged him to the window to take in the iconic rock and its pencil-thin tip.

"Click the space bar and continue!" I commanded, pointing outside, my eyes wild with excitement. A gift shop clerk looked at us with pity.

"You married a 1980s baby, didn't you?" the clerk asked. My husband nodded with the chagrin of someone too old to know the thrill of caulking a cartoon wagon.

"I used to enter the names of the New Kids on the Block as my wagon team," I told the clerk dreamily. "And then I'd murder them. Donnie has cholera! Jordan has a snake bite! Here lies Danny!" She began to back away as I stocked up on *Oregon Trail* merch, fording the river of my childhood dreams. My son found a handheld *Oregon Trail* game with the same primitive green graphics of my youth, and I beamed with delight. He would spend the car ride home lost in the absurd America of my microgeneration, inheriting its treasure trove of useless facts and dubious survival tips.

I gave Chimney Rock one last look as we headed back to the car for the ride home. I felt a twinge upon leaving, because the innocence lost was mine.

When you come from a Midwest metropolis, you can slip into every American scene, a nondescript imposter, belonging everywhere and nowhere.

People often describe Missouri as rural, and while many regions of it are sparsely inhabited, Missouri is bustling compared to the West and the Plains. Our 2019 trip shifted our expectations of space and time. We started expecting fewer people and then out-right wanting fewer, an urge that haunted us in 2020. Distances once thought long became feasible. We started calling a day trip of roughly thirteen hours "an Amarillo," in honor of our frequent overnight stop on our way to the West. Colby, Kansas, where we stopped on our way to Colorado, was one Amarillo away from St. Louis. So was Fargo, North Dakota, if we left before the sun rose.

The drive to Fargo took us up Highway 61: the Mississippi River road Bob Dylan immortalized as the heart of American music. We entered Iowa and stopped at a Waterloo diner offering a huge pork tenderloin inside a very small bun. A gigantic tenderloin sandwich is as clear a sign that you are in the Midwest as sweet tea is for the South. Down the street was a shop filled with T-shirts bearing slogans oddly attuned to my political beliefs. I discovered it was not an improbably populist boutique but Elizabeth Warren's Iowa campaign headquarters. A sad muskrat was sleeping in front of the door. We moved it gently out of the way and entered. The staff was excited and gave us a few free signs. Those signs are in our basement, next to a stash of canned goods to ride out the pandemic. March 2020 did not work out how anyone planned.

In northern Iowa, we stopped to see the place the music died. Clear Lake is where, in 1959, the plane carrying Buddy Holly, the Big Bopper, and Ritchie Valens crashed into a cornfield, killing all three. The field is now a pilgrimage site for people pretending to recall a time they never experienced, similar to the invented nostalgia shrines of Route 66. My Boomer parents are too young to remember any of the 1950s rock stars when they were alive, but they can still "remember" the day they died. My husband and I were born decades after the crash, and when our kids asked why we wanted to stop at the site, we couldn't explain it. But when we saw other visitors, it clicked: we needed reassurance that people still cared. We wanted to be links in a chain of American musical memory and ensure it remains unbroken.

A pair of Buddy Holly glasses as tall as I am stood at the front of the field, with the words "the three amigos" scrawled on it in black marker. Elderly visitors wandered around, tears in their eyes. I don't know if they were old enough to remember the crash, or if the music reminded them of the relative innocence of their youth, or if the random jolt of tragedy was sad enough in its own right, or if, like me, they were wondering about the site's future relevance.

Contrary to Boomer claims that rock 'n' roll will never die, it has been slowly strangled for decades. Songs smothered by Spotify, concerts controlled by Ticketmaster, MTV burning out and radio fading away. Clear Channel is the new Clear Lake, only everything is crashing at once. But if rock 'n' roll is going down in history, I will teach the history. I take my children to rock pilgrimage sites because I don't think anyone can understand America without understanding American music.

For years, our family had driven Highway 61 in the other direction, to the musical landmarks of the Black South: Robert Johnson's graveyard shrine in Greenwood, Mississippi; Johnny Cash's childhood home in Dyess, Arkansas; the blues and jazz hubs of Memphis and New Orleans. Quintessentially American places in a country whose leaders no longer seem to find its culture or even its existence that essential. Relics of twentieth-century America: the America of diversity and distinction, the American catalog that digital merchants wipe clean, the American sovereignty that billionaires sell. And now we had arrived at the other end of that highway, wondering what will happen when no one is left to grieve the day the music died.

We left Iowa, crossed into a small corner of Minnesota, and

then stopped in Fargo for the night. We were headed for Medora, the gateway to Theodore Roosevelt National Park at the western-most edge of the state, which meant we were going to spend the next day driving across North Dakota. This national park is one of America's least visited, and the remote location is a main reason why. I embraced the drive: I had never been to North Dakota and had no sense of what I would find. It was the most rural state I had visited. Missouri and North Dakota are roughly the same size, about 70,000 square miles. But over six million people live in Missouri while North Dakota has about 797,000. Metro St. Louis alone has more than three times North Dakota's entire population.

North Dakota is one of few American states to enjoy rapid economic prosperity in the twenty-first century thanks to oil reserves that spurred settlements in a manner reminiscent of the boom-towns of the Old West. On our second night in the state, while looking for a place to eat, we stumbled into a shale oil camp. My daughter and I were the only females in sight. Most of the workers came from Latin America and lived in mobile homes rented by the week. In a hole-in-the-wall joint in a half-finished strip mall, we found Mexican food, authentic and tailored to roughnecks. We got great tacos and curious stares. In a boomtown, everyone stays a stranger.

North Dakota is dotted with ghost towns from previous booms gone bust. We explored them on our drive west, entering crumbling, once stately homes with old-fashioned rocking chairs and piles of logs for long-dormant fireplaces. There was no sense of time—the houses could have been built a decade or a century ago. For lunch, we stopped at a diner full of dairy farmers who looked like they were auditioning for Grant Wood portraits, men who wore suspenders and straw hats and stared out solemnly over Salisbury steak. People were not unfriendly in rural North Dakota, but they were quiet, not bothering with the put-on niceties of the small-town South.

In the town of New Salem, we climbed a hill to take in the view from under the udders of Salem Sue, the World's Largest Holstein Cow, a gargantuan fiberglass heifer thirty-eight feet tall and twelve thousand pounds. Salem Sue stands defiant, gazing out at endless acres of manicured North Dakota farmland, daring you to question why she is necessary. The statue was constructed by the New Salem Lions Club to pay tribute to the dairy farmers of North Dakota.

Like so many of the roadside attractions of Route 66, Salem Sue was built in 1974, the year America broke and Americans found creative ways to convey the enormity of their loss. Road signs warned there were "livestock at large," and I wondered if they were the sole residents. I imagined ghost town cows trekking to New Salem in the dead of night, gathering around Salem Sue in a bovine mass. There are nearly two million cows in North Dakota, outnumbering people over two to one.[14] The cows would know who is really in charge, and taciturn North Dakotans could be relied on to stay silent. Before we left the Holstein shrine, I put a dollar in Salem Sue's milk can. A tithe to the udder world, just to stay safe.

In the afternoon, we made it to Theodore Roosevelt National Park, named for America's first conservationist president. Roosevelt is credited for helping introduce the idea of not destroying the earth for profit as a mainstream political proposition and for launching the environmental and archaeological protection laws that spawned the national parks system. He sought to prevent the bleak conditions of our time. To revisit his speeches is to inhabit an alternative America, one where politicians kept their promises, the daydream America I find only in the parks.

"The time has come to inquire seriously what will happen when our forests are gone, when the coal, the iron, the oil, and the gas are exhausted," Roosevelt warned in a 1908 speech, "when the soils have still further impoverished and washed into the streams, polluting the rivers, denuding the fields and obstructing navigation. These questions do not relate only to the next century or to the next generation. One distinguishing characteristic of really civilized men is foresight; we have to, as a nation, exercise foresight for this nation in the future; and if we do not exercise that foresight, dark will be the future!"[15]

National parks are aimed at the preservation of life. But Theodore Roosevelt National Park was borne of death, both personal and political. Roosevelt first visited North Dakota in 1883 to hunt bison at a time when the US government was slaughtering them to near extinction in an attempt to starve Native Americans of their livelihood and heritage.[16] Roosevelt failed to see that truth then. He was infatuated with cowboy culture, though Dakota territory ranchers were less than impressed with his outdoor acumen. But in 1884, he was hit by twin tragedies that transformed his conception of birth and death and the fragile space between them.

On February 14, 1884, Roosevelt's mother, Martha, died of typhoid. Thirteen hours after his mother's death, his wife, Alice, died in childbirth. "The light has gone out of my life," he wrote in his diary that night under a large black X. He never spoke of his wife again.[17]

The twenty-five-year-old Roosevelt left his newborn daughter with his sister and headed to North Dakota. To grieve, to heal: he did not make a distinction. He could not bring himself to write about the women he lost, so he wrote about North Dakota instead. He wrote about the places that would not leave him.

Roosevelt stayed in North Dakota for three years, becoming increasingly devoted to the preservation of the land and its wildlife. It was no longer a lark but a refuge, a break in the bravado, a land that bore private witness to unbearable pain. He lived on a ranch and served as a deputy sheriff in Billings County until a harsh winter wiped out his cattle, and the loss of fortune brought him back east.

Roosevelt credits North Dakota for restoring something in him that had gone numb and cold. He declared that without his time there, he never would have sought the presidency. Roosevelt is a man whose favorability relies on other men of the Gilded Age— most were reprehensible, so he looks good by comparison. He was an imperialist and a hypocrite but also a true lover of nature. He pioneered the parks in the way that mattered, which is to say he took the parks back from the pioneers and proclaimed them to be for no man, and therefore for all.

Now we, the inheritors of the dead future, got a taste of Theodore Roosevelt's daydream America. We entered the park near Medora, the neo–Old West town where we would stay overnight, and drove past a panorama of colorful badlands into a prairie. Wild horses leaped and bounded, dazzling the kids, who had never seen horses unbridled. We stopped to hike to a bluff overlooking the Little Missouri River, marveling that if you followed the river to the end, you would hit St. Louis. We were connected like veins and arteries in this brokenhearted land. The threat of drought beat down with the sun, a promise to break our region apart, to deliver our punishment for other people's sins. I pushed it out of my mind and held my children's hands as we watched the horses dance.

We drove on to a valley of rock mounds that resembled waves hardened into stone mid-crest, another sediment seascape: bleached badlands capped with red scoria, dotted with wildflowers and scrub grass and tufts of green brush. It was easy to see why Roosevelt had stayed, how rough beauty could heal a man. Dusk was falling, and we saw a large brown shape in the distance. A beast was stomping in the ground, creating a cloud of dirt. We drove closer and saw around forty bison moving across the river, following their leader, headed to wherever they sheltered for the night. We pulled over to watch them pass because I had never seen anything like it, and I never would again.

There is a conservation area called Lone Elk Park in St. Louis County, which, despite the name, is known primarily as a bison habitat. I had seen bison in the wild but never in a space this vast, never so many at once, never on a terrain that felt less like an approximation of North America's natural ecosystem than a continuation of it. In the late eighteenth century, there were sixty million bison in North America. By the late nineteenth, fewer than one thousand remained. Their near extinction caused a grotesque transformation of the ecosystem of a continent and its civilizations. To see them run free in the park was blissful but also heartbreaking because it had become so rare.

I watched the animals Theodore Roosevelt had first slaughtered and then decided to save. I watched the offspring of promises broken before I was born. I watched smaller bison run with what I assumed were their parents and envied all they did not know.

There are no landscapes more comforting at the end of the world than a petrified forest. That is what I told the kids the next morning as we set out on a dirt road to a remote path that led into a gulch of rounded white rock huts with orange and red stripes at the top. Scattered around the huts were glittering stumps, some brimming with quartz, some erupting with wildflowers. Sixty million years ago, this was a cypress swamp, I explained. This land was a forest, then a swamp, then an ocean, and then minerals filled the trees, hardening them into stone. The petrified forest had outlasted all the terrible and wonderful things that have come and gone, and it will outlast whatever comes next. They last *forever*, I told the kids as we wandered, lone hikers in an arboreal graveyard.

"Doesn't *petrified* mean *scared*?" asked my son. I explained that they had the same root—*petros*, Greek for stone—and that the term came about because people freeze up when they are afraid. Petrified people cannot escape or make decisions. They are locked in place.

"But in nature, that can be a blessing," I told him. "The man who helped make this park wanted things not to change. He wanted you to see the same places he did. Here, *petrified* is the opposite of being afraid, because *petrified* means you can count on it to last. The petrified survive."

The kids had never seen petrified wood, and they were fascinated. They did not understand exactly what it was—a rock? a tree? both?—but knew that it was rare and that it fit in this ancient alien landscape, these bizarre badlands divorced from even the weirdest geology of Missouri. There are parts of the Ozarks so rocky that, as the saying goes, you can't raise nothing but hell, but western North Dakota makes them seem calm by contrast. We visited Cannonball Concretions, a row of wavy white cliffs frozen in prehistoric undulation, with stone spheres lodged in narrow holes. The cliffs looked like God was bouncing a ball off the wall in boredom as he created the world, laughing at where it landed, letting it lie.

Midday, my twelve-year-old daughter and I rode horses up the ledge of a butte; my son was too young and had to settle for a coin-operated bucking bronco at our kitschy hotel. My daughter and I and the guide were the only people on the trail, granting us unimpeded views of manila cones bursting with greenery below. The canyon looked like it was carved with clay, but its floor was hard enough to kill us if we fell. Our guide looked at us skeptically, since we seemed the falling types. But we managed, steering at a near ninety-degree angle, our savvy steeds compensating for our inexperience. One reason I recommend Theodore Roosevelt to parents above other parks is that a horseback ride would be crowded or impossible or unaffordable in the popular parks. I love Yellowstone and the rest, but Theodore Roosevelt is what a family park should be.

At night, we drove to an isolated area we had staked out earlier, looked at Jupiter, Saturn, and the moon through our telescope, and then waited. "Dark will be the future," Roosevelt had proclaimed. It was pitch black in his namesake park, save the distant fire of an oil derrick. For the first time in my life, I saw the Milky Way. That starscape of ignited eyes, blurring into heraldic vision. The way it stares back at you, asking where you've been all these years.

Dark was the future, dark in the best of ways. This was the one promise that Roosevelt kept, I thought as my children and husband and I lay on our backs, gazing into a spiral galaxy that went on and on. Out of reach, for now, from the men who destroy the world.

The next day we ate breakfast at our old-timey Western hotel, which had a helpful sign that said "You cannot put gravy in waffle makers." We were up early for a long drive across a new state. Our destination was Glacier National Park. While Montana was just across the border from Medora, Glacier was at the other end, a full Amarillo away. We were taking Route 2, one of the loneliest highways in America, a sepia marathon of torn-down towns separated by cinnamon-colored fields.

Soon after entering Montana, we passed a barn painted with red and white stripes on the front and blue stars on the side, decorated like the American flag. Large parts of the barn had been painted over in black, first in neat paneled squares, like blocking out a memory, and then in a wild scrawl, like the memory had returned as a message, an opprobrium. I don't know whose barn it was. It felt like it was meant for everyone.

Our drive was punctuated by visits to prehistoric sites. We had decided to take the "dinosaur trail" across the state. Dinosaurs loved Montana because Montana is enormous like them, so they decided to litter it with their remains. My son was in his dinosaur phase, and when you have a twelve-hour drive with an eight-year-old, you appease your pint-sized fossil fiend. The dinosaurs in the museums had names like Ralph and Julie and Elvis. One dinosaur was an anonymous grinning skull who would share a name with a new brand of beer that visitors would select through a vote. We submitted a ballot because we wanted our children to get to participate in an election without the threat of a coup.

Dinosaurs seemed more at home than humans in northern Montana, which stretched like an endless void. I do not mind an endless void, I am a fan of endless voids, but I had never been anywhere as big and blank as Route 2, which made North Dakota seem flashy and Texas seem small. These were not the soaring hills of the TV series *Yellowstone* or the forested hideouts of the Unabomber—my most recent and most formative reference points on Montana—but a flatland where everyone can see everything you're doing, and you're not doing anything much.

We were staying in Kalispell, the largest city near Glacier, which means it has around twenty-five thousand people. I knew of Kalispell both as a tourist town and because mercenaries had sought out the surrounding region for training camps.[18] For decades, Montana had attracted billionaires and bombers; now it gets bombers funded by billionaires. Montana had also attracted survivalists who believed that the inlands of the Northwest were ideal to survive climate change. They built homes in preparation,

shelters that proved feeble in the face of the record-high temperatures and raging wildfires that now arrive each summer. Such was
the sucker's bet of the modern militant: they bought bunkers to
outrun the sun and wound up in time-shares of the apocalypse.

We did not know it in 2019, but we were visiting Glacier at
an idyllic time. Starting in 2020, the wildfires in Canada became
so severe, we could smell their smoke thousands of miles away in
St. Louis. We spent three days in Glacier under deep blue skies
illuminating crisp white mountains, the fresh green earth teeming
with wildflowers. There were signs of what was coming: in 2017,
the Sprague Fire had swallowed part of the Canadian side of the
park, leaving blackened trees in Alberta's ashen fields. It was a
matter of time before fire swallowed the American side too.

My children were wise to this state of affairs. Every year of
their life had been hotter than the one before. The first thing they
asked was if the glaciers were going to melt.

The answer was that despite the namesake, glaciers had always
been a minor part of the park, and most of them had already melted.
Informational booths at Glacier showcase a century and a half of
loss, with the remaining glaciers expected to vanish by 2030. Since
1950, the average regional temperature had risen by 3°F.[19] Visiting
Glacier is a journey through the damage done, a bittersweet exhibi-
tion, because what remains is still astonishing. It is a good place to
teach your children about climate change, not only because of what
has been lost but because there is so much to fight to save.

There is only one road through Glacier National Park, the
Going-to-the-Sun Road, and everyone is on it at once: a caravan
of Icaruses trying not to die while learning how to live. On a map,
the Going-to-the-Sun Road looks like a pencil scribble by a tod-
dler, random and loopy and narrow. Driving it feels like taunting
gravity. It is outrageously beautiful, literal over-the-top beautiful
because you are over the top of everything, and while there is a dis-

tinct feeling that *you shouldn't be*, you are. Above the snowcapped mountains and five-hundred-year-old cedars and bottomless blue lakes and forests of moose and bear is *you*, lucky enough to witness this gorgeous land.

You are above it all, and there are turnoffs with paths that promise to bring you higher still. These paths have names like Avalanche Trail that imply that ascending them may be a bad idea, but you go anyway. Even the more docile names belie hard-earned glory. We hiked the Hidden Lake Trail—two miles with two children on a boardwalk, how tough could it be?—and by the time we reached the eponymous lake we were gasping from a six-thousand-foot uphill hell march. The whole time we walked, we contemplated turning back, but then something miraculous would appear, like a family of mountain goats strolling by, their baby goat in tow, and our kids would follow their kid in delight.

At Glacier National Park, tourists follow animals like paparazzi, enchanted while trying to keeping a careful distance. Glacier was our family's first taste of crowds, a shock after the tranquility of Theodore Roosevelt. But it was not entirely bad. We traded tips with visitors about various trails, detailing the rewards that awaited if you toughed it out. There was a comradery among strangers making the same climb, a satisfaction in affirming that it was worth the pain as you sauntered back down. You know that if they reached the top, they would remember you when they saw those turquoise waters beneath the silver hills, like we remembered the strangers who helped us. In Glacier, we met people from around the world and found that they were good. The park brought out the best in everyone.

The kids were dazzled: they knew that even by the standards of the splendor we had seen elsewhere, Glacier was special. At an alpine lake that we hiked for hours to reach, they waded into the icy water with their clothes on, too lost in the moment to care. We joined them, feeling free, even though dozens of strangers had the same idea. We were never alone, but it seemed petty to complain about joyful, nature-loving people who needed a break.

When I think about the people we met in the summer of 2019, I wonder if, in 2020, they felt relief that they had visited Glacier then instead of waiting. I wonder if, like me, they remember it with that shaky feeling you get when you almost miss a flight.

Northern Montana was a succession of delights. I daydream about this trip often because even the most mundane objects filled me with joy. I tried huckleberries—a sweet purple berry that grows in the wild in subalpine climates—for the first time and decided I wanted them in everything. Huckleberry pancakes, ice cream, pie, licorice, milkshakes, jam, bread, hamburgers: there was no food that could not be improved by huckleberries. If there was an opportunity for huckleberry consumption, I took it. I ordered my children to keep watch for fruit stands. We made a lot of U-turns on that trip.

Montana is a state I love without understanding it. I have seen only a fraction, and it was the most glamorous and misleading part. Our relationship is like a chance encounter with a celebrity that changed your life and that they don't remember at all. Montana does not remember me, even though I am the second-most famous Polish American with a bestselling book about conspiracies to visit and the only one who did not build a bomb, but alas, this counts for nothing. I am another tourist pretending to be a guest. Montana is full of secrets you need decades of direct observation to decode.

I could belong to Montana if I had several lifetimes for it to let me in.

Glacier National Park is bordered by Native American reservations: the Blackfoot to the east and the Flathead to the south. On our way down Highway 93 out of Kalispell, we drove through the Flathead Nation, with signs in their native language, Salish. "*Čx̣ʷtpmn̓wéxʷ*" read one, and I looked it up, and found it means "passing between two ridges, where they come to an end."[20]

Salish is a critically endangered language spoken by fewer than a thousand people. The Flathead Nation was established in the ghost town of Hellgate, so named because of brutal battles between the Flatheads and the Blackfoot that were then followed by brutal battles and bitter betrayals with white settlers. I have seen Native American language signs elsewhere in the United States: the Seneca in upstate New York, the Cherokee in Oklahoma, the Navajo of the Four Corners. Every time I see these signs, I feel like a small part of the truth of this land opens up, something specific and undeniable, something that speaks to centuries of history in a way more should know.

The Salish signs of the Flathead Nation gave way to emblems of American conquest, and we found ourselves surrounded by documentation of the most mundane actions of Lewis and Clark. As a Missourian, I am inundated with Lewis and Clark lore as part of daily life—they paved the Route 66 of the nineteenth century—so this was nothing new. William Clark is buried in St. Louis's Bellefontaine Cemetery and boasts its best epitaph: "Interred under the obelisk." I plan to steal this epitaph, only unlike Clark, I will not actually have an obelisk but will inspire visitors to search the cemetery for one in vain. I imagine centuries passing and my practical joke turning into a legend, with claims of secret maps and sightings of the mysterious obelisk's ruins. This is how I would like to spend my death, with everyone who encounters me ending up on a futile quest, much like they do after meeting me in life.

From Montana, we headed to the Salmon-Challis National Forest. This route takes Lewis and Clark signage to an obsessive level even an *Oregon Trail* fanatic like me does not possess. *Here*

Clark had a bad dream, here Lewis took a shit, the signposts proclaimed, or something to that effect. As the hours passed, I got bored and wondered what did not make it into Clark's diary, what else those two got up to on those lonely nights manifesting destiny. I invented a love story, "The Erotic Adventures of Lewis and Clark," which shall not be reprinted here.

This is what happens to your brain when you have driven several thousand miles with several thousand left to go. We were at the midpoint of our trip when we crossed into Idaho, the last of the forty-eight contiguous states I had to see, and I felt great satisfaction that my childhood goal of driving through the United States of America had been realized.

I loved driving through Idaho. Bathed in soft midday light, the state had a surreal quality that never let up. The landscape looked like it was stitched from felt and glitter: shadow mountains dotted with baby green trees, blue streams turned translucent in the sun. Idaho was gentler than I had expected and devoid of people. Missouri is often devoid of people because the people moved away. Idaho lacked people because the deluge of Californians had not yet arrived. We drove along the Salmon River, looking for a place to eat, and saw only fishermen. Life seemed as it should be.

We found a diner in the town of Salmon, which had a sign proclaiming it the alleged birthplace of Sacagawea, the Lemhi Shoshone guide of Lewis and Clark. The waitress asked if we were interested in pie. I told her I was always interested in pie. I asked if she had huckleberry, and she said they did, and my children groaned.

"My mom is addicted to huckleberries," my daughter said. "You need to stop her, she's out of control!"

"Well, who *doesn't* like huckleberries!" said the waitress, a team player. "Are you folks here on vacation?"

"We're on a road trip to see the national parks," I babbled.

"And Idaho is my forty-eighth state. Now I've seen all the states except Alaska and Hawaii!"

"How exciting!" she exclaimed. I was like a child, and she was rolling with it. "And now you'll get to celebrate with some pie."

I was very happy. I like eating pie in cheap places where no one knows me, and I felt very patriotic, having checked off all my states. I looked at the giant flag on the wall and the enormous menu on the table, trying to decide which made me feel the most American.

We ordered burgers and fries. My husband told the waitress he was excited to eat real Idaho potatoes in Idaho, and at this pronouncement, our children sank deeper into mortification. But I could tell they were having fun despite my husband and I being, respectively, "cringe" and "extra." We were the opposite of cool, but we took them to cool places, and our nerdiness provided assurance that our marriage would stay stable, for clearly no one else could want either of us. We were a family, and they had a good deal.

After lunch, we got our pie. I decided to capture the moment and turned on my phone. I had vowed to leave it off the whole trip but could not resist the urge to post on Twitter that I had seen all the states. I had regressed into a childlike revelry, and now I was to be reprimanded for living my dreams. Angry replies appeared immediately.

"This is extremely insensitive to post now," said one. "You're driving through America? Have fun dying," said another.

I did not know what had happened, but I knew it was bad. There was no other way it could be in 2019.

Moments before I posted, a white supremacist terrorist had shot up a Walmart in El Paso, Texas, murdering twenty-three people and injuring twenty-three more. It was the deadliest anti-Latino attack in US history and, at the time, the sixth deadliest mass shooting in US history. The attack was notable foremost for the tragic loss of life but also for the exploitation surrounding it. There are many horrific moments from 2019 lodged in my mind, but the photo that haunts me most is of a grinning Donald Trump holding a baby orphaned in the El Paso shooting like it is a trophy, giving the world a thumbs-up after the baby's parents had been gunned down.[21]

That this image has been forgotten scares me as much as the photo itself.

American mass shootings are so common that no one expects you to remember where you are when one happens. There was a mass shooting on every day of our two-week vacation. Less than a day after the El Paso massacre, nine people were shot to death in Dayton, Ohio. There is nothing surprising about these atrocities, but I still remember where I was and what I felt when I heard about them. Part of my reaction is involuntary, an inability to shake off the horror. But part is a sense of obligation. I do not have solutions for a crisis raging for over half my life. I only know it is better to remember than to forget.

There is a difference between expecting violence, as all Americans do, and accepting violence. Politicians claiming that mass violence has been normalized are often the ones trying to normalize it. If mass shootings are shrugged off as inevitable, then they can avoid doing anything but fundraising off agony. But there is a difference between common and normal. Most Americans still react to shootings with grief. We are used to this emotion—along with fury at our useless officials—but pain does not diminish with shock.

I would rather feel the pain of remembering than forget the victims. I would rather someone take my life than my humanity. I don't think I am alone in this respect.

We paid the bill and got in the car and kept driving, and the summer day kept being beautiful, maybe to mock us, maybe to comfort us, I don't know. The summer day kept being beautiful despite the fact that the sun shone on fewer souls and on a Walmart drenched in blood. The sun shone with perverse indifference; the sun could not care less about the grieving or the dead; the sun was lighting the way to more wrong-place, wrong-time twists of fate. There were no detours left in 2019; every road had turned blind alley. The sun shone on an America where there was nowhere to hide—not the hills, not the highways, not the stores or the schools or the streets. We watched Idaho gorgeous, lit up by the sun, playing shadows with my heart, and I did not know whether to feel lucky or damned to be alive—and that, that is the most American I felt all day.

I woke up the next morning wanting to disappear, so I did.

We were at Craters of the Moon, a four-hundred-thousand-acre lava field in central Idaho. The official line on this monument is that it resembles the surface of the moon and is named accordingly. But the truth is it looks like hell, and the people who protect it know it and pay tribute with its landmarks. We began our day by climbing a mountain called the Inferno Cone, gasping at the top as we surveyed black waves of volcanic debris. In the distance, we could see the shadow-soft Idaho mountains, a limbo land next to an underworld turned inside out.

"Where are we going after the Inferno Cone, Mommy?" my son asked.

"We're going to the Devil's Orchard, son!" I answered cheerfully.

"And then we shall descend into the hollows of the earth, bereft of the slightest ray of sun," my husband said dramatically, and my son laughed because he thought we were kidding, but we were not.

I liked Craters of the Moon because it relieved me of the strain of picturing the apocalypse and let me crawl around inside it instead.

Craters of the Moon National Monument and Preserve was caused by a volcanic eruption two thousand years ago that turned the area into lava fields punctuated by large rock piles called spatter cones. In the 1960s, the landscape was used by astronauts in training, including Alan Shepard, the first American in space. In 1924, Craters of the Moon became a national monument, one of several national monuments that I hope never gain national park status even though they deserve it, because too many people would make it mad. This is a surly park that does not hide its contempt for careless visitors.

"A hundred years ago, a visiting minister declared this jumble of rocks, shrubs, and trees to be a garden fit for the Devil himself. Welcome to Devil's Orchard."

That was the sign that greeted us in a lava field of dead and twisted silver trees. A sign titled MISCONCEPTION AND MISTAKE explained that the trees had not been killed by the eruption. They were limber pines, hardy trees that thrive in volcanic soil. Over time, the trees attracted a parasitic plant called dwarf mistletoe that left their branches gnarled in tangles dubbed *witches'-broom*—disfigured but alive. But park managers wanted the trees to be attractive in a conventional way. They cut off the mistletoe and murdered the trees in the process. Now the trees formed a bucolic tomb, frozen in the form in which they were slain.

"A value judgment about witches'-broom—that it is unsightly, ugly, 'bad'—caused the death of these trees," the sign explained. The message was clear: the Devil of Devil's Orchard was man.

Craters of the Moon is a tribute to everything that is strange and misunderstood and is abused for being so but insists on surviving out of spite. The slain trees had friends. Between them grew white-green grass on which sat bright-yellow insects enjoying their otherworldly kingdom. I thought of George Washington Carver and how nature will share its secrets if you love it enough, and how at Craters of the Moon a misfit could commune with the dead.

We hiked into the volcanic fields until we reached black holes filled with snow. The snow would not melt no matter how hard the August sun beat down, and we did not know why. Craters of the Moon was not going to make sense, and its refusal to abide logic only bolstered its appeal.

We had a permit to explore the park's lava tubes and climbed to the bottom. Prisms of daylight from above cast an eerie glow, streams of violet and green beaming in like a subterranean aurora borealis.

"Should we be in here?" asked my daughter as we worked through the passages. She sounded more worried for the caves than she did for herself. I have a picture of her, age twelve, walking alone down a path surrounded by black lava fields, open-hearted and unafraid.

"I don't know," I said. "We're allowed to, but I'm not sure we should be." I was scared inside the lava tubes—scared I would break them and scared they would swallow me into a world I would not know how or seek to exit.

"These caves aren't that old," I told her. "People were living here a few thousand years ago, until one day, with no warning, their world exploded. And now here we are, wandering in the remains."

"I'm not afraid of the dark," she said. "I'm afraid *for* the dark. For all the little plants and insects who live here that people don't want to see because they won't look inside the dark. I want to leave in case something is growing and I miss it and hurt it on accident."

We climbed out and continued exploring, walking for hours

through the lava fields and their blackened twists of fate. When we departed, it felt like leaving behind a friend.

After Craters of the Moon, we headed east for the first time in a week. We crossed the Snake River—another *Oregon Trail* landmark—and entered the Teton Pass Highway. Our destination was Jackson Hole, Wyoming, a ritzy town near Yellowstone National Park and Grand Teton National Park. Jackson Hole was by far the most expensive place we had ever stayed. I was apprehensive of the cost, but that fear faded by comparison when I looked in the rearview mirror and saw the fire.

"Not again!" my daughter yelled. I turned on my phone, and it lit up with wildfire alerts. Craters of the Moon and Jackson Hole were only three hours apart, and we were close enough to Jackson to make it there. We would outrun the fire on the road. The question was whether the fire would hit Jackson and burn it down.

That was the question people were asking when we arrived at our hotel. Our first glimpse of one of the most coveted landscapes in America was of it covered in smoke. The hotel debated whether to evacuate, since the fire was only a few miles away, but decided against it. It began to rain, and we walked through Jackson Hole in a drenched daze. I wondered again whether I was with my children in a place to which they would be able to return or a place long burned to the ground by the time they were my age. In the future of my mind, every landscape was Craters of the Moon.

After the initial shock of the fire, my children loved Jackson Hole in the innocent way a child does when they don't know you paid over ten dollars for a drink. My oldest could tell we were somewhere fancy by the way people dressed and by the orderliness of the town square, and that there *was* a town square, albeit one decorated with antlers for ambiance. Fargo was cheap, Medora was kitschy, Kalispell was sprawling, but Jackson Hole was old-school posh. We'd chosen Jackson Hole for parks proximity, but it is emblematic of the kind of expensive city you often see on the coasts, where the people who work menial jobs have to live in low-quality housing far away. It is a charming town diminished by the fact that its own workers cannot afford to live there and a dark omen of national economic trends. The housing crisis has gotten exponentially worse since our 2019 stay.

Because of the expense, our time in Wyoming would be brief. We tried to pack in as much as possible. Yellowstone is known as the first national park, established as protected land by the federal government in 1872 due to the uniqueness of its geology—in particular, its geysers—and the diversity of its wildlife. The actual first national park is Hot Springs, signed into protection forty years earlier, but Arkansas's spa bath gambling den lacks a certain gravitas, so Yellowstone became the mythical standard. Ulysses Grant signed the protection act for Yellowstone at the peak of westward expansion, less than a decade after the end of the Civil War.

By the midnineteenth century, Yellowstone was famous. Images had been published in newspapers and magazines, capturing the imaginations of Americans nationwide, who welcomed the idea of federally protected escapes. After so many hard years, there needed to be a place to rest, a place to trust, an old faithful. In the region surrounding Yellowstone, Native American tribes, federal officials, and local landowners argued about the park's fate, territorial debates that continue today. But no one denies the park's majesty.

The next day, we set out for Yellowstone at dawn, and the traffic-packed drive and struggle for parking space—for any space—came as a shock. I normally avoid crowds, but this was the famous Yellowstone, and it might be our only chance. Yellowstone is renowned for much of the same wildlife we saw at Theodore Roosevelt, Glacier, Rocky Mountain: buffalo and elk and bears, sky-high geological formations, flowers so varied you stop tracking them after a while because they are seeds that sprout from dreams. Yellowstone is overwhelming, and I am glad we saw quieter versions of it elsewhere. Parks where you can take your time and contemplate nature, the way the protectors of Yellowstone had intended.

The two things I remember most from our trip to Yellowstone are geysers and people, because I loved watching them interact.

Over half the world's hydrothermal features are in Yellowstone. The geysers were formed by geothermal activity underneath the earth from a dormant super-volcano, causing fleeting eruptions and permanent pools surrounded by rock and salt. They are laid out on a wooden trail reeking of sulfur, and they have names that reflect their personalities: Depression Geyser, Economic Geyser, Spiteful Geyser. It's like Twitter as a national park.

Unlike places that I knew would require explanation to convince my family to visit—like Craters of the Moon—I had done little research about Yellowstone. As a result, I was pleasantly shocked by the geysers, their strange shapes and colors, how pretty and dangerous they were, surrounded by the ghostly white pine trees their deadly chemicals killed long ago. We walked by Castle Geyser as it belched steam in front of thundering clouds. Contrary to its all-American image, this wholesome park was maniacal. Then I decided that wasn't contrary at all. A beautiful place where everything blows up, and we watch and scream and clamor for more—what is more American than that?

Around noon, we gathered around Old Faithful, the most consistent geyser in Yellowstone, to the point that it was used as a laundry in the nineteenth century, and one of the park's most popular sites. Visitors stake out spots over an hour in advance of eruption. As the crowd assembled, I hung back, engrossed by the watchers more than the attraction. I saw a Sikh biker gang wearing matching leather jackets and turbans, busloads of Chinese tourists snapping photos, families in matching T-shirts proclaiming they were having a reunion, fellow Missourians from an Ozarks small town who told us they had driven hundreds of miles to fulfill a lifelong dream of seeing Old Faithful explode. Men pushing strollers, elderly folks using wheelchairs, babies and toddlers and teenagers and parents, families of every race and many nationalities, all waiting for hot water to burst from the ground. There were no special effects, no man-made additions. Only a geyser that had been there for thousands of years and people blessed with the primordial satisfaction of the easily pleased.

Old Faithful erupts every ninety minutes or so and has erupted over one million times since humans began recording it. When it exploded over one hundred feet into the air, we hollered and shrieked, united in frenzy. It was a magical moment that I will always treasure because I do not think it could happen now. It takes a level of trust to stand that close to strangers, and both the pandemic and the rage the pandemic stoked have broken that bond.

Maybe I am wrong. Maybe Old Faithful is so reliable it can mend even this divide. That glorious freak will remain the same regardless of what humans do to each other. Old Faithful will live in the memories of other visitors like it lives in mine. You cannot kill the daydream any more than you can stop the eruption. You cannot stop the joy of so many people made so happy by an inverted waterfall of steam gradually dissipating into air. I love that so many people from so many countries had traveled all the way to mine to see it. I love that my fellow countrymen saw it with me, sharing in a spectacle that we did not create but that caters to our innate sensibilities. An explosion of fireworks from beneath the earth, a pointless spectacle that will burn you if you get too close: that's made in America, baby.

As we drove out of Yellowstone, we saw grizzly bears eating an antelope off the side of the road, tearing its body and fighting over the meat. We watched this feast for a long time because traffic barely moved. By the time the carcass was licked clean, we decided we were done with Yellowstone and would spend our remaining days in Grand Teton National Park.

Grand Teton means Big Tits in French. This sounds like something a pseudo-French speaker from Missouri would make up, but it's true. My children never stopped finding this funny and laughed every time they saw the twin mountains in the distance.

I loved Grand Teton. Since most tourists prefer Yellowstone, Grand Teton provides a more serene escape, especially since there are over one hundred miles between it and any notable industrialization. When the surrounding land is not on fire, Grand Teton tastes like drinking a cloud from another century.

The next morning, we stopped at one of the park's few buildings, the Chapel of the Transfiguration, a log cabin Episcopal church from 1925. A sign explained that the eternal majesty of the mountains equaled that of God. It was hard not to be drawn in by the simple wooden cross in front of an ethereal mountain visible from simple wooden pews. It's the kind of setup that makes you want to convert before finding out what you're joining.

We spent the day walking trails around deep blue lakes. At the edge of a forest, we saw that someone had made a heart out of pebbles in front of the water and decided that this was where we would eat the sandwiches we had packed for lunch. We sat on a log and looked at the lake, noticing ripples in the water. They turned out to be bears swimming, and we watched in awe until a park ranger counseled us to move. We edged back into the woods and waited in silence to see what happened next.

It turned out we weren't the only family out for a picnic. A black bear and her offspring wandered down the trail about twenty feet from where we had been sitting. The ranger motioned at us to let them pass. I did, feeling that delusional kinship human mothers get in the wild, when you are feeding your children and see an animal mother doing the same and briefly relate to her until realizing that you, to the animal mother, *are* lunch.

The Grand Tetons are a sanctuary of serenity, and I wish we could have stayed longer. But it was time to go, and the next day we began the long drive southeast through the Shoshone National Forest, a red rock landscape that erupts out of the green-tinged mountains to which we had become accustomed. We drove through the Wind River Reservation, where the Eastern Shoshone and Western Arapaho tribes live. We stopped at a cemetery claiming to have the grave of Sacagawea, though this claim is disputed. The cemetery was covered in bright flowers, and after we exited, a herd of horses was crossing the road, a tribesman guiding them, and we waited for them to pass. My children remarked that they felt like they were in another country due to the dramatic scenery and that they had seen only Native tribes and their structures for hours on end.

Wyoming, which has a population of about half a million people, is often held up as the ultimate Republican state. While it is true that "land doesn't vote" and that the state is overly influential in the Electoral College given its population, many remain ignorant of the nature of that land. Over half of Wyoming's land is owned by the federal government, and significant parts belong to Native tribes. Cities are sparse and scattered, and none has a population of over one hundred thousand. Wyoming does not feel empty, nor does it feel particularly conservative. Wyoming feels left alone by necessity.

We spent our final days in a cabin near the Medicine Bow-Routt National Forest, a place without internet or many people. We saw wild horses and a double rainbow and meteor showers and a cloud that formed a frightening face in front of a near-full moon. We watched our children chase after a dog that had wandered over from a farm, running through fields that stretched for miles. I watched from the cabin window as my daughter helped her little brother out of a creek they had waded into and he hugged her in gratitude, a tender moment they would never display when my husband and I were present and they felt compelled to battle each other.

Those were the best days, the days we did nothing but be a family. The best days of our end-times summer, before solitude turned into social distancing. I wanted to stay in this daydream land where I felt safe. A place where I could love my country in the same uncomplicated way that I love my children. And feel, to my amazement, like our country loved us back.

It should not be so hard to exist in America. The gulf between the peaceful lands to which I escaped and the grim political landscape I studied should not be that vast. But the truth, the painful truth, the truth that crept on me like a spider in a cabin bed that I flicked off and flattened, is that there is no gulf. The comfort and the cruelty are part and parcel to this land and its history.

I had found where the seams of America were sewn, so soft and comforting when I did not think about them too hard. I had found a place to lay my head, and I took the opportunity, since they don't come by often, and slept a dreamless sleep.

After two days, we resumed the drive back to St. Louis. We passed *Oregon Trail* landmarks in Wyoming and Nebraska—Fort Laramie, Independence Rock, Scotts Bluff—that we knew from the video game and not from the reality. We had gotten good at playing games after two weeks on the road. Mind games, like pioneers do.

There's a feeling you get when you look to the west, and then there's the feeling you get when the center pulls you back. The center does not hold anything except illusions, but illusions are powerful because illusions spring from visions. The advantage of the center is that you can see America in every direction: north and south, east and west, past and future. You see every death and every dream and the daydreams that lie in between—because what are daydreams other than made-up memories, fictions to fill out?

You see the West burning and know that one day soon everyone will be running to the center, where the rivers meet, where escape routes abound. The Arch will greet them like a beacon, and they'll call the confluence a refuge because it will be, by comparison. Everything is by comparison when everything is a literal matter of degrees. You will greet them and remember those burned-down lands, the choked moan of lost time and lost territory. When they can manage to get out the words, you will tell them you saw it too, and it was just as beautiful as they said, and that you're sorry.

In a roadside restaurant in Ogallala, a waitress gave us the news.

"I hate to break it you," she said somberly, "but there is a shortage of ranch dressing in Nebraska." A tragedy had befallen her people. She offered us free sarsaparilla sodas to compensate, which we accepted, and she thanked us for our understanding.

We finished supper and left, feeling the wistful dread of the last-day drive. Next to our car was a puddle of chemicals, and inside the swirling rainbow toxins I could see the shadows of our faces, the four of us, a fossil fuel family portrait.

We drove through Nebraska until we could drive no more and

crashed in a cheap hotel. I don't remember where we stayed or what we saw or how we slept. I only remember waking the next morning and fueling up at a gas station called Fat Dog's. Around the edge of the ceiling looped a banner saying YOU ARE NOWHERE, YOU ARE NOWHERE. I bought a coffee and started drinking it and bought a pack of Twizzlers and started eating them and turned on my phone and it told me that Jeffrey Epstein, billionaire trafficker of children to the elite, was found dead inside his prison cell, allegedly of suicide.

"Where were you when you heard Epstein 'committed suicide'?" people would ask, and my answer was on that wall: YOU ARE NO-WHERE, YOU ARE NOWHERE. "Vacation is over," I told my husband.

Hours later, we crossed into Missouri. The kids knew I would be back to work right away because of Epstein. They saw the lurid headlines reflected from my phone onto my sunglasses and into my brain. They knew about Epstein's crimes because my children are not liars like the government is, and his crimes were so heinous and obvious that you could be in third grade and know about them. They knew I had written a book focusing on Epstein and that this trip was meant to be an escape from the horror of that book.

But in the end, it was Epstein who got away. I was not yet home, but I had exited the daydream and reentered the nightmare. I had seen the best of America while the plutocrat elite covered for the worst of it. I had protected my children while the women of my generation, the adult women who were once the children that Epstein raped, learned they would never see justice because their trafficker would never be challenged in court.

His death was a bizarre end to a family road trip. But that's the way chapters end for a mother like me. I was issued a reality check I did not want to cash.

We drove past a giant half-staff American flag commemorat-

ing the mass shooting victims who had died while we were away
and for whom our politicians would do nothing but think and
pray and fundraise and forget. I managed to hold back a one-
finger salute. I loved my country with the depth and rage of the
unrequited, wondering how a place so loved could hurt so many
so much.

At around four o'clock, we arrived in St. Louis. We entered
our home and barely left it for two years. Our daydream was over.

Interlude

Digging Stars

It is March 2021, and we are back at Palo Duro Canyon, four years after our original visit and my promise to the kids that we would return. We are staying in Canyon, Texas, a small town south of Amarillo. We skipped Cadillac Ranch because I had nothing left to say.

We were in Canyon to get a break from the plague. We drove in from Dallas, where we had celebrated a belated Covid Christmas at my sister's house. It was the first gathering of my family since 2019, my newly vaccinated parents falsely believing they were now immune. A fake Christmas, a fake cure, a fake government, a real end.

I thought 2020 was the demarcation point between Then and Now, but I was wrong. Americans could still *see* in 2020. They had 2020 vision: the ability to see through the lies of tyrants and say "no more." The fatal flaw of 2020 vision is that it fades when you close your eyes. Close your eyes or be chastised: those were the rules of 2021, when people were ostracized for grieving, slandered for sympathizing. A chorus clamoring for justice was seduced to silence by the sweet succor of a soft-focus death cult.

"It's over," people would say in 2021. I would agree without knowing the topic because there were so many options. The pandemic? The coup? The protests? America? There were so many things we were not supposed to discuss, it was hard to keep track. With the denial came the blood, the breakdowns, the rise in rage that experts pretended was mysterious. It was not. There is a saying that grief is love with nowhere to go, but grief with nowhere to go is . . . *this*.

My road trips now required careful regimens to elude death. But we took them anyway because to stay in place was to elude life. Nothing could beat the open road, and nothing could deny the pain in the eyes of everyone I encountered on it. No one could deny the horror of what had happened except for the government and the media, who denied it until the public joined in their delusion. This is not a partisan thing; this is a liar thing.

I was out for escape. Palo Duro fit my criteria: isolated, outdoors, ageless. It fit 2021's criteria too: cursed. One week before we arrived, a tornado hit the town of Canyon, causing no casualties but massive damage. I was sure we would not make it to Palo Duro, sure that I was looking at yet another promise to my children I could not keep.

But nothing could defeat rock so weathered and worn. That's how it found its shape in the first place. We got to Canyon and rented a house at the end of a dirt road, where only wild animals could find us.

Our first day at Palo Duro was idyllic. In the morning, we hiked through a maze of sun-colored hoodoos, each more enchanting than the next. In the afternoon, we rode horses along the canyon edge, the site of brutal battles between the Texas government and the Comanche in the 1870s. The sky was a brilliant blue, the canyon a cauldron of history and color—and I felt nothing. I felt as empty as the plains around me—not like I was disappearing into a void, as I desired, but like a void was disappearing me.

In the evening, my husband grilled dinner outdoors while the children played nearby. I could hear them through the window. I kept away because I wanted them to be happy. They had spent most of the past year in virtual school, praised for their efforts for the "quaran-team." When school reopened, my daughter would gather her books and her violin and a plastic bag marked BIOHAZ-ARD that contained four vials of our saliva to be tested by doctors at Washington University for a deadly disease. This was our life now.

I wanted my children to explore the world without fear, and Palo Duro gave them that chance. I wanted them to be free. But I wanted to be free too, in a way that did not benefit anyone but myself, so I stayed inside. I loved my children and did not want them to see me eyeing the canyon edge like a temptation, like a conclusion.

I paced the house, browsing the owner's books in an effort to distract myself from bad ideas. They told the history of this slice of Texas, this panhandle of sorrow and survival. One of the books was a collection of letters by the artist Georgia O'Keeffe, whom I knew best from her paintings of New Mexico. But it was in Palo Duro that she'd lost herself and found her vision.

"I don't know how to begin—don't know that I have anything to say—only all inside I'm crazy and I don't know what over—how—why or anything," she wrote.[1] I stopped pacing and began to read.

"What in the world is the matter with me these days anyway," O'Keeffe continued. "I feel full of wheels and empty spots—Out of kindness to the rest of the folks I ought to leave everyone alone—I feel like a curse to everyone I talk to."

O'Keeffe's letters were written in 1917: during her world war, her pandemic. She wrote with increased desperation as World War I raged and the Spanish flu lay in wait. Hired to teach art at West Texas State Normal College, she was swept away by the beauty of the plains, comparing their vastness to "what comes after living." She stopped painting city streets and started creating southwestern color.

O'Keeffe made New Mexico her home in 1949. But West Texas settled in her art like a permanent prelude. In the book, her letters were accompanied by her pictures of Palo Duro, jolting in their familiarity. She spent three years climbing the canyon walls, painting landscapes that "looked like Hell let loose with a fried egg in the middle of it."[2] She dreamed of having the freedom of a man, "so I could hunt for that big loneness—away from folks—I don't think I'll have the courage to go as far as I want to alone—being a woman—I wonder—is it much different?"

I read her mind like a time traveler gone full circle. Sometimes a book takes you to another place, and sometimes it clarifies where you are. O'Keeffe longed for a "dust-colored vacation," and I did too. *Ashes to ashes*, I thought, and watched smoke rise from the grill.

As night fell, I put the book back and joined my family outside as my husband served dinner. I pretended I was fine, and I was not convincing. He knew I was in a bad place, but no one knew the depths because I could not fathom them myself. For the first time, I was out of words. The sun vanished into blackness, and I looked up for glimmers of hope and felt none of the wonder that had marked my previous sightings of the sky.

I had spent a year blocking out memories. The gulf between past and present was too painful to process. But as I gazed into the night, my family by my side, memories forced their way back. Memories of the same Texas sky in 1998, in 2007, in 2017, emerging like stars when your eyes adjust to darkness, at first few and dim and then bright and all at once, leaving you wondering how you did not see them before. I felt something—a crack in the numbness, a wave of grief waiting to be unleashed, an ache I welcomed because it meant I could still feel. The constellations had not changed. My mind gripped them like an anchor.

"I want to pick holes in everything folks call Art," O'Keeffe wrote in 1917. Her colleagues did not understand: not her paintings, not her pain. She left Canyon one year later. She became sick during the pandemic, and her father died. But she never questioned the purpose of her time in Palo Duro.

"I'm not trying to do Art," she explained. "I'm digging stars."[3]

6
Route 66

Coming Home

It is March 2023, and I am back on Route 66, determined to get back what I lost. Now, I am with two teenagers who have seen too much and not enough. They have seen thirty-six states and eighteen national parks and dozens of museums and scores of mass shootings and one pandemic and one attempted coup and a million unpunished state crimes. America has not yet ended, and they have their own road trip routines, their favorite snacks and sites and scenery. My son loves beef jerky and war museums and towns with signs in a foreign language. My daughter loves Little Debbie Cosmic Brownies and street musicians and long hikes to hidden ruins in the woods. I have only two years before my oldest child will leave me and maybe less before my country does.

We usually do not repeat our routes, but I make an exception for Route 66 because it is the keeper of dreams and decline. There is always new forensic evidence to be found in my search for who killed America.

In spring 2023, we were seeking to recapture the wholesome joy of our 2019 national parks journey and decided to take the kids to the Grand Canyon. This turned out to be impossible because of an unprecedented atmospheric river hovering over the southwest like a sodden UFO, a mass that burst midway through our trip and left us fleeing floods in Flagstaff. In 2023, Route 66 had new gigantic attractions: America's Biggest Climate Crisis Cloud side by side with America's Worst Western Drought. Together they created the West's Weirdest Weather, rendering the Grand Canyon an invisible hole.

"How can a hole be invisible?" my son asked when I told him we couldn't see it. His question stuck in my mind. It reminded me of something, but I couldn't figure out what.

By 2023, we had found every way to leave Missouri. We exited in every direction, zigzagging from the center like light rays in a plasma lamp. North to the Great Lakes, south to the Gulf of Mexico, as far east and west as we could go before running out of money and time.

Now we were heading to Arizona, retracing an old route in a very different America. This was the kids' first trip to Arizona and my husband's and my first return since 2007. We set out on the familiar drive southwest at dawn, determined to get to Amarillo by night.

We drove through the farm town of Bois D'Arc—that's "Bo-dark" to you—to the ghost town of Plano and watched the sun rise from window-size holes inside a stone roofless building next to a golden field. The building had allegedly been a coffin factory until there were no longer enough residents left to die to make it a viable business. We continued on through the district of Mike Moon, a Missouri state representative in the news that week for his belief that twelve-year-olds should be able to marry,[1] passing a large sign that said WHATSOEVER A MAN SOWETH THAT SHALL HE ALSO REAP. We passed a town called Albatross followed by a town called Rescue.

We drove through La Russell, a town of 134 people, named after a guy named Russell. The "La" was added to make it sound French. In La Russell, there is a cherished water pump that sits in the middle of the street and has caused multiple traffic accidents, but is too beloved to be removed. Every year it is festooned with Christmas decorations while residents bask in its glory. This has been going on for over a century.

La Russell is near the old Route 66 town of Red Oak. But Red Oak no longer exists, so we headed to Red Oak II, twenty miles away.

Red Oak II is the painstaking creation of artist Lowell Davis, who returned to the Ozarks from Dallas in the early 1970s and found, to his horror, that his hometown had atrophied out of existence. In 1974, Davis relocated and rebuilt over three dozen landmarks of his childhood—colorful Phillips 66 stations, the general store run by his father, the blacksmith shop run by his grandfather—and arranged them in a townlike formation in a large field. The day we visited, Red Oak II also seemed abandoned, or at least empty. Its layers of loneliness left me unnerved. We wandered by midcentury replicas of small-town life like a family of extras on a canceled series.

Davis had no desire to make Red Oak II a living re-creation, with actors and reenactments, or a commercial venue. He just wanted his memories back.

In November 2020, Lowell Davis died at home. He was buried in Red Oak II, per his request.[2] At eighty-three, he had lived inside the reconstruction of his childhood far longer than he had lived in the original Red Oak. Davis died during a global plague in the middle of one of the most violently contested elections in US history.

But in Red Oak II, nothing had changed. His tombstone is a sculpture of an owl he had fashioned out of old washers, gazing out at the still point of the unturning world.

A disproportionate number of roadside mega-objects were built in the 1970s, particularly during the turbulent years of the Vietnam War and Watergate. Many, like Red Oak II or Cadillac Ranch, are cloaked in nostalgia. Others, like the Giant Praying Hands of Webb City or Salem Sue, are pleas for things to stay the same, for no attacks to arrive on milk or prayer. This is counter-counterculture art, objects whose physical enormity compensated for their cultural obscurity. They mattered to the people nearby and sent a message to the people passing through.

But some mega-objects are personal gestures of love that stood the test of time. After crossing the border into Oklahoma, we stopped to see the Blue Whale of Catoosa. Built in 1972 by zoologist Hugh S. Davis as a gift to his wife, Zelta, who collected whale figurines, it now sits in a public park as Catoosa's main attraction. The massive Blue Whale wears a tiny white baseball cap and a wide, toothy grin. On the day we visited, a small boy stood inside its open mouth, fishing in the pond, content in his cement world.

We kept on Route 66 until we reached the World's Largest Totem Pole, part of a landscape of attractions built by folk artist Ed Galloway in rural eastern Oklahoma. Constructed between 1937 and 1948, the ninety-foot pole was allegedly conceived in commemoration of Indigenous nations forced off their native lands. Galloway intended it as a gesture of solidarity to the Native American communities in his region.

But there are no tribes from Oklahoma who use totem poles,

nor did any symbols Galloway painted reference local cultures. According to a signpost, the pole is decorated with "four nine-foot Indian chiefs" at the top, with creatures resembling aliens and animals beneath them. My daughter at first assumed Galloway's art was thoughtless, like other cheap impersonations of Native life on Route 66. She was surprised when she wandered into another Galloway creation: an eleven-sided "Fiddle House" displaying hundreds of hand-carved violins. Whatever Galloway had been trying to do, it had not been done in carelessness. Intrigued by his craftsmanship, my daughter, a violinist, glanced at the garish Totem Pole and shook her head in confusion, absorbing the contradictions of a man and his era.

"All my life I did the best I knew," Galloway explained on his deathbed. "I built these things by the road to be a friend to you."

We continued on through old-school Oklahoma and its Dust Bowl vestiges. A crumbling stone building with an American flag outside and a laminated note attached to the outer wall, stained and barely legible, beckoned from the road. The note explained that we were inside the remains of a filling station that had been used in the 1930s to produce counterfeit money after one of Al Capone's gang members came to shake down victims of the Great Depression, including the filling station's owner. Desperate for money, he agreed, only to be caught and taken to prison, crying, "It wasn't worth it!" The site was abandoned and became a body dumping ground for the Mafia.

"So be careful entering this fragile old building," the note concluded. We were careful; we always were. Since our Bonnie and Clyde excursion six years prior, we had visited other remnants of early twentieth-century crime. The bars frequented by mobsters in Hot Springs, Arkansas. The hotel room where Capone was held in luxurious captivity by the feds in Chattanooga, Tennessee. Wall Street in New York City. The United States was a road trip crime spree, glamorized and forgotten and replaced with planes that carry the criminal elite through the skies, where they commit slicker crimes from safer distances.

I wish that the conspiracies I believed in were simple and wrong. I wish I were more afraid of chemtrails than of the people in the planes. When you study transnational organized crime from the vantage of the Midwest, you are always searching for the precise point when your region transitioned from a powerful political crime hub to a disposable resource grab for foreign and domestic elites, because understanding that helps clarify other strange events that followed. Route 66 was my escape, but it was a drive into the past—a search for answers, not a reprieve from questions.

An hour west of Oklahoma City, a town popped up on Google Maps called Dead Women Crossing. Being a Missourian, I had seen my share of strange town names—Licking, Bland, Humansville—but nothing this grim. There was not enough internet access in western Oklahoma to look it up, so we looked at it head-on. We drove through a residential neighborhood over a graffiti-covered bridge beside a cow pasture, seeing nothing out of the ordinary. There was no indication that in 1905 a schoolteacher named Katie DeWitt James had tried to get a divorce, fled with her baby, and was allegedly murdered by a local sex worker, who then allegedly ingested poison, killing herself. The sex worker was said to be an associate of the husband whom James was trying to flee. James's skull was found four months later under the bridge, next to a revolver, and her baby was raised by the husband who likely had her killed.[3]

I did not tell my children this story, even though they were teenagers and had heard worse. It bothered me too much: the viciousness of the crime, the casual way the name showed up on GPS when there was no memorial or marker on the site. It left me wondering how many other dead women crossings we had unknowingly passed.

We reached Cadillac Ranch as the sun was setting, arriving at golden hour. My son did not remember his 2017 visit, and my daughter recalled hers only vaguely. But they ran into the field like little kids, accepting spray paint cans from strangers, laughing and ducking between other families from across America leaving their marks. Cadillac Ranch was an oasis of community in an alienated land. I sprayed THEY KNEW, the title of a book I wrote, across the hood of a car, and a man in dark glasses said, "Damn right they did." I nodded from behind my own dark glasses, the comradely gesture of the conspiratorial. He did not know what I meant, and I did not know what he meant, but we were standing on common ground and that was enough.

My children spray-painted shout-outs to St. Louis and a "get well soon" greeting to my father, who had been diagnosed with cancer the week before, and gestured to my husband to take their photo with their words so they could text it to him. I felt my throat tighten, and I wandered into the field, not wanting to ruin their good time. I watched the scene from a distance, Americans coming and going, Americans speaking and writing in different languages, knowing that what they wrote did not matter because it was all one message in the end: *We were here, and now you are here too.*

I wondered if I would see Amarillo again, and if I returned, who would be with me. I wondered what I would have to say and if I would be allowed to say it. I had long treated every place like I was seeing it for the last time, every journey like a last-chance ride.

If Route 66 teaches you to do anything, it's that.

Over half of Route 66—roughly 1,372 miles—cuts through Native American land. Most of this territory is in Oklahoma, home to thirty-nine Native American nations, and New Mexico, where it passes through or near ten pueblos before reaching the territory of the Navajo, Hopi, and Hualapai people.[4]

Caught within the actual Indigenous lands of Route 66 is a funhouse mirror, a series of tourist traps white Americans created to capitalize on caricatures of Native American iconography. Plastic statues of Natives placed in doorways, fake tribal insignia on walls, motels called *tepees* and *wigwams*. These midtwentieth-century landmarks are faded because white America has learned to be quieter about their desecration.

But there's a lingering horror of being the original inhabitants of a land, suffering extermination or exile, and then having your oppressors market you as their mascot. Route 66 is the road of the ridiculous, but this particular commodification is not kitsch. It is in keeping with the naming of US military equipment, cars, and sports teams after Indigenous targets of state slaughter. It is the dehumanization that follows genocide, the mythmaking that covers crimes.

Drive through New Mexico and you will veer from fake representations to real people, from the retro novelty shop Tee Pee Curios in Tucumcari to the old stretch of Route 66 past Albuquerque that leads to the Laguna Pueblo. In Laguna, we stopped at a pottery shop that sold frybread tacos and saw tribal residents gathering near the seventeenth-century mission at the center of town.

As we ate, the owner of the shop told us it was a holiday. Locals walked past wearing traditional clothing and covid masks as they prepared for a celebratory feast. The masks were required because Native American covid deaths are disproportionately high, and they were taking no chances. The feast was closed to nonresidents without permission, and signs forbade photography. We were invited and declined because we were short on time and also did not want to intrude, but we were grateful to be asked. Families strolled hand in hand, elders guiding children, and I was glad for them. This is a land of survivors holding on to what they have, aware of how cavalierly it can be stolen. Theirs is a history from which every American could learn, which is why so many politicians seek to ban it from being taught.

After Laguna Pueblo, we left Route 66, switching to the Trail of the Ancients, a scenic byway of ancient geological and archaeological sites from New Mexico's first inhabitants. Lured by signs for the Bandera Ice Cave—as Missourians, we have no choice but to submit to bombastic billboards announcing cave adventures—we drove to the longest lava tube in the United States and hiked through black fields lined with firs and pines. We climbed down until we could see the ice cave floor, its surface a greenish glass of Arctic algae. The ice was first mined by Zuni tribes, and then by Spanish colonists, and then by American bootleggers in the 1930s who turned the prehistoric cave into a saloon to cool their beer, until it was left alone in the 1940s to be a tourist attraction for everyone.

This is the fabled New Mexico "land of fire and ice," a land that revels in the paradoxical, a land that advertises coexistence and then reflects it back in tales of greed and violence. New Mexico is one of America's newest states, but it has some of the best-preserved proof of habitation, a millennium of human history carved in stone.

At El Morro National Monument, farther down the Trail of the Ancients, we walked to a desolate red-brown rock tower. On its walls were centuries of graffiti: ancestral Puebloans' seven-hundred-year-old etchings of hunting scenes and smiling suns, nineteenth-century Anglo-American travelers' names in simple block script, paeans of seventeenth-century Spanish conquistadors to the throne and to themselves. The symbols and signatures lined the walls at random intervals, like a sandstone Cadillac Ranch.

"General Don Diego de Vargas, who conquered for our Holy Faith, and for the Royal Crown, all of New Mexico at his own

expense in the year of 1692, was here," read one Spanish inscription. We were startled to see a photo of this exact etching a few
days later at the New Mexico History Museum in Santa Fe, which
had an exhibit on de Vargas: how he had conquered New Mexico
by recruiting Pueblo allies and then waged war against them two
years later. In June 2020, de Vargas's statue was removed from
Santa Fe as part of the broader movement to take commemora-
tions of colonizers out of public parks.[5]

That movement seems surreal in our era of contrived out-
rage over "critical race theory" and serious attacks on freedom
of speech. The most surreal part is that back then, the activists
usually won. In 2020, I watched warily as the monuments were
taken down, assuming politicians were allowing it because remov-
ing statues of dead tyrants is a great cover for a plan to do nothing
about the ongoing oppression of living people. Remove the statues,
keep the statutes.

In 2023, I gazed at El Morro as Native populations struggled
with covid-era losses of jobs and health care, as Spanish-speaking
migrants continued to be separated from their parents or forced
to labor in captivity, as a country of panicked citizens attempted
to recover from an attempted coup by neoconfederates that the
government refused to prosecute and from a pandemic they falsely
claim has ended.[6] I gazed at El Morro and read the writing on
America's wall.

The sins of the past linger. Only the records change—digital
deletions and banned books but also collective memory marred by
inaction toward tragedy. In 2020, there was a movement to demar-
cate America's heroes and villains and remove the villains from
public prominence. On the whole, it was well intentioned and
motivated by traumas that are hard to parse because they never
stopped happening. The real villains, the worst villains, are the

officials who respond to protests with performative applause while quietly continuing the crimes.

That is how you make a hole invisible.

We drove north to Gallup and stayed in or near Navajo territory for the next few days, moving between New Mexico, Arizona, and Utah. We followed the remains of Route 66 through the Painted Desert and the Petrified Forest National Park, through striped mesas of purple and blue next to pink logs of ancient wood tinged with ice. This was a geology to which I could relate. Missouri has some of the oldest rocks in the world, billion-year boulders expectorated from the earth's core. Navajo land has that same strength and fire but more vivid, so alive you can lose yourself in the landscape and still feel part of it.

I let my children run alone in the Painted Desert, navigating prehistoric debris. I let them lead me and my husband because they are older now and have hiked so much that they know what they are doing. Respect the trail, leave no trace, treasure solitude. We are always the first to arrive at any park, no matter how early, because those are the best hours: when it is only you and your family and the land, ever so briefly, to yourselves. And then the joy in sharing it as new families arrive, families with little kids who make your heart ache for bygone days and wide-eyed first impressions. The comfort of geological time is its slowness, the way your children grow and change as the rocks stay stalwart and still. These are parent parks.

On a thirty-degree morning bright and clear as summer, we went to Monument Valley Navajo Tribal Park. Due to the large number of movies filmed there, the rock tower silhouette landscape of Monument Valley has long been synonymous with how the public envisions the American West. But it is Navajo sacred land, shut down for years due to covid, and I felt lucky to see it at all. The atmospheric river had left its mark: red dirt roads ran ragged, sparse vegetation coated in ice. But the sun-colored pillars remained, erupting out of the desert in intervals like a sprawling city planned by forces beyond human understanding. I could have stayed there for weeks, moving deeper into the dust and never stopping. Monument Valley did not feel dead or alive but something in between, transcendent and otherworldly.

The night before, we had driven to a remote area of Navajo territory in Utah and were shocked by the number of stars. It took no time for our eyes to adjust to the dark, for there was no darkness to be found. The stars were everywhere, shooting through the sky one after another, glimmering balls of white heat. They had a frantic, pulsating glow that would have made Earth seem trite had the landscape around us not been so magical. The wildness of the night was mirrored in the red-orange desert I walked the next morning, aware that there was much more to it that I could not see, land that is not mine to wander because it is open to its original inhabitants alone. I am fine with this. To share the sky is enough.

The next day, we had exited Monument Valley and were heading south when I saw a sign: VISIT UNIQUE WWII NAVAJO CODE TALKERS DISPLAY AND NAVAJO CULTURE CENTER AT BURGER KING! Of course we had to follow it.

Kayenta is a small Arizona town in the Navajo Nation about twenty miles south of the Utah border. The Burger King Museum of the Navajo Code Talkers serves up fresh Whoppers and historical truths. Glass cases are filled with rare mementos from Navajo soldiers and memorabilia from World War II. Signs on the wall educate Burger King visitors about the Navajo language and culture.

Code talkers were US citizens employed by the government to carry out classified communications in languages the enemy could not understand. Other members of Native American tribes, including the Cherokee and the Choctaw, had worked as code talkers during World War I. But during World War II, the Navajo played a more prominent role, transforming their complex language into the only military code that remains impenetrable to this day and helping ensure an Allied victory.[7] The relics of their military prowess are now preserved in Burger King. There were plans to move the Museum of the Navajo Code Talkers elsewhere, but they have not come to pass. As a result, the Kayenta Burger King, owned by the son of a code talker, contains more code talker artifacts than the Pentagon.

The Burger King Museum of the Navajo Code Talkers was the second exhibit about Native American life we saw in a fast-food chain that year. In Vinita, Oklahoma, we stopped at the World's Largest McDonald's. It is technically called the Will Rogers Archway Oasis but is best known for being a *really* big McDonald's, one that spans the entirety of Interstate 44, the highway that replaced Route 66. On the top floor, you can sit in a booth next to a glass window and position your fries so they look bigger than the 18-wheelers below.

If someone asked me to take them to the most American place in America, I would head straight for the Will Rogers Archway Oasis, which, true to form, half hides its Native roots.

Will Rogers was once the most popular entertainer in America, boasting the number one radio show and newspaper column and dominating the vaudeville and silent film industries. To explain the popularity of Will Rogers to children requires explaining what radio shows and vaudeville and silent films and, yes, newspapers are. Born in 1879, Rogers grew up on an Oklahoma ranch, learned how to lasso from a newly freed slave, debuted in a Wild West show at the 1904 World's Fair in St. Louis, and spent the rest of his career embodying a folksy cowboy persona, as quick with his wit as he was with a rope. He is the originator of the famous "I am not a member of an organized political party; I am a Democrat" quote. He was, in many ways, a successor to Mark Twain.

He was also a member of the Cherokee tribe who became a US citizen in 1898, after the Curtis Act disbanded the tribal government of his birth. His father had been a Cherokee war hero—for the Confederacy. Rogers did not deny his Cherokee roots—another of his well-known aphorisms is "my ancestors didn't come over on the Mayflower, but they met the boat"[8]—but he was careful how he displayed them. He walked a fine line, detesting politics but relentlessly commenting on them, running a mock presidential campaign in 1928 and nudging politicians toward policies that helped the underdog. At the height of his popularity in 1935, Rogers set out on a world tour and promptly died in a plane crash.

Reporters compared the magnitude of the public response to his death to Abraham Lincoln's.[9] Shocked Americans demanded the government build tributes to their fallen icon, which is why it is difficult to travel through Oklahoma without encountering something named after Will Rogers. In the McDonald's, a bronze statue of Rogers wearing a cowboy hat and carrying a lasso stands below a wire Corvette floating from the ceiling, representing Oklahoma's other fallen icon, Route 66. Video displays of Rogers and an exhibit case detailing his life round out the experience, which you pass on the way to the restroom.

There are almost no Americans old enough to remember Will Rogers when he was alive. The media in which he thrived are dead. Folks often say America is a young country, a statement that ignores the millennia of habitation that preceded European conquest. Will Rogers—part Cherokee, part white, all-American—embodied America's multifaceted history. If anyone should have retained cultural cachet, it was him. But by the 1960s, scholars were remarking that Will Rogers was already being forgotten.[10] Nowadays, many Oklahomans admit that they have no idea why he was famous.[11]

The notion of a wildly popular entertainer being far enough in the past to fade from collective memory is new in the United States. There is something unnerving about an American icon so easily deleted from national consciousness. This was not the intentional erasure of marginalized groups or the cancellation of a controversial celebrity but the slow lurch of a star fading until he is known as that guy with the lasso you look at while eating McNuggets. Will Rogers belongs to Route 66 now, another roadside ghost. I am glad they built him an explanatory display.

I am also glad they put him in the World's Largest McDonald's. If anything will survive the end of America, it is that.

It was time to head home. On March 25, 2023, we began a two-day drive from Santa Fe to St. Louis, retracing Route 66. We loaded up at the travel megaplaza in Clines Corners, where, seeking a change of pace from the Amazing Zoltar, I gave a mechanical alien one dollar to tell my fortune. It read me for filth instead.

"Recently you have made a mistake that you are dwelling on," said the green card spit out by ALIEN SPEAKS. "I am here to tell you that no amount of guilt can change the past and no amount of anxiety can change the future." The alien ordered me to "jump off the endless hamster wheel of guilt, forgive myself, and move on." *Forgive myself for what?* I wondered, then, *Why are you taking advice from a gas station alien?* But I kept the card in my wallet all the same.

From New Mexico we headed east on Route 66, the mountains

and mesas fading, Texas a flat plain lined by more bizarre attractions. We passed the Leaning Tower of Texas in the town of Groom: a water tower set at an angle mimicking that of the Leaning Tower of Pisa to draw tourists to a truck stop. We drove through the town of Alanreed, named for two men called Alan and Reed but originally called Gouge Eye after a saloon brawl.[12] In McLean, we spotted a sign for a place called the Devil's Rope. We decided to visit after discovering that it was a museum dedicated to barbed wire, located in an old bra factory.

Inside awaited the Smithsonian of barbed wire: thousands of displays on cattle branding and "fence cutter wars" and prison camps. On the entryway wall, a poster of a man wearing a fedora and smoking a cigar explained—in a barbed wire font, of course—that Joseph Glidden was "the father of barbed wire" and that religious groups deemed his creation "the work of the devil." The photo came from the August 1976 issue of *Barbed Wire Gazette*, a magazine that once had enough of a readership to exist.

I had so many questions and so many distractions. Barbed wire art lined the halls: cowboys and hats and hearts coiled from a metal meant to stab you. Past the barbed wire halls was a re-created Route 66 diner with a large plastic cow called the Original Steer in the middle. It was donated by the Big Texan, the restaurant where we had eaten steak in Amarillo. The fake Route 66 diner had a Route 66 mannequin waitress with a beehive hairdo, eternally taking orders inside a 1950s barbed wire cage.

The Devil's Rope is free. A cashier told me that it was made possible by donors who "really, *really* like barbed wire." I felt like I should contribute something, so I bought a small triangle of barbed wire as a souvenir. I emerged from the gift shop to find my children lying on a bench, giving me the side-eye.

"This is it," said my daughter. "This is the weirdest place you've taken us. This is even weirder than that psychic dog."

In Marshall, Missouri, there is a memorial garden for Jim the Wonder Dog, a Llewellin setter who predicted lottery numbers and sports races in the 1930s and whose psychic powers were verified in a solemn decree by the Missouri state legislature. Today, a bronze Jim stands surrounded by plaques detailing his many impressive feats.

"You'll, uh, appreciate it when you're older."

"Why? Am I going to be branding cattle?" my daughter asked.

"Or running a prison camp?" said my son.

"You'll appreciate someday that your mother took you to a place called the Devil's Rope: A Tribute to Barbed Wire and that you could just walk in, that no one gave you any hassle, that a bunch of people strangely enthusiastic about barbed wire put all this together so folks can learn something new, and that you can take any meaning you want from it."

"Including that barbed wire looks scary and painful and kind of sucks?"

"Yes."

My daughter laughed. "I don't need a museum to tell me that."

"But you'll look back on this time. I hope you do. That we could drive around on a nice spring day and go where we want, and think what we want, and just be a family, out for a ride in America."

"Even in middle-of-nowhere Texas?" said my son.

"Especially in middle-of-nowhere Texas," I said. "What is the middle of nowhere? You talk to people on the coasts, they say Missouri is the middle of nowhere. You come here from Missouri and say that this is the middle of nowhere. The middle of nowhere is the most interesting place in the world because it's full of things you couldn't conceive. You gotta look out for the middle of nowhere. You gotta protect it. Because you'll miss it when it's gone. You'll want it back, but people will tell you it didn't matter, or worse, that it never existed, that you must have imagined it. Because it was just the middle of nowhere—nowhere people living nowhere lives. They mean lives they don't appreciate for whatever reason. They say it about the cities, they say it about the country, they say it about any place and person they want to devalue and dismiss. All I know is when I get to spend a week with you two in the middle of nowhere, it's the most special, beautiful thing. There is not one moment I take for granted."

"This isn't really about the barbed wire museum in the bra factory, is it?" asked my daughter, taking my hand, and I shook my head no as we walked to the car.

On the first day of our Route 66 trip, the media announced that Donald Trump would be indicted that week. I did not believe them because I had heard this claim every year since 2016 and throughout my 1980s and 1990s childhood, when reporters were more straightforward about his ties to organized crime. Trump had been under federal investigation since before I was born.[13]

The year 2023 marked a half century of the Department of Justice opening an inquiry and then doing little about it. With every year his impunity grew, and with it his cruelty. He pushes and pushes, as if frustrated with the ability of the United States to contain its worst instincts, which are embodied in himself. He pushes and pushes, as if testing whether people are as weak and hypocritical as they seem, and no one in power pushes back, which means he is probably right. Trump ended the week he was supposed to be indicted by holding a fascist campaign rally in Waco, Texas.

I knew the rally was coming, and I knew why he chose Waco. When the ATF stormed the compound of cult leader David Koresh in 1993, killing eighty-two people, including twenty-eight children, I was fourteen years old. I remember the shock of coming home from school and hearing almost everyone had died, and starting to cry. My mother initially assumed I was crying about Koresh and thought I was crazy, but of course it was not over him: it was over the deceived, the innocent, and the torment they endured. I had been following the case, and I could imagine how terrifying it was inside that compound for a child besieged by multiple forces. It seemed the cruelest way to die.

I was upset by the coverage because the media kept implying it was wrong to grieve people killed by the government. We were told these were not casualties who mattered: the same lie I heard on television two years before during the Gulf War. I refused to accept that because every death matters—especially that of a child. I was a child myself, and it scared me to see the casual dismissal of the killing of innocents.

I look at the middle-aged men and women at Trump rallies, so different from me in many of their views, and wonder what they thought of Waco when they were young. If they saw the same callous reports that I did and felt the same disgust. And then I see them under the sway of another cult leader, a criminal politician with no regard for their welfare, one who feigns contempt for the very forces that supported him for a half century—the FBI and its institutional apparatus.

I wish they would leave him for their own sakes. I don't like cults, and I can't stand the government, but I loathe cults of the government most of all.

Oklahoma City is on Route 66 halfway between Santa Fe and St. Louis. It is a natural place to break up a drive for the night. I did not know that I would be in Oklahoma City on the day of Trump's rally in Waco. I do not know whether, had I arrived on another day, I would have reacted differently to what I saw or if what hit me hardest was the brutal banality of American horror.

Sometime in the twenty-first century, a day with a fascist rally

or a mass murder became just a day. I do not know the exact tip-
ping point, only that I cannot stop searching for it, like if I knew
where it started, I could undo it. I want to unwind our century and
cut the cord, let that alternative America spin off into the darkness
and live instead in the future that never arrived.

We got to the Alfred P. Murrah Federal Building Plaza as the
sun was setting. We climbed up a stairway from the street and
entered a platform overlooking a field filled with chairs made of
steel and glass. Behind the field was a pool bordered by two hulking identical bronze archways. We walked down the stairs to the
field and the sun hit the chairs, making them glow, and the sun
dropped behind the archways, making them dark, and the pool
reflected everything. The pool reflected everything: 168 chairs to
represent 168 victims, the archway with "9:01" engraved on it to
signify their last moment of peace, the archway with "9:03" engraved on it to signify the first moment of recovery, the redbuds
blooming in defiance, the sun flooding the field with its final light.
The pool reflected everything like a parallel reality, a before and
an after, the future and the unfathomability of its erasure.

At the Oklahoma City National Memorial, you are left forever
contemplating time. You are left forever wanting 9:01 to come
back.

On the side of the pool is a building with a spray-painted message: WE SEARCH FOR THE TRUTH. WE SEEK JUSTICE. THE COURTS
REQUIRE IT. THE VICTIMS CRY FOR IT. AND GOD DEMANDS IT! It was
written by an Oklahoma City rescue team member on April 19,
1995, the day that Timothy McVeigh and Terry Nichols committed the deadliest domestic attack in American history by blowing
up the Murrah Federal Building and much of the surrounding
area with a truck bomb. The building on which the message was
painted was one of few that remained; it is now a museum about
the bombing. McVeigh claimed the attack was in retaliation for

the ATF siege at Waco on April 19, 1993, exactly two years before. He expressed no remorse that his own attack had murdered
children. In the memorial field, there are nineteen small chairs to
represent the nineteen children he killed.

After the attack, the children of Oklahoma City drew pictures. Those pictures are now preserved in tiles on a wall. They
drew rescue workers and families holding hands. They traced the
outline of their state and drew hearts and Band-Aids inside. They
called Oklahoma "the broken heartland." They struggled for
words. "I feel very sorry," wrote a twelve-year-old. "I'm sorry,"
wrote a ten-year-old. "Fix the hurt," one child wrote in small,
wobbly print.

I walked back to the pool, where my husband was standing with
my children, all with tears in our eyes. My children knew the history
of the bombing. But it is one thing to know it and another to be
where it happened. My husband and I were overwhelmed, even as
adults who had lived through terrorist attacks ourselves. But I was
grateful that our children, who had seen so much horror in their
short lives, could see the memorial because what they had not seen
enough of in America was compassionate commemoration. They
knew all too well that life could change in an instant, but they had
rarely seen an official declaration that it mattered, that we should
grieve together as a nation, and that acknowledging the pain can
make it hurt less.

I wanted them to know that this was America too. That there
was a time, not that long ago, when it was considered so important
to remember the dead that a stunning memorial would be created
in their honor. That of course Americans from across the country
would grieve for Oklahoma. We live in an era of mass violence
and pandemics and a government that tells us to move on, to look
away, to abandon each other, to weaponize our pain for their politics. They tell us that we brought this upon ourselves. But ordinary

Americans have not had the power to bring things upon ourselves for a very long time.

This is not a partisan matter but the prevailing attitude of American institutions. The line from the Waco siege to the Oklahoma City bombing to Trump's Waco speech is a circle. McVeigh and Nichols were part of a network of domestic terrorists that the federal government did not investigate, one that remains active today.[14] The refusal to investigate spanned every administration, Democratic and Republican. The officials who participated in that obfuscation have been installed in office for decades. It should not be children writing on walls that they are sorry. It should be them.

That refusal of officials to atone for horrific mistakes, to confront their own failures and hold the perpetrators accountable, is how rare acts of violence and extremism became common. Americans are told to abandon the pursuit of truth because truth forces accountability, and accountability reduces fear. It is easier to control people who live in constant terror—not only of violence but of apathy. The fear of being killed, and being forgotten.

The Oklahoma City National Memorial is designed to make you appreciate life as you honor those from whom it was stolen. It is impossible to visit and believe that America is beyond redemption. Because good Americans never forget the victims. They never abandon them, even in the darkest hours, even when there seems no light ahead, because they are the light.

For twenty-five years, I have driven Route 66 looking for escape. If you asked me what I was seeking, I could not have answered other than a way out of the paralysis of the present. Escape to the time when the past lives and breathes. Escape from a surveillance state into barren lands where you feel unreachable. Escape to places that make you feel very small only because they are very large—in a purposefully ridiculous way or in a naturally awe-inspiring way. When you feel small, you feel like less of a target. You can fit inside the cracks, and you can see what caused them.

Route 66 is a road through the cracks of America. Americans have long driven this road in the aim of freedom, lost in imagination— but others are out there imagining things too. Their ideas are as big as yours, only they are violent and cruel. From Chicago to Los Angeles, they drove what became Route 66: Al Capone and Bonnie Parker and Timothy McVeigh and J. Robert Oppenheimer and the colonizers and conquistadors and con men. They all left their mark on this road. It is fitting that Ronald Reagan decommissioned it, because he tried to decommission American memory and replace it with vacant dreams.

I have driven Route 66 in grief—in 2007 for members of my family, in 2017 in grief for my country, and then, in 2023, in anticipatory grief for both. I drove through the middle of the country at what should have been the midpoint of my life, wondering what tragedies I was bracketing. I navigated Route 66 looking for history, but memories found me instead. They jolted me when I was driving, illuminating guilt and pain from the last time I came around.

Everyone's backstory is on the backroads, including mine. I try to forgive myself, like the truck stop alien suggested, and move on. On Route 66, you get good advice in stupid places.

The gift and curse of Route 66 is that nothing can be forgotten. The evidence is all over the road. The evidence is absence: blank signs, empty buildings, ghost towns. The evidence is presence: the ubiquitous graffiti, the tributes and shrines, the unique creations of Americans who share their private worlds, who express their reverence and sorrow and let you bear witness. Route 66 is the Mother Road because it welcomes the orphaned and abandoned. It is not such a lonely road when so many of us are lonely together.

7
The National Parks

New Nightmares

July 2020: The Indiana Dunes

It is strange to look back at 2020 years later, because that year, at the time, brought such uncertainty and heartache. Had the pandemic ended, I would consider it one of the worst years of my life. But since the pandemic continued while the worst of "real life" returned—economic exploitation, rising autocracy—along with a horrific loss of public empathy, I look back at 2020 with something not quite approaching nostalgia (the year is too sad for that) but nostalgia for *possibility*. For the belief that we had hit rock bottom and that the world would either quickly burn or radically improve. Either way, we would get resolution.

Instead, we live in the worst of all worlds, the world that ends too slow.

In the late 1990s, there was a show on FOX called *Millennium*, made by the creators of *The X Files*. It was about an elite global secret society and an investigator with an uncanny ability to predict atrocities without being able to stop them. In its second season, FOX announced *Millennium* would be canceled. In response, *Millennium*'s producers decided to end the world. The series finale depicted shadowy government groups releasing a deadly pandemic, initiating the apocalypse and killing off most of the main characters.

But then the unthinkable happened: FOX decided to renew *Millennium* after all. The show returned for a third season as a police procedural with a mostly new cast. The characters who survived season two treated the pandemic as a trifle, ignoring that the world had ended. The shadowy groups returned to the shadows, their mysteries rarely mentioned and never solved. *Millennium*'s audience was baffled not only by the show's makeover but by its audacity: were the people running things really going to pretend the death and destruction of the previous year had never happened?!

This is what it feels like to live in America during the Biden administration and its denial of the horrors of the years that preceded it.

In 2020, my goal was still to rescue my children from daily hell, not impending hell. I was too exhausted from navigating the present to fathom the future. But I wanted my children to know that America was worth saving, that miracles occurred even in the worst of times. I did not trust America, but I loved it, and love mattered more than faith. My love would endure even if my country did not. I looked for things no one could take and everyone could treasure. I searched for places that would outlast the end of the world, in case it had already happened, and we would learn of our cancellation after the fact.

The Indiana Dunes is that kind of place, doing right by me time and time again.

The first time I went to the Indiana Dunes was in 2005. I was supposed to be studying Uzbek in Samarkand, but my summer language program was canceled when Uzbekistan's government massacred hundreds of protesters that May. I then wrote an academic journal article exposing the conspiracy behind that massacre and got myself banned from Uzbekistan. Professors had advised me to stay quiet, saying controversy hurts careers. I refused on principle, arguing that government crimes must be quickly exposed. But the truth is, I did not think I had anything to lose except my integrity. I had a strong hunch there was no such thing as a career left to hurt. The 2008 economic collapse proved me right.

A hunch and a conscience are a dangerous combination. People mistake your survival for sacrifice and your sacrifice for survival. You know too much about what has already been stolen and what is still left to lose. No one wants this information, even you.

Due to Uzbekistan's political crisis, I was spending the summer of 2005 in Bloomington, Indiana, where I was a graduate student. My husband and I did not yet have children or much money. But we had a car, and we were a three-hour drive from Indiana's only beach. My husband had grown up in Chicago. He knew about the Indiana Dunes, though he had never been there. He had seen them from the highway near the rotting smokestacks and shuttered factories of Gary, Indiana.

"No one goes to Gary, Indiana, for vacation," my husband told me when I proposed this trip, and I said, "People whose first choice was Uzbekistan do."

We drove north, singing little ditties about Jack and Diane, as is required by Indiana state law, until we arrived at the semipolluted waters of Lake Michigan. I say "semipolluted" because northern Indiana deserves points for trying. Gary produced the Jackson Five and steel and glass and a Black middle class and in return got white flight and decaying streets and predators like Donald Trump, who ripped off the city with a casino scam in 1993, one of many coastal vultures picking at the corpse of Gary's dead dreams.[1]

Every Midwest city has a long-distance villain. St. Louis's is corporate raider Carl Icahn, who destroyed Missouri-based airline TWA in the 1980s, stripping the state economy of its stability from his New York base. Every Midwest city gets blamed for these homewreckers, even though they arrive uninvited. Every Midwest city, not coincidentally, has a large Black population that bears the brunt of the pain. These dynamics prompt national pundits to ignore the invaders and blame the locals. Pundits love telling Black Midwesterners that they don't deserve anything good.

But Gary still had something to envy. It had the beaches of the Indiana Dunes, despite multiple attempts to destroy them. It had a lake that looks like an ocean, with waves you can ride and a skyline that won't quit.

In 1966, Indiana Dunes became a national lakeshore, officially protected by the federal government. There are few national parks in the Midwest but many national lakeshores and national scenic trails, designations created to preserve the ecological diversity of the regions. Indiana Dunes's status was the hard-fought victory of local activists, mostly women, who worked through the 1950s and 1960s to prevent industrialists from destroying their shores.

"We are prepared to spend the rest of our lives if necessary to save the dunes," proclaimed local English teacher Dorothy Buell, a Republican founder of the Save the Dunes movement.[2] Buell was inspired to save the Indiana Dunes after a 1949 trip to White Sands, New Mexico, which she saw as inferior to the dunes in her backyard.[3] She fought until officials saw Indiana her way: not with scornful dismissal but with respectful reverence.

Some national lakeshores and national monuments shun national park status, fearing over-tourism. But in 2019, Indiana Dunes embraced it and became America's sixty-first national park. The result has been an explosion of visitors, a more sophisticated ecological protection program, and panic about how to keep the park's precarious dunes and bogs safe. Between 2019 and 2020, the number of tourists increased by 60 percent.[4] My family was among them.

A new national park I already liked was now only four hours from St. Louis, making my 2017 vow to take the kids to all of them seem feasible even in a pandemic. I was wary because covid laced every venture with potential disappointment. But in June, I heard news that solidified my desire to go. The brightest comet since 1997, NEOWISE, would be visible in July. I had told the kids the story of Halley's Comet the previous month while we were stargazing in Mark Twain's hometown of Florida, Missouri. Since then, my son had fantasized about seeing a comet and also going to an actual Florida-style beach instead of my cheap, cheeky facade.

I wanted my son to see a comet. I wanted his view to be spectacular. I wanted, in the year everything broke, to make him a promise I could keep.

On a hot July weekend, we drove to northern Indiana, arriving in the evening and heading straight to the main attraction: the dunes. I had learned the hard way that there was never time to waste. One look at what had happened to the park since 2005 confirmed it.

The first thing we noticed from the parking lot were the footprints. They led up a dune to a tree half submerged in sand and continued to a lake so vast it hit the horizon. My husband and I knew this view of Lake Michigan: we had seen it before, in the old America, before the sands of time had shifted. We had seen this tree too, before its branches came to resemble the outstretched arms of the drowning.

Our kids asked how the tree had become trapped, and we pointed to the footsteps in response. Human beings were no longer supposed to climb a dune this delicate, and there was a sign telling visitors to keep away. But it was 2020, and people were having trouble doing what they were told.

The kids stayed off the dune, even though their instinct, too, was to climb it. They were anxious to see a real beach, to feel a semblance of summer normalcy after the shutdown of pools and camps and everything else that marked the season. We told them we would be back to swim the next day. They bounced into the car, high on anticipation, and we headed to our hotel.

In an unfortunate coincidence, the hotel floor was covered in carpets with a pattern resembling the coronavirus molecule. We shrieked at the sight: we had been inside too long and had gotten jumpy. Since March, we had been binge-watching *Lost*, relating to the baffled characters trapped in a dystopian hellhole, yet also jealous that they could go swimming. The desire to swim through the apocalypse was part of what inspired our journey to the Indiana Dunes.

I reminded the kids that we would be outside, where the virus was far less likely to get us, especially if we were alone. Seeking the safety of solitude, I woke us the next day at dawn. Indiana Dunes National Park has multiple beaches, and I'd spent weeks doing research to find the least popular one. My plan worked: for a whole morning, my family had a beach to ourselves.

The water felt like ice, but the kind that wakes you out of a stupor. I floated on my back, eyes closed, as the rising sun warmed my body. I opened my eyes on occasion to catch the sun lighting up the dunes and driftwood, my heart pounding from cold and gratitude. My children played nearby, relearning how to swim with my husband's help because it had been too long. They were retracing the motions of summer childhood, happy to gain back one day of a lost year. I swam low, where my tears mixed with the lake water. I was grieving stolen time while thankful for this defiant, peaceful place where the inherent goodness of nature refused to concede to the mistakes of mankind.

Over the next two days, I began to feel human again. When it was sunny, we went swimming. When it was cloudy, we hiked through sandy forests. There was a "three-dunes challenge" that we ignored, having learned our lesson from Colorado. We were there to relax, to live slow, but on our own terms instead of the government's. We went to a nature trail and strolled a wooden boardwalk through marshes and savannas as birds sang above us and wildflowers sprouted below. Gary, Indiana, was beautiful.

Afterward, as we ate dinner at a burger shack in town with other tourist families, I thought about how during our 2005 visit I had dreamed of having children and taking them here. How nonchalantly I had envisioned a safe future, even though I was studying foreign massacres. How I had never imagined we could lose the whole world at once and would have to try, through small gestures, to get it back.

We made side trips, giving the kids the lay of the land. We crossed the Indiana border to Michigan to pick the best blueberries in America. We wandered around the college town of Valparaiso, where we posed on a bench with a statue of Indiana popcorn mogul Orville Redenbacher, a hero to my popcorn-loving children. We drove through Amish country, where horses and buggies ruled the roads, and bought baskets and honey from Shipshewana shopkeepers in stores without electricity.

We navigated microcosms of America that form no coherent whole, a crazy quilt that still warms you at night. My children were not old enough to have expectations of Indiana, but I liked knowing that every place we visited defied them, that any stereotypes of Indiana my children would encounter now came pre-refuted.

The comet arrived on our final night. The dunes were full of people: Lake Michigan was an ideal place to greet a celestial guest.

Across the lake were the towers of Chicago, a distant silhouette of dead architects' visions of what the future should be. That night they were bathed in the purest gold, a divine admission that their ideas were right. Last-chance sunshine raced in ripples across the water, yellow and orange and pink and purple glittering balls that exploded into waves at the shore. Waves that hit with rhythm and repetition, waves that beat like the music of the Great Lakes, the Motown music of Gary and Detroit and Chicago. The music was in the water, the music was in the sky, the music was the tempo of time running out. In that summer of suffering, the waves wailed too.

We craned our necks to look for 2020's other unexpected visitor, the one we actually welcomed. My son squeezed my hand as we waited. And then it happened, blazing through the night like the reverse of a curse and flooding me with relief. I had kept my word: my son would see something greater than the world we had been dealt. NEOWISE was here.

I was worried about ambiguity, but there was no mistaking it. NEOWISE was a bright and burning streak, slicing the sky and seeming to move while staying still. *Get a look while you can*, it seemed to say, *I'm giving you a show, I'm showing you a sign, I'm granting you a second chance, take it, oh God, please take it.* Mosquitoes swarmed the shore, drinking our blood, but no one cared. We were hypnotized by this transient presence that confirmed there was still such a thing as a pleasant surprise.

For one night, there was an omen so good it could not be ignored. For one night, we could forget what we sought to escape. My children ran to the water like they were chasing NEOWISE, and eager adults followed; everyone becomes a child when a comet is in town. We clapped and cheered like subjects of the sky as the night waves lapped up our applause.

The next morning, when we returned to the beach to say

goodbye to Indiana Dunes, the water was cold and calm and clear, and the footprints had washed away, as if none of it had happened at all.

October 2020: The Great Smoky Mountains

There were a lot of small heartaches in 2020, but the one that broke me was Zoom Orchestra. Every day I heard the violin through the door of my daughter's bedroom, where she played alone, able to see other students only on a screen. I heard her teacher trying to hold the middle school musicians together, to hold *anything* together, but it was impossible. My daughter lives for music, so I composed a libretto of lies. I told her nothing could take away her music, not even the pandemic. I reminded her that for centuries, violinists had played in the worst of times, conveying and soothing the pain of the masses.

She reminded me that, by definition, the masses got to be together.

In 2020, every duet was a solo, every stage a screen, every audience an avatar. When my stoic daughter asked in a quavering voice if she would ever play live music again, the pain of her query astounded me, because her wish was so simple and ancient and impossible.

My children's public school went virtual in March 2020 and did not reopen until August 2021. We did not complain because compared to other families, we had it easy. My husband and I worked from home and our incomes were not interrupted. Our lives were not put in direct risk like the parents of their classmates, many of whom worked customer service jobs. My daughter powered through Zoom school despite hating it. My son, a fourth grader, struggled to focus. I told him not to worry about grades. He could learn fractions when the plague ended.

But the start of the virtual school year was terrifying, regardless of one's position on school closures. The start of school marked the moment when Americans wondered if this was not merely a dystopian present but the future—and, worse, the future of our children. This is why I feel for every parent, no matter where they stand, and for every exhausted educator. There were no easy decisions, and there was no good advice. Parents and teachers were caught in a web of contradictory lies.

The one thing we knew was that childhood had been stolen. As lost time kept ticking, pain turned into rage, and rage was converted into fuel for political wars. But grief was what filled the air that we were not supposed to breathe. Grief gripped us in a fall stripped of milestones, a pantomime of parenting and education that was exhausting to uphold.

By October, it all seemed pointless. I found reprieve in nature: the way the leaves fell with flamboyance, forcing you to notice their demise. I started imagining what the trees looked like elsewhere in America and if this was my last chance to find out. You could never be too careful in 2020. You could never be too reckless either.

"Let's go on a road trip," I said to my husband. "The Great Smoky Mountains at the height of fall. New national park, nine-hour drive. Less than an Amarillo away!"

"What about Zoom—" my husband started to say as the kids yelled, "We hate Zoom school!"

"I don't know what this is," my son said, "but I will do anything as long as it's not on Zoom."

"Even get eaten by a bear?" asked my daughter.

"Yes, because a bear can't talk and won't tell me to turn on my camera as it eats me."

The kids had a three-day weekend. We added a day, figuring we had two for driving and two for exploring the park. We drove east, through Illinois and Kentucky and Tennessee, through red and yellow and orange streaks of arboreal flame. Fall is the season of death, and that year it was as vibrant as the flowering births of spring. The spring of 2020 had been uncannily gorgeous, and we have not had a spring like it since. Sometimes I wonder if it was earth's grand finale or humanity's final warning.

The fall had a similar surreal sense of Technicolor doom. I could not get the pandemic out of my mind—and why would I? The death toll was climbing. Autumn leaves drifted to the ground like eulogies.

We passed Nashville, where, two months later, a bomber would blow up several blocks of Second Avenue on Christmas morning while blaring Petula Clark's "Downtown" on repeat. Most people would forget it happened because it was not even in the top ten strangest events of 2020.

We arrived at night in Asheville, North Carolina, which we made our base of operations. The Great Smoky Mountains are the most popular national park in America, in part because cities like Asheville and Knoxville are near it and smaller towns are inside. For residents of Tennessee and North Carolina, the Great Smoky Mountains are the local park. In 1940, the government transformed 187,000 acres of land into federal property in order to protect the region from logging companies, forcing many long-time residents to abandon their homes and traditional ways of life. Parts of the park are dedicated to showcasing the hardscrabble heritage of the Americans who inhabited and then lost the land first stolen by the US government from the Cherokee and other tribes.

For Americans outside the region, the Smokies are synonymous with thick forests and misty mountains and Appalachian culture. It is a region of ancient trees and wild animals that is surrounded by tourist traps, a place where you can see a black bear and a historic log cabin and then return to your hotel, which is near a museum commemorating Cooter from *The Dukes of Hazzard*, or visit Dollywood, the rural-Tennessee-themed entertainment center of beloved singer and philanthropist Dolly Parton. The region is similar to the Ozarks, and being there feels like walking into a Missouri mirage, one where people admit they live in the South and know how to profit from it.

We were visiting at a glorious time—clear blue skies, cool mountain air—and we were not alone. The rest of America had the same idea. I remember the tourists of the Great Smoky Mountains more than I do its nature, in part because the park looks so much like the Ozarks that the scenery pleased but never astounded me, but mostly because it was my first experience with pandemic crowds. The park was mobbed, and the visitors were angry.

If Yellowstone and Old Faithful were an exercise in how love for nature could unite humanity, the Smokies during covid showed how we fall apart when we are told to stay apart—or told not to. Thanks to conflicting advice from the government and media, no one was clear on what to do, and that confusion was maddening. Strangers fought over parking spaces and masks; they stumbled drunkenly through hotels; they cowered instead of waved. They had palpable rage for obvious reasons: everyone was desperate for relief. Everyone went to the Smokies for a diversion only to find that the most ferocious wildlife was man and it was a pervasive predator. I got used to seeing people's faces fall when they saw us coming. I could feel my own doing the same, even though I didn't mean anything cruel by it.

On Saturday, we went through the motions of a family vacation. We ascended the park's highest peaks, climbing Clingmans Dome and hiking the Appalachian Trail, exploring gulches and streams and pathways of ancient stone. But to my shame, the best moments of that trip were in the car, where I could be with the only three people I trusted, even if it meant separating myself from the natural world. My daughter retreated into her headphones, looking blankly out the window as music played in her head. I wondered if it mattered to her where we were.

On Sunday, we decided we were done with the Smokies and went to check out the Blue Ridge Parkway. We left so early that fog made the scenic drive almost imperceptible. That felt fine; I was done bearing false witness. But then light pierced the veil, revealing the region's deep blue mountains, the highest peaks east of the Mississippi, and my old daydream desires returned. We drove a winding road toward an insistent sun that dissolved the clouds and impressed upon us an earthly grandeur, daring us not to be dazzled. We pulled off at scenic overlooks with wild legends and sensible names—the Devil's Courthouse, said one, as if there were any other kind.

As the day went on, we stopped at trails that got increasingly crowded and tense. Travelers were friendlier than in the Smokies, but they kept their distance. That's what we Americans were supposed to do to each other now, right? Not *for* each other, but *to* each other—that was the new way. Keep our distance: from each other, from answers, from empathy. The old feeling of camaraderie in nature, of mutual appreciation of something simple like a golden tree against an indigo sky, was fading. It had still been there at the Indiana Dunes, in the early days when there was hope. But covid had become a way of life, and no one knew how to handle it, only how to try to escape it, and it turned out we were not much good at that either.

We passed a waterfall on our way out of the park, weeping without reservation, and I appreciated its honesty.

I do not regret going to the Great Smoky Mountains. But I was kidding myself when I thought it would be a break. I saw exhaustion in everyone's eyes—backpackers, families, workers, locals. The exhaustion of looking for an ending that wasn't a finale. It was fall now, but the wrong kind: *we* were the fall, we were the leaves turning from bright to brown, we were the canceled Thanksgiving and the rotted cornucopia, we were the great American fake-out, the trapped tourists of the national imagination who took to the road to get away from ourselves—and failed.

I came to the park to see wildlife. But everywhere I looked, I saw ghosts. I looked at my fellow Americans, and I saw ghosts. The ghosts rose from the mountains in great plumes of smoke, white billows filling the air, begging to be recognized for what they were. The ghosts haunted me in the rearview mirror, merging into the mountains as we began the homeward drive west, where winter and worse were waiting.

July 2021: Congaree National Park

In March 2020, we were supposed to take a trip to the southeast, a region we had not seen outside Destin. In January, I had created an itinerary that was part history tour, part beach vacation: Charleston, South Carolina; St. Augustine, Florida; Chattanooga, Tennessee; and then home. In March 2020, this trip was canceled with everything else. It was not until May 2021 that we felt safe to travel for a week again, because the government had proclaimed that covid was over. We made hotel reservations during the most convincing period of their lie.

As we left St. Louis in July, Delta covid spread from Missouri into the south, trailing us state to state like a tailgating demon.

We did many things on our trip to the southeast. We ate shrimp and grits and went to a museum about slavery and saw Gullah Georgians selling sweetgrass baskets in an outdoor arcade in Charleston that used to be an open-air slave market. We took a boat to Fort Sumter six months after an attempted and unpunished coup against the United States, one the former president initiated and the current president didn't seem to mind, and watched the American flag wave from behind a cannon.

We saw placards naming the secessionists who lived in Charleston's grand historic homes, signs that reminded us that when seditionists tried to split this country, they did it with the backing of big money. We went to a cemetery overgrown with Spanish moss and saw the tomb of Charleston native John C. Calhoun, the proslavery vice president who learned how to be a shrewder racist at Yale.[5] There are rumors that Calhoun's body is not inside the tomb; since he did so much damage to America, people wanted to kill him even after he was dead.

After two days, we left Charleston. The city had worn us out: everything in 2021 had become both more expensive and more lethal, and what did not kill us made us poorer. We were outrunning the plague and headed for that special slice of America where drinks and shame are bottomless. Tall, skinny pines shimmied on the highway, a verdant gate beckoning us to a wilder land. We drove through Georgia and bought nothing but peanuts. When we drove past a combination drive-through liquor and bail bonds store, we knew we were in Florida.

It was pouring in St. Augustine, the oldest European settlement in the United States. We headed to the historic district, a combination of ancient Spanish relics and tourist-trap malls, and watched a Florida Man play the accordion accompanied by Noodles, the World's Greatest Singing Dog. The Florida Man and the Florida Dog wore matching straw hats, so we gave them five dollars. We went to see the settlement explorer Ponce de Leon had dubbed the Fountain of Youth in 1513 because conquistadors and colonizers believe their bastard creations live forever, but it was closed due to covid. We climbed the Castillo de San Marcos, a beachside fortress, and saw the rooms where captives were chained, and watched the rain slap the ground to its senses.

After three days of swimming in the storms—a reckless but inevitable move, for what are Missourians if not landlocked Floridians?—we left St. Augustine and began the drive back home. We paid tribute to Ronnie Van Zant at his memorial park outside Jacksonville and drove north until we arrived at the hotel in Chattanooga where the feds let Al Capone have a luxury stay before arresting him. Capone's captivity room is left as a shrine, complete with his fedora and federal warrant. I listened to Ronnie Van Zant sing "Free Bird" and thought about how some birds you cannot change, which is why they are coddled by the federal government. I had too much America in me, and it was making me feverish.

I also possibly had covid. According to the tests, I was clean. The government said breakthrough cases were rare. But since nearly every vaccinated person we knew got covid anyway, we did not trust this line. We did not trust much of anything except that pain was hard to heal when denial was hard to break and that this nation, past and present, thrived on both.

We were all feeling bad. Though we had other plans for Chattanooga, we decided to be safe and head home. I never did test positive for covid, but you know me—I'm negative on everything.

On the drive back to Missouri, I thought about the start of our southeast trip, which taunted me like an unheeded warning. We had begun the trip seeking adventure, and that meant visiting a national park. The only one on the way was Congaree, one of the least popular national parks in the contiguous United States,[6] located on the outskirts of Columbia, South Carolina. Maybe if I weren't so stir-crazy, I'd have felt different about Congaree, but it was what it was—a daydream deferred.

Congaree National Park is a forest of hardwood trees on a floodplain with a wooden walkway that lets you walk over a swamp. I had not yet learned to love swamps, not in the way George Washington Carver described, where the plants spill their secrets if your love is pure. If Congaree's plants had words for me, they are too obscene to print.

We went to the information desk to get maps. As I reached for one, a monstrous creature crawled by, and I screamed. I did not catch what it was because I had covered my face with my hands, and it still looked bigger than both.

"Oh, that," the park ranger said. "That."

"That!" I exclaimed. "What the hell was that?!"

She looked at me, and at my family, and at her coworker, and at the creature, and then at me again.

"Y'all have fun now," she said.

"We will! Thank you so much for your help, and have a terrific day!" my husband said midwesternly. In the small Wisconsin town where my husband was born, they implant a cheese curd where your amygdala should be so that this is the automated response to imminent peril.

We entered the boardwalk trail. The air was thick with steam, like we were fresh ingredients for a long-boiling stew. Pine trees shot past the sky and into orbit, cypress knees poked through the water like mutant eyes scouting for prey, and all around us buzzed the secrets of the swamp dwellers, little spies that watch and sting and hide.

We saw the web before we saw its keeper. It came into view like a slowly unfolding map of a portal to hell, stretching across one side of the walkway to the other. On its side, swinging on a fencepost, was the largest spider I had ever seen, black with a yellow center, its legs twitching in anticipation.

"That's the thing! That's what I saw at the desk!" I screamed, walking backward and then stopping, scared of what I was walking into.

My husband grew very quiet. Then: "Did you see the rest of the boardwalk?"

And that's when I saw it: web after web, spider after spider, a series of sticky nets guarded by gargantuan monsters. Outside the arachnid doom loop were colorful trees and flowers that bloomed in obnoxious defiance, daring me to withstand these rancid conditions. I wanted to see Congaree, but that would be possible only by entering the maze of fear. Sweat poured down my back, and I became sure it was spiders, certain they were crawling all over me. I swatted frantically, and my son started to panic along with me. My daughter stared coolly ahead, analyzing the situation.

"This sucks, but there's nothing we can do but keep going," she said, which summed up 2021. She ducked under the first web, and we followed her.

The national parks are America's daydream lands, and Congaree is its token nightmare. Maybe I am wrong; maybe there's a season where the spiders vanish and you are left with only sweetgum and persimmon and loblolly pine and other trees that sound like festive desserts.

But I don't think I am. Congaree National Park is haunted, and new ghosts keep coming.

In the early nineteenth century, escaped enslaved Black Americans hid in Congaree's swamps, choosing a terrifying life in freedom over the cruelty of South Carolina captivity.[7] There were signs on the boardwalk describing their fate. I imagined the escapees wading in the murky water and climbing the trees, surrounded by insects and snakes. I imagined Black mothers trying to convince their children that this place was the safe one.

After the Civil War, the swampland of Congaree was among that given to Black South Carolinians. Land was power, land was self-sufficiency, and this was the type of land they got.[8] While the US government gave white immigrants free fertile farmland, southern Blacks toughed it out in swamps, only to have their fragile gains eroded by Jim Crow. Eventually they left, and in the 1960s the region became a favorite of local conservationists. In 2003, following decades of activism, Congaree was made a national park.

Congaree is not unique in having a tragic history. Nearly every national park does, since they are all built on stolen Indigenous land and often mapped by exploited workers. But Congaree was the rare case where—for me, at least—the landscape suited the backstory instead of providing reprieve from it.

But as I made my way down the two-mile boardwalk, something strange happened: I found myself adjusting. The spiders did not seem as frightening once I had seen dozens and learned how to dodge their webs. After a while, I came to almost respect them. They laid their traps with care, meticulous and blatant. These invaders did not mind who noticed them. They knew that they would catch and kill, and no one would stop them. Everything else was incidental.

I learned that the spiders were new to the park. No one knows the precise date of their arrival, but they showed up sometime around the 2016 election.[9] They had come to Congaree in droves as a result of climate change, which caused wildlife to mutate and travel, to the horror of locals.[10]

I had resigned myself to a bitter slog when I had no choice but to forge through. But when the boardwalk end became visible, the old fear flooded back, along with resentment. I hated the spiders. I hated how they wedded themselves into a landscape that was not theirs. That they held the state's ancient beauty captive, interrupting life fighting to be free, making it impossible to move. I hated their domination, and I hated how easily I had let myself adapt to it.

In the parking lot, we checked each other for contamination. You could never be too careful. A family like ours fits in so well, we could get used to the most god-awful things. A family like ours blends into the scenery, and that is what scared me about the Deep South, with its sweet tea smiles and seditionist secrets and easy acceptance of the worst of ways.

I'm not trying to pick on South Carolina, which is no worse than Missouri. Like Missouri, it is a beautiful state with plenty of good people. But that summer, I did not feel like being one of them. All I wanted to do was destroy the webs.

On the way home to St. Louis, we drove behind a silver delivery truck. It had not been cleaned in a while, and on the back, someone had written GET WELL SOON, AMERICA in the dust. It did not say from what America should be recovering. I could not guess because there were too many options. I held my head in my hands and started to cry. I wept for the losses, and I wept for the lies. But I cried most because someone cared enough to write that message. We followed the truck as far as we could, until it exited the highway, and we were alone again. That was okay with me. I did not want to see the driver of the truck give up and wash those kind words away.

August 2022: Pictured Rocks and Sleeping Bear Dunes

On August 2, 2022, one week after the once-in-a-millennium flood that destroyed much of my neighborhood, we lent our home to my sister-in-law and drove north. My in-laws needed a place to stay, and we needed a vacation. In an ironic move, we decided to take it at the largest body of water in America, the Great Lakes. We wanted to be engulfed in water, but voluntarily this time.

There is a place I visit in Missouri that is too special to name. Most of the time I believe that writing things down preserves them, that words are eternal even when places are destroyed. But I rely on this place too much to share it with the world. It exists in the wild and is fed by my mind. When I go there, my imagination meets my expectations in a seamless courtship, and I know why I am alive.

I don't know if every state has a place like this. But I know Michigan has plenty, and that its sanctuaries are safeguarded as fiercely by Michiganders as I protect mine in Missouri. This may be why two of Michigan's largest federally preserved lands—Sleeping Bear Dunes National Lakeshore and Pictured Rocks National Lakeshore—were never made into national parks, even though they are more magnificent than some places with that designation. My guess is that upper Michigan would like to avoid the fate of Indiana Dunes and its tourism explosion. I don't know for sure, because I was not around long enough for a Yooper to trust me, but I think I am right.

But just in case: if you go to northern Michigan and find these special places, leave no trace and shut your mouth.

I became interested in northern Michigan the way all Americans do, which is by looking up the book Dalton was reading in *Road House* and discovering the Upper Peninsula—a.k.a The U.P. or Yoop a.k.a. the home of Yoopers—and author Jim Harrison. Harrison wrote about upper Michigan even when he was not writing about upper Michigan because his books are infused with seething observations of humanity, deep reverence for nature, and a keen desire to be left alone.

"I'd say ninety-nine percent of my hiking, I never saw another human being. Which is the way I liked it," Harrison said of his life in the Upper Peninsula.[11]

I have found some of the more isolated parts of upper Michigan, and I am not sharing their location. But I will pay tribute to Michigan because it saved my life.

After the flood in St. Louis and the painful years that had preceded it, I was lower than low. Over one week's time, my family drove north along Lake Michigan until we were nearly in Canada, then crossed the Mackinac Bridge to Lake Superior. At the terminus of our trip, we found ourselves in a land resembling the Mediterranean: turquoise water and soft tan beaches with swirling stones. Lake Superior was freezing, but according to a local, we had arrived during the three-week period where it is not cold enough to kill you, and we jumped in and swam. We swam through fog that rose off the icy water, fog that rejected the sun, fog that preserved our privacy. This is not a sunny place; it's a tranquil place.

It is a place to drown your problems before they drown you.

We spent the first two days of the trip near Sleeping Bear Dunes, farther south on the Lake Michigan side. As a family, we have never set out looking for dunes like we do for caves and national parks. It's only in retrospect that I realize how many we've seen. Maybe it's because at heart we are drifters, so of course we are attracted to mounds of shifting sand. Or maybe we craved the relief of being on top of a dune, towering over water instead of watching water threaten to tower over us and climb the hill to our home.

We spent the rest of the week in Munising, an unassuming town on Lake Superior where you can buy cheap fish sandwiches and Cornish pasties and Finnish snacks. Munising is the base for Pictured Rocks National Lakeshore, one of my favorite places in the world. It combines so many things I love—cliffs, caves, water, wildlife, and art—into one mountainous seascape. It is best visited from the water, where you can dart in and out of passages and see everything up close.

My daughter and I shared a tandem sea kayak covered with a sea skirt tarp because, unlike the lazy rivers of Missouri, Lake Superior does not mess around. We went with a guide and a group, a situation I usually reject but that was necessary for my safety because I was out of my league. Awe made me uncharacteristically obedient; I would do anything they said if I could stay longer. My daughter and I navigated Pictured Rocks together, and for the first time in ages, I felt pure joy. After a year of disasters worse than even I could have anticipated, I was in a paradise beyond my wildest daydreams.

Pictured Rocks are so named because they contain every color: the green-blue of rusted copper, the gold of sandstone, the red of iron, the black of manganese, and on and on. They are, essentially, a Missouri cave turned inside out. Missouri was once covered by an ocean, and the caves that I explored are the vestige of that era. The Upper Peninsula is what Missouri looked like in prehistoric times, and I felt like there was a geological continuity that recognized me like a relative and welcomed me there to heal.

Later, we went on a boat trip at sunset because I wanted to see what Pictured Rocks looked like at dusk. I wanted to see what Pictured Rocks looked like at every hour. I wanted to stare at Pictured Rocks round the clock, doing nothing but chasing shadows and tracking color. Black cliff towers streaked red like dripping blood, orange rock melting into scream-shaped holes, sandstone crevices with mysteries too high to fathom but that dangled like keys.

I pointed at the cliffs and told my kids, "You can come here in ten years, twenty, fifty, and these rocks will look the same. Remember them, because they won't let you down. Everything else might crash and burn, but they will stay, and you can come back to them."

My daughter leaned her head on me and said, "Come back with us."

And we lay on each other, content, because even though we were surrounded by water, we were safe.

June 2023: Cuyahoga Valley National Park
Once upon a time, there was a river that caught on fire.

One month before man landed on the moon, the Cuyahoga River in northeast Ohio burned. It was not the only Great Lakes regional river left to burn following decades of industrial pollution: the Rouge River in Detroit burned that same summer of 1969, and the Buffalo River had burned the year before.[12] But the Cuyahoga's floating inferno of trash and sewage, caught on camera before being quickly extinguished, captured the nation's attention. The nearby city of Cleveland, which had also burned after riots, became known as "the mistake by the lake." The Cuyahoga River became part of a national joke that Ohio did not find funny.

Today, the Cuyahoga River is renowned as a site of ecological triumph. According to the legend, its horror jolted the conscience of America and became the catalyst for the modern environmental protection movement. This is how people like to frame crises after they are considered resolved.

The reality was more complicated. In 1970, the first Earth Day was held. Cleveland Democratic mayor Carl Stokes, a leader in cleaning up the Cuyahoga River, gave a speech. While applauding activist efforts, he added, "I am fearful that the priorities on air and water pollution may be at the expense of what the priorities of the country ought to be: proper housing, adequate food and clothing."[13]

He was grateful the river was saved—but for whose enjoyment? Stokes was the first Black mayor of a major US city. He understood that ecological disaster was inseparable from racial discrimination and civil rights. His legacy endures in the environmental justice movement and in the failure of officials, both federal and regional, to provide clean air and water to Americans.

Stokes died in 1996, before the worst effects of climate change were felt. He died having witnessed the abandonment of what was known as the Great Lakes Rust Belt—Black-majority cities like Gary that are scorned and rejected, or cities like Detroit that are gutted and gentrified while impoverished residents are denied basic resources like drinking water.[14] But he saw victories as well, especially for Cleveland.

The Cuyahoga cleanup was a locally led effort, one that insisted the Midwest mattered. It was therefore opposed by both multinational corporations and the federal government. But ordinary Americans pitied Cleveland and recognized its conditions in their own cities and towns. Chemical pollution had become a mainstream concern throughout the 1960s, spurred by Rachel Carson's 1962 bestseller, *Silent Spring*. Alarm over Cuyahoga was aided by an inadvertent publicity blitz. The river was featured in an issue of *Time* magazine with a cover story on the mysterious death of Ted Kennedy's girlfriend, an issue that flew off the stands. Overnight, millions of innocent Americans were exposed to environmentalism.[15]

The initial Cuyahoga cleanup was accomplished through volunteer work, litigation, and the humiliation of the powerful. Corporations accused of violating the Water Quality Act of 1965 were forced to scale back their use of the river as a dumping ground. The establishment of the Environmental Protection Agency in 1970 and the Clean Water Act of 1972 added further federal regulations.

But the strongest defense arrived in 1974, when the land surrounding the Cuyahoga River was made a national recreation area. The year 1974 is also when strange nostalgic shrines began appearing on Route 66 and elsewhere. There is a continuity to these efforts: an insistence that ordinary Americans would be the ones to define America.

Ohioans tried to make the Cuyahoga region a national park. They did not accomplish this until 2000. In 1974, they succeeded only in pissing off President Gerald Ford.

"The area possesses no qualities which qualify it for inclusion in the National Park System," the Ford administration scoffed. "Interior is strongly recommending veto and we concur with their recommendations. This bill is just the first of other urban parks which Congress will serve up next year. If this bill is signed, the precedent will clearly be set for an urban recreation area near every large city."[16]

An urban recreation area near every large city? Fresh water and protected wildlife and a place for families of all backgrounds to play? The horror, the horror!

I wanted to see Cuyahoga Valley National Park because I wanted to see what it looks like when the good guys win.

Cuyahoga Valley National Park is exactly halfway between my children's hometown of St. Louis, Missouri, and my hometown of Meriden, Connecticut. My husband and I realized this was the midpoint as we set off on a sixteen-hour drive to see my father after he was diagnosed with lung cancer. I was too afraid to fly because flights were expensive and unreliable. My daughter needed her violin, and I needed my laptop. We needed comfort and control in times of sorrow, and we needed to be alone for the ride. We filled up the car with mementos and took off for a family gathering we worried would be the last.

The summer of 2023 is infamous for its wildfires and record heat. But the week we visited my parents in early June, we woke every day to a sky cool and clear and blue, a reprieve of fresh air for my father, every breath a gift.

We saved Cuyahoga for the drive home to St. Louis because I knew I would need the consolation only nature can provide. After an eight-hour drive, we stopped for the night near Cleveland. We drove to the park and hiked to a waterfall streaming over red and yellow and green rock. It was pretty but unremarkable at first glance. I sensed Cuyahoga was a park that needed regular visits: a place that if you love it, it will love you back and share its secrets.

I have experiences like this often in Missouri. The Midwest is like that. If you stick with it, it will reward you. I've been disappointed in the Midwest, but I've never been betrayed by it, because it wears its heart and its wounds in the open.

The next morning, we walked along the boardwalk surrounding Beaver Marsh, a junkyard restored into a wetland over the latter half of the twentieth century. Humans healed the earth, beavers returned to the water, birds came back to breed. We entered the park when the birds were waking, cooing reassurances. I saw many I see in Missouri—red-winged blackbirds, cardinals, great blue herons—and others I could not identify, but I did not care because I was lost in their song.

I spent 2023 in anticipatory grief: for my father, for my country, for the planet. What I felt in Cuyahoga was the opposite. It was anticipatory hope, the idea that someday, things could get better. The evidence that this was possible was all around me. The Cuyahoga River was a lost cause that people found and refused to abandon, nourishing it back to life. This is an unusual ending nowadays. It's not a magical ending. There is no happily ever after in the climate change era. But there is a path forward if you are willing to confront fire and flood to take it.

Cuyahoga Valley National Park is a place to go not to escape reality but to affirm that reality can change. It is not the most dazzling park, but it is the most humbling. It is the ultimate daydream land, the one where the deepest dream came true, the dream people are afraid to speak: the dream of life after death.

March 2024: Death Valley National Park

Death Valley is alive.

I had heard the rumors, but it is one thing to imagine and another to see. There are not usually flowers in Death Valley, the hottest place on Earth, but it happens from time to time.

We drove to California over spring break because it had been another hard year, and I wanted my children to see Death Valley bloom. I wanted them to know that life can persist in the harshest conditions and that walking through the valley of the shadow of death can be a pleasant stroll if you've got good company.

Our route took us through Nevada, a state, like California, that my children had never seen. We stopped for a night in Las Vegas. I was glad when we left because it reminded me of the government. I had liked visiting Vegas decades ago—the artificial antiquities, the gung-ho glitz—but now it felt federal. Too many places were named after corrupt political donors; the underworld was just the world. We stayed in a cheap hotel with windows that made everything look pink. My room looked out at planted palms and people-less lots: a candy-coated apocalypse strip, an inferno too weak to go red. Some cities come to life the more you know them, and some die a slow, sad death the same way.

I wasn't after a simulacrum of perdition: I wanted the real deal. I took my family to Death Valley because Earth is on life support. I wanted a place where time is so vast that you don't need to borrow it. I wanted confirmation that we are living in hell, and I knew Death Valley would deliver. Even its toponyms dare you to turn back: Funeral Mountains, Coffin Peak, Dante's View.

Death Valley is the largest national park in the contiguous

United States. It is also the driest, the hottest, the lowest, and the most dangerous. It is an international Dark Sky Place where you see more stars than people. There is no cell phone service and unreliable GPS. Some roads are impassable unless your vehicle can handle ultra-rough terrain. Unprepared travelers are often hospitalized in summer, when temperatures can reach as high as 134°F.

As a result, Death Valley's appeal lies in its mountains and minerals: a geological vortex with almost no habitation. The sun is your enemy in Death Valley. But it is also your guide, giving you different views hour by hour, its shifting shadows rewarding your mind's eye. This is what the world looks like stripped to its elements. Beauty posing as bleakness, so that no one gets too close.

Death Valley is a good place to defy the odds. By definition, you are starting from the bottom, as low as a person can go. I appreciated its straightforward inhospitality, its steadfast disregard for mankind. Death Valley had rejected humanity before humanity could take its final shot.

Or so I thought, until we got there.

We left Las Vegas in the morning and headed west. I had been to Vegas and to the California coast but never to its eastern deserts. This was my first time in that fool's-gold stretch, the place where Mark Twain fled when he dodged the Civil War.

"Some people are malicious enough to think that if the devil were set at liberty and told to confine himself to Nevada Territory, that he would come here—and look sadly around, awhile, and then get homesick and go back to hell again," Twain wrote to his St. Louis friends.[17] It did look like hell, but I found this flavor of hell comforting—and familiar.

My family had left Missouri in spring, when dogwoods and

redbuds fill the forests, and traded it for brown desert dirt. But there is a bond between Missouri and Death Valley, and it is geology. When I saw California's billion-year-old boulders, I felt at home. I had gone from one land of ancient rock to another.

America is one continuous nation, no matter our faults.

In the border town of Pahrump, Nevada, we stopped to stock up on supplies for our excursion. Pahrump is a town of brothels and Bitcoin: Nevada's past and future scams. On the way to Walmart, we passed a military-style complex with wild horses roaming in front of it. We pulled in to discover it was a park.

As the kids watched the horses play, I found a familiar face on a plaque. It was a portrait of Art Bell, host of *Coast to Coast AM*, the conspiracy radio show my husband had listened to in the long hot nights of 2006, when a derecho knocked out St. Louis power. Pahrump was Bell's base of operation during his 1990s peak, and he had returned before he died in 2018. His fans commissioned a memorial for a curious man who had become a curiosity himself.

My husband and I liked Art Bell because he never dismissed anything out of hand. If the caller sounded deranged, he wanted to know *why* and would hear them out, for better or worse. He was a relic from a time when it was harder to weaponize conspiracy theories for politics and profit. It made sense that Art Bell was from Pahrump, a border zone between the lawlessness of Las Vegas and the impenetrability of Area 51 and the illusions of Los Angeles.

A road stop to a wasteland where, even though it could kill you, at least you knew what was real.

The first major site upon entering Death Valley is Zabriskie Point, a lake that dried up five million years ago, leaving waves of sediment behind. We stopped and stared, trying to process the undulating gold in every shade we knew existed and some we had never seen. With every passing cloud, the colors shifted, like a looming Lazarus raising the gilded dead.

We drove south, twisting through passages of rainbow stone. Death Valley reminded me of Pictured Rocks in its diversity of color and of Craters of the Moon in its alluring desolation. Glittering borax and puzzle-piece breccia enticed us to look closer; marbled mountains beckoned from afar.

Near an area called Furnace Creek, we saw fields of yellow flowers on black rock hills. Sometimes, after heavy rain, a "superbloom" covers Death Valley. That didn't happen in 2024, but I didn't mind. I'd grown up searching for wildflowers in sidewalk cracks, and now I was seeing them in no-man's-land. Slender stems, standing strong in the shards. They belonged here same as everything else, I decided. They were like the hoodoos of the Kansas plains or the sand dunes of Colorado—who is to say what is an anomaly and what is right at home?

We pulled into a parking lot in Badwater Basin, the lowest point in North America, 282 feet below sea level. It is endorheic, meaning it is not supposed to retain water. Under normal circumstances, it looks like a field of white salt in a grid of interlocking honeycomb shapes that extend to the mountains on the horizon.

I wouldn't know, though, because I saw a lake instead.

Twelve thousand years ago, Badwater Basin was home to Lake Manly, which was about six feet deep. Ten thousand years ago, Lake Manly disappeared. In 2024, it came back.

While the return of Lake Manly was not entirely unheard of—it made a fleeting shallow appearance after heavy rain in 2005—it had never been so deep in modern times that people could kayak and swim, which they'd been doing before we arrived. They could do this, perversely, because of climate change. The atmospheric river that derailed our Grand Canyon trip in

March 2023 reappeared in February 2024. It filled Badwater Basin until the lake reemerged, five times saltier than the ocean.

That was not the end of its climate twists. In early March, sixty-mile-per-hour winds blew Lake Manly two miles from where it had formed.[18] The lake that was not supposed to be there in the first place had pulled a fast one. No one knew how to explain how the reemergent lake had relocated mostly intact. Rangers decided to curtail the kayaking. Who knew what trick the lake would do next?

We were excited to see Lake Manly. It was spectacular, and we knew we were the first generation of humans to see it in ten thousand years. But nothing captures the feeling of walking into something so right and so wrong at once. So beautiful in its visage and so devastating in its implications.

When my son saw Lake Manly, he asked, "Is this what Death Valley is going to look like in the future? Because of climate change?"

"What's more likely," I said, "is that the rest of the world is going to look like Death Valley."

We walked to what looked like a white sand beach and realized it was a ragged shore of salt. Beyond it were snowcapped mountains mirrored on a sudden sea—a rapture, a rupture; nature's revenge and mankind's reward.

My children ran barefoot to the water, and I followed them as my husband hung back, taking photos. My daughter ditched all of us to explore alone, and I let her. She was sixteen now and wanted to be on her own. My son and I waded together, the thick water rising until it covered our ankles and approached our knees.

Badwater Basin was popular by the standards of Death Valley. But the farther out we walked, the more alone we were, to the point that we could look in three of four directions and see no one but ourselves: two foggy phantoms in a lake that should not exist—or should it? Humanity was behind us, and ahead loomed a void: an ancient resurrection, a freakish novelty. Time melted in Death Valley. After today, either we would never see Lake Manly again or it would return regularly after more catastrophic storms. Neither prospect was reassuring.

I stared at the lake and made up a story. The mourning earth had wept so hard, it formed a lake of saltwater tears. I was wading in a warning. I held my son's hand and focused on the present; the past and the future were wrapped inside it anyway.

Later in the week, we would visit Joshua Tree National Park, home to the famous large yucca plants that the government of California is now chopping down to make way for solar panels.[19] After Death Valley, Joshua Tree was pleasant but lacked the dark drama I had come to crave. The exception was in the visitors' center, where notecard messages hung on strings. Visitors from around the world had written down the changes they had witnessed in their environments over the past decades. I read each handwritten note, from New Orleans ("We're sinking") to New Zealand ("Glaciers are melting"). People told of how their homelands were lost to urban development or climate catastrophe. Poland, the Navajo Nation, Holland, Alaska: no place was spared.

I thought of Lake Manly, already evaporating even though mere days had passed. The way the mountains seemed to move away the more my son and I tried to reach them. The way that brimstone oasis cut my feet, and I didn't realize how badly I was hurt until I returned to shore and mopped up the blood. The way my wounds were worth it. I was in a special place at a special time, and my children were with me.

It took a while for my son and I to agree to leave Lake Manly. When we were knee-deep, and clusters of salt floated by like little knives, he announced it was time to go. We wanted to run to shore but instead moved with hesitation. We could throw caution to the wind, but who knew what the wind would do in response? Maybe it would pick up Lake Manly again and blow us all away.

My daughter met us on the shore, ecstatic. She told me Lake Manly was the most amazing thing she had seen. I felt a pang in my heart: I didn't know how many trips we had left together, for a variety of reasons. I wanted this visit to be special, and it was, bittersweet like a mother's tears.

My husband, wise enough to stay out of the water, helped us clean up. He was wearing sunglasses, and I could see our shadowed reflection in them: the three of us laughing, bleeding, covered in salt and mud. I looked at the mountains reflected in the sunglasses and sea, the double illusion of an endless horizon.

California has an otherworldly feeling that extends beyond its landscapes. Many stores no longer take cash, an impediment to my continual surveillance dodge, and UFO lore is an industry. In the town of Baker, home of the World's Largest Thermometer, we stopped at the Alien Beef Jerky Store, where jerky is made from cows abducted by extraterrestrial beings. Inside, there is a robotic Alien Donald Trump who will tell your fortune if you feed him money. That is how the actual Donald Trump works, so I was not surprised.

In California, even the skies are captured by robots. When you gaze into the night on remote terrain, Starlink appears like a dotted line dividing our divine primordial past from a future designed by Elon Musk. Maybe it is not as terrifying as it seems, if you are used to it. Maybe people getting used to it is the terrifying part.

I had never been to the California desert, even though of course

I had seen it, like every American, in movies set in galaxies far, far away. At night we climbed Death Valley's Mesquite Dunes, where they had filmed the original *Star Wars*. We were on Tatooine, Luke Skywalker's home planet. We lay on our backs and waited for darkness to reveal the Milky Way. When it appeared, my heart filled with familiar elation.

That is, until Starlink slithered across—and suddenly this galaxy no longer felt like mine. A Death Star had interrupted my reverie. Nothing can fully destroy the joy of the Milky Way, not even SpaceX's satellite internet constellation. But you are supposed to watch the sky; the sky is not supposed to watch you back.

I know why Lake Manly jumped two miles, I thought wildly. *Like all of us, it's on the run.*

8
A Cave State of Mind

You know you are in the best parts of Missouri when the ground starts to sparkle as you walk. There is a secret buried in our sorry state, a hole in the heart of our earth. This is not a bad thing. You can fill it with freedom.

Inside the secret place, time slows to a stop. The temperature stays steady no matter how fast the outside world is ending. Walls sparkle and drip, breeding creations that bend your mind and soothe your soul. You want to touch them but you cannot. They will not break, but they will bear the mark of your offense somewhere hidden and deep, and that is worse.

There is not enough light here for you to have a shadow. You surrendered that when you agreed to come inside. There is only enough to know how much you cannot see, and the fragmented view fits you fine. You can always come back for more. Anticipation is the greatest gift of the secret place. Here, the future is solid. No matter how far you descend, it never lets you down.

It is hard to destroy a secret place. You know because so many have tried. Men left behind their tools and their dreams, and the underground resumed its ancient ways: life masquerading as death, heaven hiding as hell. The internet cannot find you there. The world cannot either. Sanctuaries still exist, even in the twenty-first century. You can afford to be a romantic where it's too dark for anyone to see your face.

My family has searched for sanctuary from the pain of this century, and we have found it in America's caves. We have tried to be good in a country gone bad. We have tried to be honest without losing ourselves in the grief of truth. I cannot separate the caves from our national plight any more than I can separate that plight from my need to escape it, and to take my children with me. A cave, in the end, is a reliable shelter. So is a parent, if they are doing it right.

I never want to leave Missouri. But if I had to move to another state, it would have to be over a karst formation. This is the only acceptable option. I need to know that at any given moment, I can disappear hundreds of feet beneath the earth.

Karst topography is formed from the dissolution of rock over millennia, which creates enormous caverns and caves, primarily of limestone, gypsum, and dolomite. The karst coexists with groundwater, the slow drip of which creates stalactites and other formations that seem complete but are slowly growing, taking decades to show the slightest progress. My children have stalactites they plan to check on in fifty years, to see if they grew half an inch as promised.

Caves allow children to make future plans they can keep: a rarity nowadays. That is why I have been taking my children to caves since they were old enough to walk. My children are Missourians, and in caves, they will always be home.

Missouri has two nicknames: the Cave State and the Show-Me State. The nicknames work together because the best things in Missouri to show are the hardest ones to see.

Missouri has over seven thousand caves and some of the world's oldest geology, stretching back nearly two billion years. The land-scape is formed from ancient volcanic debris and the fossilized remains of its time as an ocean in the Paleozoic period. Because of its geological diversity, Missouri became a leading state for min-ing. Now many mines are closed, as they should be, after polluting the land and water. But their gleaming remains lay everywhere, beckoning like a wink. Minerals are the corollaries of caves, clues telling you there is more to life beyond the surface.

My family has a rock collection from our adventures in the forests and mines. They took a skilled eye to find and a careful touch to clean. They glitter on our shelves like a prehistoric photo album. I should give some away, but I can't, because every mineral is a memory. Every stone is a story as old as time, and we have become a chapter.

When you enter Missouri, passing the fireworks stands that mark the state border, you are greeted by billboards directing you to a show cave. It does not matter if the show cave is several hundred miles away: its existence must be noted and relentlessly advertised. This is a hangover from Missouri's Route 66 heyday, when a show cave called Meramec Caverns became the highway's first big tour-ist draw. Missouri's treatment for hangovers is to keep on drink-ing, and its cave hype is no different.

Every show cave has its own formations and legends, but there are some ubiquitous traits. Speleology slang like *cave popcorn* and *soda straws* and *cave bacon*. A fake sluice mine where children "pan for gems" planted in dirt by the owner. A gift shop selling mood rings and geode lamps and Bigfoot swag. A sign saying that you have arrived in the long-lost hideout of a legendary outlaw. A tight passageway called something like Fat Man's Squeeze that also squeezes the skinny man.

These oddities are not limited to Missouri. You'll find them in any state with a show cave. I know because I have spent the last fifteen years trying to visit them all. Wherever we went, if a show cave was near, we took the detour and the tour. Show caves are tacky, but they come by their spectacle naturally. Speleology is God's revenge on boring people.

A few caves offer classier fare, bigger on science and facts and lower on "Ozarks truth." These are the caverns that became national parks, forcing the proprietors to refrain from inserting strobe lights and plastic skeletons dressed as dead miners. There are four cave national parks in the contiguous forty-eight states: Carlsbad Caverns in New Mexico, Mammoth Cave in Kentucky, and Wind Cave and Jewel Cave in South Dakota.

My family has seen only two. We are saving the caves of South Dakota for the future, to convince ourselves that there is one.

Carlsbad Caverns is one of my favorite national parks, and I try to go whenever I am in New Mexico. Visiting it was a formative experience. I went with my husband in 2007, a detour on our Route 66 journey. I was aching from a rough pregnancy, and I remember descending into the coolness of the cave and feeling my body and mind ease at once. Descending a cavern is like wading through an ocean of air into a passage of stone embroidery that tricks you out of pain. The sublime surrounds you on all sides, a self-contained galaxy of innuendo. Walls flow with motionless tears; ceilings erupt with sticks of memory. Your private torments become small in the shadow of primeval creation.

In Carlsbad, I felt my daughter kick, and I wondered if my womb soothed her like the caverns did me. I wondered if she could sense the change, the cool serenity I downed like a prisoner who did not know she had been dying of thirst. Caves are like channels that adjust my senses to where they should be. They heighten perception while dulling the white light fever forever flashing in my mind. I have never entered a cave and not felt immediate psychic relief.

By the time we took the kids, ages nine and six, to Carlsbad in March 2017, they were veterans of the underground. They had toured Missouri caves and were well behaved on tours because I had told them an appealing lie. I pride myself on being an honest parent, willing to answer difficult questions, but I have also been a wrangler of wayward toddlers. My children grew up believing that the mall was not full of toy stores but untouchable "toy museums," that Build-A-Bear Workshop was "a holding pen for kids who aren't allowed to go to Mrs. Fields," and that Gerald Ford was a wizard whose presidential library is full of magic clues that appear if you stay quiet. (There is no other way to entertain a three-year-old at the Gerald Ford Museum.)

Usually, the kids would forget whatever nonsense I had made up on the spot. But there was an exception, and I realized it when the Carlsbad tour guide asked if we had any questions.

"Yes," my daughter said. "Does Carlsbad Caverns have a baby dinosaur? Because at Meramec Caverns, there's a secret room with a baby dinosaur. They only open the room if you're good on *all* the cave tours. Then they'll let you see it."

I buried my head in my hands while my husband frantically signaled at the tour guide not to answer.

"Well, I wasn't expecting that!" the tour guide said brightly. "No baby dinosaurs here, I'm afraid. Where did you say you were from?"

"Missouri," I groaned.

"Mmmm-hmmm," she said. "Well, you folks in Missouri are going to have to figure that one out on your own!"

My daughter looked at me imploringly. "So, was I good?"

When my daughter was three, she was afraid of having nightmares, so every night I would decide her dream in advance. The dream was always about two animals who were best friends. I would choose a different combination of animals each time so her dreams would never be boring. When I went away on business trips, I would write the dreams on pieces of paper and put them under her pillow for her to find. She would always claim the next morning that she had dreamed exactly what I invented, and that the dream was wonderful.

But she was nine now, and my ability to dictate reality was waning.

"Both of you were very good!"

"So we'll see the baby dinosaur soon, right?" she pressed. "Right?"

"Um, well, we're not done seeing all the caves in America yet. We'll have to wait and see!"

She gave me a knowing look.

"I'm going to find out the truth about this."

"Me too!" her six-year-old brother announced happily. "I'm going to see the baby dinosaur!"

My daughter got ready to speak, and I gestured at her brother with pleading eyes. Suddenly my little girl was my accomplice.

"Mommy," she said, shaking her head. "You are lucky that I like caves too."

Later that year, we continued our national parks cave quest with a weekend trip to Mammoth Cave in Kentucky, a five-hour drive from St. Louis. It was December, so we stopped in Santa Claus, Indiana, along the way. The town of Santa Claus was originally called Santa Fe. In 1856, upon learning that there was already a Santa Fe in New Mexico, residents took the natural next step, which was renaming their town Santa Claus[1] and restructuring the entire economy around Christmas.

In downtown Santa Claus, there is a post office where children can write and mail letters to Santa with the promise that he will read them at the North Pole and his elves will reply. My children composed their letters with great care and included a missive from our dog. A week later, everyone, including the dog, received postcards from Santa Claus—the myth, the man, the town. My children were delighted, their faith in Santa affirmed.

Volunteers in Santa Claus, Indiana, have been answering children's letters since 1914. They respond to as many as twenty-five thousand a year.[2] This holiday tradition is among the sweetest I have witnessed.

After visiting Santa Claus, we stopped for lunch in Bowling Green, Kentucky. The city had gained pseudo-infamy earlier in the year when Trump advisor Kellyanne Conway referred to "the Bowling Green Massacre": a fake terrorist attack Conway invented while trying to justify the administration's anti-Muslim travel ban.[3] At the Smokey Pig Bar-B-Que, my husband wolfed down a rack of ribs with a side of mac and cheese and proclaimed his triumph "the real Bowling Green Massacre," prompting us to explain Conway's comment to our baffled children.

Santa Claus, the Bowling Green Massacre, a baby dinosaur in Meramec Caverns. My children learned that all adults are liars, and it's the motive of the make-believe that counts.

We drove on to Cave City, passing concrete motel tepees built in the 1930s: the same era fake Native dwellings arrived on Route 66. Kentucky's concrete tepees are misnamed *wigwams*, and they sit on the stolen land of the Cherokee Nation. Our hotel was a few miles away, near the charred brick ruins of Bell's Tavern, an internationally famous resort built in 1830 for Mammoth Cave tourists. Enslaved Black Americans were forced to construct Bell's Tavern, and after it burned down during the Civil War, they refused to rebuild it, because they were free.

Like most of America, Kentucky is a land of white lies: lies told by white people to mask the truth about who inhabited or built the region. Mammoth Cave is the story of white exploitation of Black exploration. The longest cave system in the world, Mammoth Cave was first navigated around five thousand years ago by Indigenous people. Around 1200 BCE, it became the home of the Southeast Woodlands people, who left behind petroglyphs and artifacts. The cave was then uninhabited for centuries for reasons that remain unclear. In the 1790s, as Kentucky became a state, parcels of land containing the caverns were purchased by European settlers, who forced enslaved Black laborers to mine them for saltpeter used to make gunpowder.

Even today, Mammoth remains somewhat of a mystery: a sprawling series of caverns in which new passages are still found. The first person to map it was an enslaved Black man named Stephen Bishop. Bishop was brought to the cave in 1838 by lawyer Franklin Gorin, who had bought Mammoth from Pennsylvania financer and human trafficker Hyman Gratz, who owned seventy-five slaves.[4] Along with the Mammoth property, Gorin purchased the then-seventeen-year-old Bishop.

Forced to give tours, Bishop began to explore Mammoth's uncharted territory. He taught himself to read and write and became an expert in geology and minerology. He discovered the fancifully named passages on the tour today—Fat Man's Misery, Tall Man's Misery, and the Great Relief Hall you enter after surviving the former two—and created the first map of Mammoth in 1842. Bishop drew the cave from memory after being sent to work at the Locust Grove plantation near Louisville, an extravagant compound that catered to US presidents while using slave labor. While there, he met an enslaved chambermaid, Charlotte, whom he married. In

1843, they had a son, Thomas. Upon his return to Mammoth, he resumed giving tours, including to prominent Americans like Ralph Waldo Emerson.

Before the Civil War, European travelers considered rural Kentucky an exotic luxury destination. Mammoth Cave was the jewel in its crown. The first travel guide to the region, Alexander Clark Bullitt's *Rambles in the Mammoth Cave, During the Year 1844, by a Visiter*, describes Bishop as inseparable from the cave.

"And now, this first and most important preliminary to a traveler settled to his perfect content, he may remain for weeks and experience daily gratification, '*Stephen* his guide,' in wandering through some of its two hundred and twenty-six avenues—in gazing, until he is oppressed with the feeling of their magnificence, at some of its forty-seven domes,—in listening, until their drowsy murmurs pain the sense, to some of its many water-falls,—or haply intent upon discovery, he hails some new vista, or fretted roof, or secret river, or unsounded lake, or crystal fountain, with as much rapture as Balboa, from 'that peak in Darien,' gazed on the Pacific; he is assured that he 'has a poet,' and an historian too. Stephen has linked his name to dome, or avenue, or river, and it is already immortal—in the Cave."[5]

In the narrative of the book, Stephen Bishop, the enslaved explorer, has no last name. But in a rare show of respect, Bullitt added Bishop's 1842 map and gave him full credit. It was the first map of Mammoth Cave ever published.

Bishop was admired, adored—and still enslaved. By 1852, he was making plans to flee with his family to Liberia. In 1856, Gorin agreed to end his captivity. He lived only one year as a free American before dying of unknown causes.

Bishop was the most prominent in a long line of Black Americans who explored Mammoth Cave. They found themselves in a contradictory and painful position: respected by white locals as experts inside the cave and treated as property outside of it. The enslaver of a Black guide named Mat Bransford sold three of four of Bransford's children, and he never saw them again. Heartbroken, Bransford sought solace in the caverns. At the end of his life, Bransford remarked that Mammoth "seems most like a child now, you know, we've been together so long."[6] He taught his one remaining son about the cave. For the next century, five generations of Bransfords worked as Mammoth guides, basking in the pride of their expertise while still enduring discrimination.[7]

After the Civil War, many Black Americans worked as Mammoth guides, earning wages for the work they were once forced to do for free. But as Reconstruction collapsed, Black intellectuals and adventurers were forced into menial labor while white men took their places. Black explorer Ed Hawkins, a surveyor of Mammoth's Cathedral Dome, was given a new job peeling potatoes.[8] Their skills were unappreciated in their time and remain little known outside Kentucky.

On the tour of Mammoth, I thought of Bishop and other Black men who navigated this paradoxical world. In the hollows of the earth, inside a vast tomb devoid of human life, they were treated as men. And then they emerged, and the dream of freedom, so vivid in the dark, dissolved in the light of America.

After visiting Mammoth, we headed south to Diamond Caverns, a privately owned cave with a ceiling like twisted teeth and a floor like an altar of ooze. Diamond Caverns was discovered by another enslaved American, their name unknown, who noticed that the ground near the entrance sparkled like diamonds. Like most show caves, Diamond Caverns was owned by a white family. The cave was hot property, used to host weddings and parties in addition to tours. Thanks to Mammoth's fame, caves became major tourist attractions until the Civil War, when they briefly ceased operations.

They reopened after it ended, only to face a new bloody and bizarre episode: the Kentucky Cave Wars.

From the midnineteenth century until the designation of Mammoth as a national park in 1941, Kentucky cavers went to battle: in advertisements, in courts, and in shoot-outs. Competing cave owners would stake out roads to other caves, seeking to sway visitors by claiming their intended destination had imploded. Schemes frequently ended in tragedy. One cave owner claimed that a trapped explorer in a competing cave was faking his plight for publicity until the trapped man, Floyd Collins, died an agonizing death seventeen days later.[9] (This highly publicized case prompted Mammoth to be taken over by the National Park Service.) Rival proprietors sabotaged each other's caves, their impulsive capitalist rage causing permanent damage to formations that had taken hundreds of millennia to form.

The Kentucky Cave Wars were rooted in both greed and despair. Karst topography is bad for crops, and commercial caves were a way out of poverty for an impoverished region. Caves were family property, passed down through generations. But as the caves lured tourists, they also fueled Appalachian stereotypes. Clan violence over cave tourism was compared to the infamous feuds of the Hatfields and McCoys. "The 'cave men' of Kentucky are now reverting to the chief pastime of their ancestors—war," wrote a Pennsylvania newspaper in 1928.[10]

But being slighted by the northern media was a boon for publicity, and Kentucky cave owners rode the bloody wave. The Cave Wars were incorporated into marketing campaigns that emphasized outlaw bravado, a tactic polished over time like rocks through a tumbler. All across America, show cavern tour guides began to boast that their caves were used by bootleggers and bandits. This tactic continues to the present day. Famed Ozarks and Appalachian criminals are mentioned with pride, as if the region should be honored that their subterranean enclave met the exacting standards of a jackass.

Foremost among these criminals is Jesse James. James was a racist, a crook, a murderer, and a traitor. He was lauded as a folk hero in his time and remains revered by some over a century after his demise.

The continued veneration of Jesse James explains a great deal about the United States in the era of Donald Trump.

Jesse James was born in 1847 at the western edge of Missouri's Little Dixie: the same stretch of slaveholding territory that Mark Twain inhabited at its eastern edge in Hannibal. The two Missourians were contemporaries. But they lived foremost in the American imagination, challenging public conceptions of freedom and virtue. Twain wrestled with the moral decrepitude of slavery through his writing; James stole and slaughtered his way to infamy while relying on the press to portray him as a populist. James lived as a myth and died as a murderer; Twain shattered the American Dream in prose and, in doing so, gave birth to a new one. Both spent their childhoods exploring Missouri's caves and their adulthoods immortalizing them in lore.

In September 2022, while driving back from Lawrence, Kansas—a town where in 1863, James and his brother Frank had helped Confederate mass murderer William Quantrill kill scores of civilians[11]—my husband and I passed through James's hometown of Kearney, Missouri, where he remains revered. We passed the Jesse James Park where they hold the annual Jesse James Festival before arriving at Mt. Olivet Cemetery. The grave of Jesse

James was covered in flowers and a Confederate flag. His visitors were recent and approving.

After Twain, James is the most ubiquitous historical figure in Missouri. His childhood homes are lovingly preserved. The banks he robbed are marked with plaques of pride. The caves he visited—or did not visit—are advertised as his hideouts. This veneration extends beyond Missouri into all the states he is said to have terrorized, whether it happened or not.

"If every cave that claims Jesse James had been there was valid, Jesse James would never have been on the surface," noted Katie Cielinski, the proprietor of the Lost River Cave in Bowling Green, yet another cave proclaimed to be visited by the James Gang.[12]

In the heated years after the Civil War, James realized cloaking crime as politics would endear him to lingering Confederate loyalists, and he exploited those officials' craven goals. A wealthy racist, James repackaged himself as a Robin Hood for the benefit of political elites bent on destroying the progress of Reconstruction. His robberies were whitewashed as social revolt instead of thrill-seeking thievery.

The legend of James grew after he was killed in 1882, an episode Springfield, Missouri, native Brad Pitt glamorized in his 2007 film *The Assassination of Jesse James by the Coward Robert Ford*. Pitt played James, following James Dean in giving the Confederate killer a handsome cinematic face lift. The legend of James, far more than his actual life, taps into a particularly American pain combining genuine economic precarity with a vicious, often racist lust for impunity. Critic Roger Ebert described Pitt's film as portraying "a time when most men were so powerless, they envied Jesse James even for imposing his will on such as they."[13]

The movie was a box office bomb. Pitt should have waited a year for the global economy to collapse and a Black president to be elected. For the dynamic that built the cult of James—the desire to see someone act on their worst impulses, even if their actions benefit no one but themselves, so long as they pretend to hurt the powerful—is the same force that created the cult of Trump.

The first cave to brag of being the hideout of Jesse James is Meramec Caverns, the same cave where I first lied to my little children about a secret room with a dinosaur. The five-mile cave is shaped by the Meramec River, a tributary of the Mississippi River known both for float trip fun and for being "the river of death."

The Meramec River is where my family drifts on steamy summer days past charcoal cliffs filled with flittering cave swallows. The Meramec is also where at least one unlucky soul tends to drown each year. The drownings often happen near a bucolic region nicknamed Zombie Road. The area is plastered with signs warning visitors not to go in the water. Eventually, officials gave in to local lore and added signs about the zombies too.

Zombie Road is in a defunct railroad town called Glencoe where the Union Pacific train crossed the Meramec a century ago. The tracks are still there, peeking through the thick of the forest. The area is called Zombie Road because at night, the undead are said to stalk St. Louis County suburbanites foolish enough to traverse the area. Native Americans, Civil War soldiers, and others who perished in Glencoe are among the zombies spotted by locals. Some zombies are said to be the reanimated corpses of train robbers who hit Glencoe in 1910—one of whom was, of course, the son of Jesse James.[14]

There have also been sightings of what one researcher called "a shadow nest of children" staring out from the hillsides.[15] Officials close off Zombie Road at sundown. St. Louis County has enough problems without a shadow nest of children getting involved.

There is a tunnel near Zombie Road under the old railroad bridge. Built in 1930, the tunnel is painted with the phrase "The Route of the Scenic Limited" in a bloodred art deco font. The Scenic Limited is the name of a train that traveled from St. Louis to San Francisco. But for modern travelers, it is also a sound piece of advice. The scenic limited is the best way to see Missouri, for what is a zombie but brain-dead history rising from the earth, racing to reclaim the remains of your rationality? The scenic limited is the edge of reality, and it flows with the river to a land of lore so bizarre you have to pace yourself in absorbing it.

The Meramec River meets the Mississippi River near Zombie Road, originating in the town of Salem and running through the Ozarks roughly parallel to Route 66. Along both rivers are numerous Missouri caves, but none so influential as Meramec Caverns— both for the cave tourism industry and for the invention of the American road trip. For a few years, Meramec Caverns was the Mother Road's central attraction, an innovator of the inane. It is now a sprawling nostalgia complex.

Meramec Caverns is four hundred million years old and promises visitors a trip through time. It does not tell you that the time you are traveling to is 1950.

Launched as a tourist attraction in 1935 by local entrepreneur Lester Dill, Meramec Caverns is the consummate American show cave. It drips with stalactites and hyperbole in equal measure. The flamboyant Dill, frequently photographed grinning in a leopard print suit, managed multiple caves in Missouri, nearly destroying some of them as he paved routes for guided tours. But Meramec was his meal ticket. The caverns became a Route 66 staple, and while its natural beauty was enough to attract visitors, that did not suffice for Dill.

Lester Dill was a master of publicity. He started local, bribing farmers with whiskey to paint MERAMEC CAVERNS on the roofs of their barns. Many of these barns can still be seen today. He printed MERAMEC CAVERNS on small pieces of cardboard and had employees he nicknamed "bumper sign boys" tie them to the cars of visitors, who then unwittingly advertised the caverns as they made their way down Route 66.[16] This is how Lester Dill inadvertently invented the bumper sticker.

In 1953, Dill bought another cave, Onondaga. It had nothing to do with the Onondaga tribe of New York; he just liked the name. He gave it a theme song—"If you want your eyes to go gaga, come and visit Onondaga!"—and proclaimed it to be in a Kentucky-style cave war with Meramec. He asked tourists to visit each cave to judge which was better, never revealing that he owned both. Only through multiple visits with multiple admission fees could a proper verdict be reached.

In the 1940s, Dill's son-in-law, Rudy Turilli, went to the top of the Empire State Building dressed as a caveman and threatened to jump unless the whole world visited Meramec Caverns. Dill did not get the whole world, but his stunts attracted millions of tourists, including Hollywood producers and government officials. According to Dill, there was nothing that could not be accomplished inside Meramec Caverns. You could film a heartwarming episode of *Lassie*. You could sell Cold War fallout shelter coupons. In Meramec Caverns, the dreams and dread of post–World War II America collided.

Over the decades, legends about Meramec Caverns changed with the times. But its one constant was Jesse James, the hype man for the Lost Cause and the power brokers who sanitize it.

The first thing you see upon entering Meramec Caverns is a small wooden shack with a neon sign proclaiming that it is the long-lost cabin of Jesse James. Once the tour begins, the tour guide informs you that the sign is nonsense and that you are actually looking at the shack of a random moonshiner found floating in the Meramec River. The fake hideout sits under a disco ball dangling from the ceiling and across from a broken pendulum measuring nothing.

It is easy to get swept up in the magic of Meramec Caverns, where the speleothems are as steadfast as the folklore is flimsy. Twisted passageways offer elaborate drapery around each bend, surreal towers as tall as the tales they tell. For millennia, living stone grew silently into an architectural marvel beneath a blank slate of Missouri farmland.

It's enough to make you believe in America again: if Stanton, Missouri, boasted a secret underground primeval metropolis, surely other implausible things could be true. Maybe democracy wasn't dying; maybe it just went underground! Maybe accountability is supposed to grow like a stalactite, one inch every millennium! Maybe you should stop thinking and surrender to the charmed timelessness of the cave, that most ancient of illusionists, with puddles of water that look as deep as oceans. Look into the water and see your reflection in a place both so fake and so pure, everybody can belong. Look into the lie, and love it, like an American.

The tour culminates in a stone theater of stalactites and stalagmites against which a red, white, and blue light show flashes as Kate Smith's rendition of "God Bless America" blares from a loudspeaker. Everyone is asked to support the troops, and also the gift shop.

Down the street from Meramec Caverns is the Jesse James Wax Museum. Created in 1964 by Turilli, it is premised on the idea not only that James was an American hero but that he did not die in 1882. According to the museum, James instead lived out his golden years on the grounds of his favorite hideout, Meramec Caverns, and died in 1951 at the age of 103.

The legend of Geriatric Jesse James, Cave Dweller, was launched by Dill and Turilli as the ultimate publicity stunt. It was not enough for Meramec Caverns to be the hideout of Jesse James. Every cave claimed that. He had to *still live there*.

Dill and Turilli's hoax was inspired by an Oklahoma man named Frank Dalton. He announced in 1948 that he was the real Jesse James, that the coward Robert Ford had killed an imposter, and that he had been living in hiding under the pseudonym Frank Dalton while dodging the law.[17] He claimed he sang hymns at his own funeral while officials buried Ford's real victim, a sucker named Charlie Bigelow. These stories tapped into preexisting mythology and a twisted longing for James to return. For decades, rumors spread that James was still alive, to the extent that his corpse in Kearney had to be moved for fear of grave robbers.

News of "the real Jesse James" broke in the May 19, 1948, cover story of the *Lawton Constitution*, an Oklahoma small-town paper. The editor included a small addendum that the entire story may be a fabrication. But, he noted, truth is not the point of journalism.

"There's a code among the kith and kin of that lost generation of Americans who lived by the staccato bark of a flaming six-gun as they took from the people 'who had it, and distributed their loot to those that didn't,'" gushed writer Frank O. Hall. "That code, never spoken, but always understood, makes it an offense punishable by death to reveal the hand of a man whose past failed to meet with the dictates of the law."[18]

That there is no evidence Jesse James robbed for any reason but his own enrichment made no difference. It's the thought that counts—not the thoughts of James but the longings of the low-down for a loser who emerges a secret winner. The desire for a Civil War that was a war against power rather than a referendum on the abuse of it. The irresistible fantasy of a notorious bandit defying officials and time to live a full century on his own terms.

If that were possible, what bright American future awaits? Better yet, what bright American *past* awaits?

Anything is possible in America if you ignore the constraints of logic and law. No one understood that better than Lester Dill. In 1948, Dalton agreed to Dill and Turilli's offer for him to live for free on the Meramec property in exchange for telling tourists he was Jesse James. A raging alcoholic, Dalton made national headlines for his claims, appearing on popular television programs and attracting even more tourists to the caves. The ruse, which Dalton likely really believed, became increasingly elaborate. Dill tracked down other geriatric men claiming to be lost-lost fugitive outlaws and invited them to Dalton's 102nd birthday party, which was held, of course, inside Meramec Caverns.

All that remained was to make it official. In 1950, Dill petitioned a Missouri court to legally change Dalton's name to Jesse James, showing up in the courtroom with a stretcher on which lay the febrile Dalton. The court declined, and Dalton died soon after on a visit to Texas.

The Jesse James Museum does not depict this story as a stunt but as the plain truth. The museum claims, with straight faces frozen in wax, that Jesse James died at age 103. Frank Dalton is not mentioned by name but is referred to as Jesse James.

Proof is offered via a photo of his tombstone in Texas, where Dalton is buried under the name Jesse James, to the dismay of the actual James family. The grave in Kearney, where the corpse of Jesse James was verified as authentic in a 1995 DNA test, is ignored. There is no mention of Stella James, the eighty-five-year-old daughter-in-law of Jesse James, who sued Turilli in 1967 after he went on television offering $10,000 to anyone who could prove the now-dead Dalton *wasn't* Jesse James. Instead, there are somber tributes to hoax accomplices. "Witnesses" that Turilli and Dill rounded up are immortalized as figurines. Turilli presents himself on video as a neutral arbiter of truth instead of the guy who owns the museum.

While visiting the Jesse James Wax Museum in 2023, I flinched in recognition: media ruses abetting lawless wealthy racists felt too familiar. But I started to feel better about the dinosaur lie I'd told my children eight years before. Worse things had been made up here for worse reasons. Clearly, as a Missourian, I could not control myself in a cave. My story was not a lie, I told myself, but a tall tale in the fine tradition of Lester Dill and Mark Twain. And when you think about it, kind of true!

"There *was* a dinosaur hiding in Meramec Caverns," I said, pointing to the shriveled wax dummy of a centenarian imposter. "And his name was Frank Dalton!"

My teenage children looked at a doll-size sculpture of Dalton smiling from inside a glass box, and then back at me, shaking their heads.

"You were lucky to find something that dumb to make you feel less guilty about my poor baby dinosaur," my daughter said.

"Luck's got nothing to do with it," I said. "You were born on a bedrock of bullshit, and I just follow the road." I bought a beer koozie that said "Get Your Sips on Route 66" and exited the liar's house of lore.

The makeover of Jesse James was part of a broader midtwentieth-century rehabilitation of slave owners, including Daniel Boone and Davy Crockett. Their biographies were rewritten by Hollywood's "cowboys and Indians" culture, softened to appeal to ten-year-old boys and to the ten-year-old boy inside every man. The mythology was insidious. James, the most vicious of the lot, was forgiven for his crimes. He was white, entertaining, and an alleged foe of the government: in other words, an ideal American.

There is a darkness in the caves of Middle America. It is not the absence of light but the traces of saltpeter, the substance used to create gunpowder for war—first for the war of 1812, and then for the Civil War. The ceilings were scraped for battle, and the floors were paved for crime. Caverns have natural air-conditioning that is ideal for storing alcohol and corpses. They played a key role for everyone from the Confederate Army to the Chicago Outfit to Missouri beer barons, who hid their illicit wares in caves under the streets of St. Louis during Prohibition.

Caves are where miners first dug out the minerals that powered the plants and poisoned a nation. Missouri's caves are where the US government keeps billions of pounds of emergency cheese, for reasons they have not explained.[19] Missouri's caves are also where the US government stores the national archives under the belief that the outside world will be destroyed—a fair assumption, since they are among the ones destroying it.

The karst belt stretches across the region most divided during the Civil War: Missouri, Kentucky, Illinois, Tennessee, Pennsylvania, Virginia. It extends south into Arkansas, where criminals entranced and terrorized America in the 1930s. Caves are where white supremacist terrorists met before emerging aboveground in sheets and then in suits and ties.

Caves attract people who are not afraid of the dark, whether the introspective adventurer or the unabashed outlaw. Caves were mankind's first home, its welcoming womb. Caves accept everyone, and that is their danger and their appeal.

The use of caves for serious crimes, particularly violence centered around race, is often omitted from show cavern tours. Fantastic Caverns in Springfield, Missouri, is known as "America's only ride-through cave." Visitors board a Jeep-drawn tram that slows down to showcase inspirational relics like the signatures of the brave teenage girls who first explored it in 1867 inscribed on the wall. Fantastic Caverns is a hit with small children, who enjoy seeing giant stalactites from a tiny train. They are not told that they are in a cave that from 1924 to 1930 was nicknamed the Ku Klux Klavern due to its tenure as the meeting place of white supremacists.

Civil War caves are a particular point of controversy, especially in states like Missouri where people fought for both the Union and the Confederacy.

In December 2022, on the road back from our Arkansas crime scene vacation, my family went on a tour of Smallin Civil War Cave in the southwest Missouri Ozarks. It had been mapped in 1818 by explorer Henry Schoolcraft, who married an Ojibwe woman and then felt so guilty about the sins of westward expansion that he wrote an epic poem called "The Groans of Missouri" written from the perspective of minerals stripped from the earth.[20] Smallin had been the home of the Osage, the Cherokee, white settlers, and Civil War soldiers. It was now managed by Kevin Bright, a Missouri cave expert who had purchased Smallin with his wife, Wanetta, a decade before.

We were the only visitors that day due to the freak snowstorm of December 2022, which had created a rare ice stalagmite in the cave entrance. Bright's tour focused on the cave's unique ecology, including fossils of a starfish and a giant prehistoric worm. The gaping outdoor entrance meant that, unlike other caves, Smallin could host living animals, including white-blue cave crawfish and sleeping bats. But when my husband asked about the cave's role in the Civil War—its alleged selling point—Bright nodded toward my children and shook his head. He was right that in 2022, in a Missouri roiling with vicious political rhetoric, the story would have scared them. It was too familiar.

Later, the Brights told us the tale while the kids played with farm animals outside. After the Civil War, Smallin was the hideout of feuding bandits called the Bald Knobbers—nicknamed for the treeless "bald knob" hills in the area—who operated as vigilantes after the collapse of local law enforcement. At first they were embraced for restoring a semblance of order, but the Bald Knobbers' lust for power proved deadly. This was the group that drove the Trumans and other families out of the Ozarks. Civilians were whipped or shot for merely criticizing the vigilantes, who covered their heads with masks to remain immune from accountability. Impoverished and remote, the Ozarks were left to mob rule that ended only with the public hanging of Bald Knobber leaders in 1889.

This history looms over the Ozarks, contributing to wariness of authority and the knowledge that anyone can cloak themselves in a badge or a government position and use it to abuse citizens.

Some Ozarks residents compare the Bald Knobbers to the KKK. Others compare them to the FBI. And then there is Branson, which for sixty years boasted a country music comedy show called the Baldknobbers Jamboree, for there is no carnage that Branson cannot commercialize.[21] Its inimitable talent for combining violence and showmanship is what makes Branson a favored Trump campaign stop. Branson is located in Taney County, named for Roger Taney, the Supreme Court justice who deemed Dred Scott less than human.

Yet in the midst of this chaos is the cave itself: a geological wonder, a community archive, a spiritual shrine, the stomping grounds of the best and worst America has to offer. In a self-published book, Wanetta Bright reminisces on finding a Bald Knobber chieftain's inscription carved into the wall:

"I remember how I felt the first time I found the signature in the beam of my flashlight; a feeling of dread washed over me, and the hair stood up on the back of my neck as I imagined the presence of vigilantes all around me in the darkness of the cave.

But then I looked away from the signature, to the beautiful, sunlit entrance behind me. As I turned, I quickly shook off the 'ghosts' of the past. What struck me at that moment as I enjoyed the reassuring, welcoming view of remarkable beauty that stretched out before me, is this . . . The blessing, and the 'gift' of Smallin Cave is its presence as a peaceful sanctuary in the lives of good people who have encountered it through the ages, and who still encounter it today."[22]

My children saw a cave for the first time in the fall of 2014. I have photos of them dwarfed by four-foot stalagmites, wide-eyed with wonder. We had gone underground, as Missourians had done since time immemorial, to escape.

My children were three and seven. During their short lives, the global economy had collapsed, first graders had been massacred in the worst school shooting in US history, and voyeurs had converged on St. Louis to witness the violent police suppression of the Ferguson civil rights protests. Their earliest memories of Missouri are of a state of grief, a state whose leading export was pain, a state the rest of the country emulated and then exploited and then abandoned. My daughter was sent home from second grade with a "riot packet" as police gassed protesters during the week of the Ferguson grand jury decision.

I wanted to assure my children that Missouri was good deep down, but I had no proof, so in desperation I took them to Meramec Caverns. At the end of the tour, we were sold star-spangled sagas about America, and I felt my own urge to believe. Not in the goodness of America's government or politics but in its stalwart beauty, the defiant life of the underground. Here, we could love America without irony or regret.

I had told the kids that the rest of America was also good deep down. I could not decide if I was lying or sliding by on a technicality, but I figured we would find out. And so, like a subterranean parallel to our national parks quest, our show cave journey began.

—To Alabama in March 2018, watching the sun rise over Cracker Barrel and Larry Flynt's Hustler Club as we drove to Selma and Birmingham and Montgomery to teach the kids about civil rights before it became illegal, and stopped at Cathedral Caverns on the way home. Cathedral Caverns is in the town of Grant, named for Ulysses S. Grant because this northern area of Alabama supported the Union. We gazed at Goliath, the World's Largest Stalagmite, and followed Mystery River to the Crystal Room, past shark teeth fossils and flowstones until we emerged outside into an America where the president was being investigated for crimes as white supremacists cheered him on—

—To Cave of the Mounds in southern Wisconsin in June 2018, wading through water as we stared at a giant fossilized cephalopod formed hundreds of millions of years ago when the cave was a sea, and I wondered what fossilized remains my children's generation will witness once our cities sink into the oceans—

—To Blanchard Caverns in northern Arkansas in September 2018, where we descended into a primeval silver and white rock forest as ethereal as the blue springs above and entered the Ghost Room with its luminous hulking flowstone, a past so vast it could make you believe in the future, and then surfaced to a parking lot of cars decorated with Confederate flags—

—To Natural Bridge Caverns near San Antonio in December 2019, after we had seen the Alamo and asked if it had a basement and when we learned it did not, we decided to explore nature's basement, back when you could make stupid jokes without too much worry, back when things were bleak but not yet broken in Texas—

—To every Missouri cave as the aboveground America plunged

into political misery; to the ethereal Onondaga that my children take me to on Mother's Day; to Jacob's Cave, where piles of flash-bulbs from decades of tourists lay in tribute to the time the whole country loved Missouri; to Bridal Cave, where the Osage Nation held weddings under an ancient stone altar; to Stark Caverns, home of prehistoric bears and modern moonshiners—

—To an Ozarks cave I cannot name because we went in 2020 when it was supposed to have closed for covid but stayed open because, as the proprietor said, "The law don't matter here, and we won't tell no one if you don't," and we knew we'd be fine because Missouri has a poor track record of catching families of outlaws in masks—

—To Fisher Cave near Meramec Caverns, where, in 1908, a ten-year-old Lester Dill got his start giving tours.[23] Dill never sig-nificantly altered Fisher Cave, which was across the street from his family farm and which he came to own; what my children saw there in 2023 is more or less what he saw as a child a century earlier, and the cave can be explored only by lantern with park rangers to ensure that it remains pristine. Meramec is Dill's legacy, but his heart resides elsewhere. In the 1970s, Dill helped block a dam project that would have destroyed the Ozarks cave systems, including his beloved Onondaga. When Onondaga Cave State Park opened in 1981, it was with a dedication to Dill, who had died the year before, and this is what I mean when I say Missouri is good deep down—

—And to so many caves over so many years; and how each time, regardless how bleak our circumstances, there were mo-ments of bliss and clarity and wonder; how my children gripped my hands when the guide plunged the caves into total darkness and all my senses heightened, including gratitude and reverence and love; how I was reminded how short our time was both by the immense geological sweep of the caves and that I was walking through them with two children who somehow had become taller than me; and how I longed to live at the speed of cave time, to have my children grow as slow as stalactites, to have every second with them last a millennium, to have nothing break or end.

"It was said that one might wander days and nights together through its intricate tangle of rifts and chasms," Mark Twain wrote in *The Adventures of Tom Sawyer* in 1876, "and never find the end of the cave; and that he might go down, and down, and still down, into the earth, and it was just the same—labyrinth under labyrinth, and no end to any of them. No man 'knew' the cave. That was an impossible thing."[24]

Mark Twain "knew" his cave as well as anyone could. He grew up exploring it as a boy in Hannibal, when it was called MacDougal's Cave. He knew the cave in that he knew he would never *really* know the cave but understood that its mystery was its appeal, that the narrow dark passageways held an unlimited inventory of imagination. When a character in *Tom Sawyer* shouts, "Who's ready for the cave?" the answer is, of course, "Everybody."

Today MacDougal's Cave is known as Mark Twain Cave and is part of Hannibal's Mark Twain tourist industry. The Mark Twain Cave holds three claims to fame. Opened for official tours in 1886, it is the longest running show cave in America. It was an *actual* hideout of Jesse James, who wrote his name on the wall in 1879, along with members of his gang like C. E. Tucker, an alibi-destroying renegade who scrawled his name over 250 times after robbing a nearby train. And it was the actual hideout of teenage Twain, whose cursive "Clemens" was discovered and authenticated in 2019 after over a century of speculation.[25] Inside Mark Twain Cave, all tall tales turn true.

In the 1880s, Twain returned to Hannibal to research *Life on the*

Mississippi. He contemplated entering the limestone caverns now bearing his name but decided against it. He had a valid reason.

"In my time the person who then owned it turned it into a mausoleum for his daughter, aged fourteen. The body of this poor child was put into a copper cylinder filled with alcohol, and this was suspended in one of the dismal avenues of the cave. The top of the cylinder was removable; and it was said to be a common thing for the baser order of tourists to drag the dead face into view and examine it and comment upon it."[26]

This anecdote, the inspiration for the grave-robbing legends in Twain's Tom Sawyer series, is another example of the unrelenting weirdness of Missouri. Joseph Nash McDowell was a St. Louis doctor with a side hustle as a grave robber. Along with his students from Missouri Medical College, McDowell snatched bodies to chop them up and see what was inside. He dressed in a suit of armor and kept a thousand rifles, several cannons, and a live bear in the building for protection.[27] After the college was stormed by a mob in 1849 in an event known as the Anatomy Riots, McDowell fled to Hannibal.

Shortly after his arrival, his teenage daughter Amanda died of pneumonia. The grief-stricken McDowell believed that traditional burial blocked communication between the dead and the living. So instead of burying Amanda in a cemetery, he tried to preserve her corpse with chemicals and suspended it from the cave ceiling.[28] This unusual approach was nothing new for McDowell, who buried his wife at Cahokia Mounds so he could spy on her grave through a telescope from his St. Louis office across the river and see if anything interesting happened.[29]

Hannibal residents were spooked—at least until 1861, when McDowell was made the surgeon general of the Confederate Army, and his reputation was restored by people who had more of a problem with free Black people than with corpse-snatching maniacs.

McDowell was a Kentucky native and graduate of Transylvania University. His dream was to be buried inside Mammoth Cave, where he had carved his name into the wall, allegedly while on a tour with Stephen Bishop. He instead was buried in St. Louis's Bellefontaine Cemetery like a normal person. His daughter allegedly remained tied to the cave ceiling and became a tourist attraction, as Twain described, until she was finally taken down. Missouri Medical College was turned into a prison for Confederates until the Civil War ended, after which it became, and remains, the headquarters of the Purina dog food company.

Unlike most Missouri caves, the Mark Twain Cave does not have stalagmites or stalactites or large open rooms. Its walls are barren and its passages tight, like halls in a prehistoric office building. It is easy to get lost and was especially so in the 1800s, when visitors used candles or lanterns. Today, the cave is wired with electricity to display the over 250,000 signatures on the wall. Everyone from Norman Rockwell to Twain's childhood friends to an assortment of plutocrats and gangsters have left their marks, and Twain's signature is easy to miss in the morass.

I had walked by it myself every time I visited the cave and did not see it until 2023, where it is now protected inside an illuminated frame. No one is sure of the exact year Twain wrote his name, but it was likely when he was a teenager. He was oblivious that this place would inspire the books that made him revered, unaware that by visiting, he was becoming both an inventor of America's story and a part of it. He was just a kid in a cave.

My children looked at the signature with curiosity and continued down the clay path, unsure of what loomed ahead. They were just kids in a cave too.

This was their second visit, nearly ten years after the first. I have photos of them in 2014 getting ready for the tour, wearing fake coonskin hats and the oblivious smiles of people who literally cannot read the writing on the wall. They did not know about Twain or McDowell or James. But as the tour went on, they learned that this was a place where adults did terrible things, a place where a child grew up and turned the terrible things adults did into stories, and those stories turned into lessons and lore.

Stories are what we have to hold on to when the United States collapses, as it did in the midnineteenth century, during the prime years of the cave's exploration, and as it is doing now, in the twenty-first century of my children's youth. Stories are the air of the underground, relentless in their preservation of the truth that the world above wants you to forget.

Between their two visits to the Mark Twain Cave, my teenage children had witnessed an attempted and unpunished coup, a global pandemic, the destruction of our neighborhood in a flood, and record-setting heat waves every year. We passed the Mississippi River on the drive to Hannibal: it was disappearing again.

My daughter asked me if I loved America, and this is what I said. I know it is what I said because she made me write it down.

"I love this country more than anyone I know," I told her. "But you have to love it honestly. This country has done acts of incredible evil, almost unparalleled evil. And you have to be honest about that. In order to love it, you need to be honest. You can only love the good things and then be honest about the rest. Then your love will be honest too."

She nodded and said she understood.

"But you have to be that way about people too," I said, my voice breaking. "And that is the hardest thing."

In June 2023, my husband and children and I drove on a gravel road past a city dump, crossed a crumbling wooden bridge, disappeared through a rock tunnel, and arrived at a parking lot next to a cavernous hole in a towering sandstone wall. A dozen people stood near the hole, bundled up even though it was summer, handing dollars and waivers to an elderly man. We were at a cash-only operation, as trips through abandoned mines known for lead poisoning tend to be.

There is no Riviera in Festus, Missouri. But it does have an official twin city, called Crystal City. Both Crystal City and Festus border the town of Herculaneum, named after the Roman city buried by the eruption of Mount Vesuvius.

In the nineteenth century, Herculaneum opened its first mines, whose minerals were used to create glass for celebrated monuments like the Eads Bridge. The mines made the town prosperous while slowly poisoning generations of residents.

By 2001, the smelter from Missouri's Doe Run Company mining plant had caused the ground to have a concentration of lead 750 times exceeding the minimum hazardous level.[30] Fifty-six percent of the children within a quarter mile of the smelter were diagnosed with an excess of lead in their blood.[31] Outraged locals sued Doe Run, who unsuccessfully tried to argue that oxygen was also a toxin, if you breathed it wrong.[32] The residents won, the smelter closed, and the empty mines gaped like an exit wound.

One of those mines was our destination: Crystal City Underground.

Crystal City Underground is, like so many Missouri attractions, a nightmare trying to become a dream. I live halfway between Crystal City Underground and the Nuclear Waste Adventure Trail, a concrete stairway that brings you to the top of a giant mound of buried radioactive material, upon which you gaze at the cement landscape of Weldon Spring, Missouri, and its birds and animals, scouting for ones with three heads. The government says that the Nuclear Waste Adventure Trail is safe. But the government says that about a lot of things.

Over the last century, the St. Louis region has endured secret chemical experiments performed on residents during the Manhattan Project; a slow-moving underground fire headed toward a different pile of buried nuclear waste; and a region of cancer clusters due to toxic waste poisoning a local creek. Many of these environmental atrocities were initially denied, and almost none have been remedied. Our state of natural beauty is frequently left to fend for itself—abandoned by the federal and state governments, and shunned by Americans who think Missouri deserves harm.

Documentation does not work, voting does not work, and activism, though admirable, does not work fast enough. Corporate morality works, but that is as real as the dinosaur in Meramec Caverns. This has left Missouri with but one recourse, at which we excel: recreation. The ability of Missourians to transform *anything* into recreation is both a perverse admission of our powerlessness and our refusal to abandon the autonomy of our reckless lives. If our fate is to be killed, might as well enjoy our poison.

The site that became Crystal City Underground started as a silica mine for the Pittsburgh Plate Glass Company in 1870. In 1991, it closed down, and the six-million-square-foot underground labyrinth was left to trespassing revelers. The site was then revived by Missouri entrepreneurs in the spirit of Bob Cassilly and Lester Dill, which is to say, people with limitless imaginations and a free-spirited notion of safety. People like Tom Karr, a self-described nutcase who bought the mine for $800,000 in 2005 with the dream of making it a training ground for Olympic athletes, but settled for a subterranean recreation center instead.[33]

By 2014, Crystal City Underground had Frisbee golf and pole vaulting. It hosted an underground Jeep Crawl inspired by Dill, who used to hold car races through the opening of Meramec Caverns. But that was before the floods. Located near the Mississippi River, Crystal City Underground filled with water whenever there was torrential rain. In the era of catastrophic climate change, those storms were becoming more frequent. By 2019, floodwaters had wiped out the complex.

The owners of Crystal City Underground responded by declaring that the disaster zone was now a kayaking adventure.

This was not an original idea. It says something about Missouri that Crystal City Underground was not our family's first float trip through an abandoned mine. Our initial foray was at Bonne Terre Mine, a Lead Belt adventure land that boasts, among other things, a scuba diving venue and a terrarium. At the entrance to the mine is a fake safety record list, including gems like "Folks We Blowed Up," "Folks We Jest Plain Lost," and "Folks Et by Critter." I used to post photos of the sign and say that it was the CDC's covid casualty record, but Bonne Terre keeps better track than the CDC. I first went to Bonne Terre the day after Trump was inaugurated, a day I was afraid America was jest gon' get blowed up.

Crystal City Underground is more ramshackle than Bonne Terre, which, thanks to the pricy professionalism of the scuba divers, has edged toward respectability. While Bonne Terre transports you on a pontoon, Crystal City Underground expects you to paddle on your own for three hours and assumes you will survive. If not, well, that's what the waiver is for. The kayaking tours began in 2012, when Don Marsan, a proud veteran and outdoorsman, began bringing Crystal City Underground visitors through a flooded section of the mine known as the Lake. When new floods turned the whole complex into the Lake, Marsan started a kayak tour through the ruins of ruins, a float trip buoyed by audacity.

Inside the mine, we were given gear—life jackets, headband lights, two layers of gloves, and Hefty garbage bags we were told were our "sea blankets." We each took a kayak and a paddle. There are no lights in a mine four hundred feet beneath the earth. If you drifted down the wrong passage, it seemed doubtful you would return. I could see the endless mirror of the dark and my shadow reflected in the floodwater. My children wobbled in their boats, struggling to stay close to my husband and me. Our breath was visible in the frigid air, little ghosts escaping from our mouths, our words echoing to the point of indecipherability.

The week we kayaked through the mine marked one year since the Missouri state legislature signed away my bodily autonomy. That was followed by the destruction of my neighborhood in the flood and then by my dad's terminal cancer. Within this six-month time frame, other things happened, but I barely remember them. Life passed like an invisible wind between brackets of tragedy. Every now and again, something would make me feel safe and alive, and it was never anything normal. We were in Crystal City Underground because I wanted to see something made out of nothing, and I wanted to do it in the dark. I had been walking around with eyes so hollow that you could see straight to my soul, and I wanted that view obscured. It was Father's Day.

We set off with two guides, one in front, one behind, to keep our group of paddlers together. The mine was as still as a tomb, a maze of repetition with none of the formations of Missouri's natural caves and no current to propel us. There were no signposts but endless options for where to turn: in this respect, it resembled the ruthless labyrinth of Mark Twain Cave. The silence was broken only by the nervous laughter of paddlers and the enthusiastic explanations of our guides, who shone their flashlights on relics of good-time days: a sunken chunk of machinery, a wall of graffiti saying WHAT AM I DOING HERE. They were enamored with the abyss, and so was I. There was nothing left to do but drift through it.

Two hours in, we hit a section nicknamed the Squeeze Box. We had been warned about this at the start, but I had navigated too many Fat Man's Squeezes in caves to take it seriously. I should have paid attention: the passage required me to lie completely flat in the kayak, pulling my paddle close to my body, and let the guides push me forward as the ceiling of the mine grazed my hair. If I lifted my head even slightly, I would injure myself. If I tried to move to a wider passageway, I could make a wrong turn and drift into the void.

There was no choice but surrender. The Squeeze Box was not a quick turn, it stretched on and on, and I gave up, feeling a strange sense of relief. I would go out the way I'd gone in, looking for adventure to distract from the pain. I would move and move and move until moving suffocated me or left me lost, because the pain ran too deep to keep me on course.

But gradually the gap widened, and when the ceiling was a few inches above my head, I pushed my gloved hands against it to propel myself forward. Gradually the mine rose to a level where I felt safe enough to lift my head, turn my kayak around, and see if my husband and children were still alive. They were there beside me, laughing in terrified relief.

We lined up our kayaks, pulling each other close until we were in a row, our hands linked across the water. It was cold, but I felt fine; it was dark, but I felt free. I was floating on a pool of wreckage, and it was where I belonged. This was what we would need to survive the future, I thought. Not to live underground, not to hide out from the world for eternity, but to hang on to each other tight no matter the peril. To recognize that these wayward places had been abandoned like we were and reclaim them together as something beautiful and true.

I want more for my children's future than survival. But in a world of existential threats, a life that is more than survival hinges not on hope but on imagination. If our fate is to be the real-time archaeologists of humanity's demise, then at least let the trip be interesting. If once-prized places are tossed aside as ruins, then band with others who refuse to be forsaken. There is a reckless resilience to both Missouri and America that is difficult to stomp out. If I cannot help but find heaven in other people's idea of hell, then I am all the better for it.

My children did not inherit this trait so much as have it impressed upon them: that people and places are almost never what they seem. Never as steady, never as strong, never as boring, never as clear. And that the pathway against prejudice is not merely travel but the willingness to explore with an open mind. Contrary to the old adage of Mark Twain, travel is no longer fatal to prejudice—not when people journey for the purpose of turning the lens on themselves and living as a brand, quantified by clicks and likes. Travel is by nature a ruminative activity. But the goal was rarely to be the backdrop, as it so often is now. "Leave no trace" works not only as an environmental mantra but as a philosophical guide. If you are studying your surroundings, you are looking less at yourself and, in the process, learning to understand both.

Travel is a barrier to deception in a digital age when the past has never been so easy to erase or rewrite. Travel makes you a direct witness instead of a distant voyeur. Children may not remember the details of what they saw correctly, but they remember the *feeling* of seeing it, and sense memory is beyond the scope of artificial intelligence. You cannot summon serendipity; you cannot clock revelation. An algorithm cannot catch you in a cave or circumvent your view of the stars. It is not a coincidence that the Dark Sky Places where you can see the stars are the same places where your phones do not work.

I parent through the American apocalypse by showing my children everything from every vantage point: the rivers, the woods, the mountains, the dirt roads and highways, and the caverns beneath the ground. It is the last that is my favorite, for it feels most true. That when you descend into the earth, you are met not with the cruel yielding dirt of the grave but with crystalline unbreakable mazes. Worlds that prompt you, upon returning to the surface, to wonder what else you are missing.

It is as impossible to know America any more than it is to know a cave. There are too many backstories that remain unread, too many backroads undriven. But it is worth a try. If on your travels what emerges of the past, as it does so often in America, is a horror story, then that should increase empathy for its victims. Compassion is not just moral but wise, since whoever is left in the future will look back at us with the same pitying gaze.

Didn't they know any better? they'll ask, and our wasteland ghosts will answer, *We had to invent our own better, because all we were handed was worse.*

When we left Crystal City Underground, it was pouring. We raced to the car, afraid of water on land despite having floated through a pitch-black waterway for hours. Our senses, sharp beneath the ground, were dulled by instinctive panic. It was out here, in the open air of America, that the walls felt like they would close in.

We drove through the tunnel and over the rattling bridge and past the dump until we reached Festus, where we pulled into a gas station called On the Run. It is a good name for a chain store. Americans used to live on the road, and now we live on the run.

Inside, the kids and I wiped off the rain and poked around the aisles, looking for treasure. You never know what you will find at the gas station. We bought snacks and coffee and went back outside, where my husband was filling up the car. The rain slowed, the clouds parted, and a rainbow appeared. I took out my phone, trying to photograph the rainbow before it vanished, but I got a picture of a billboard for a gun show instead.

We stared at the arc of color shimmering above Festus, becoming lighter as the sun got brighter and vanishing into mist. It was only noon. The tank was full; the day was open. We could drive in any direction from the center of an America that does not hold, navigating its cracks, finding comfort in the ingenuity of countrymen who transform them into passages. We were a good country, deep down. But we had buried our grace along with our sins.

My family did not know what to do with the rest of our empty Sunday, but that was okay. The greatest source of comfort is the company we keep. The moments you miss most tend to be the ordinary ones—the days you take for granted until they are gone. The trips you relive on the backroads of your mind, guarding them from the nemesis of time. *They won't be with you forever*, a voice in my head whispered, but a good thing about living at the end of the world is that forever never comes.

I pulled my husband and children close, and we fell, like an empire, into each other's arms.

Acknowledgments

I wrote this book in 2023 and early 2024. It was a labor of love, and I mean that in the purest sense, since it's about the places and people I love and my desire to protect them. And it required a lot of labor! I appreciate everyone who put up with me while I put my heart on the line.

First, tremendous thanks to my readers. I am very lucky to have such an engaged and thoughtful audience, and I never take it for granted. You made my first book, *The View from Flyover Country*, a grassroots hit, and my other books into bestsellers. Your feedback and friendship have been invaluable to me during difficult times. I hope to see you on the road soon! Also thank you to Left Bank Books in St. Louis, and especially to Shane, for your continual support of my writing.

Thank you to my agent, Robert Lecker, who signed me when I was freelancing for the *Globe and Mail*. He insisted I could write a book even when I was skeptical, and as usual when it comes to my doubts, I was wrong and Robert was right. Robert has been a source of great support over the past eight years. I appreciate his creative feedback as well—and I'm glad I was able to write something less terrifying and more entertaining this time.

Thank you to my editors, Bryn Clark and Zachary Wagman. Bryn had been my editor since 2017 and while I was sad to see her leave Flatiron Books in 2024, I'm thrilled for her hard-earned success in publishing. When Bryn left, Zack took over, and I am grateful for his thoughtful editorial feedback and willingness to take on a work in progress and pave the way to publication. I am also grateful to the copy editors and production team at Flatiron Books and to Michael Cantwell for making legal review as fun as legal review can be.

Thank you to my in-laws, Sally and Phil, for helping our family through difficult times, and especially to my sister-in-law, Liz, for emotional support. Thank you to my sister, Lizzie, for moving to Texas and creating intriguing new road trip opportunities! Shout-out to my four favorite nephews and nieces: Kay, Julia, Jack, and Kate. And love to my muse, Twizzle the dog, who kept me company as I worked.

Special thank-you to my parents, Barbara and Larry, who always encouraged me to read broadly and critically. My mom is the funniest person I know and behind her sarcasm is a kind and loving heart. Mom, me and Pete—just kidding, *Pete and I*—will be here for you in the years ahead. Dad, it is hard to write this because I don't know what will happen by April. Thank you for giving me all those James Lee Burke novels when I needed them most. I'm now going to pay tribute to you and stop talking!

A huge thank-you to my children, Emily and Alex, for accompanying me on my adventures and letting me document them. I am so proud of both of you for being the kind, imaginative, wonderful people you are. You have made me happier than I can express, and our years as a family have been the best of my life. I hope we have many more adventures together, and that they are in the America you deserve.

Finally, thank you to my husband, Pete. My best friend, at-home editor, canoe partner, fellow adventurer, and so much more. The World's Greatest Dad, for real. Whatever happens with this book, I am glad I wrote the good times down. We have packed a lot of lifetimes into one. Thank you for reading dozens of drafts, for helping me find the coffee lids at QuikTrip, for decades of road song duets, for being there when things got dark, and for following my elusive dreams, which are not so elusive after all, because they all lead back to home and to you.

Notes

1. The Great River Road

1. Sarah Fenske, "Bob Cassilly Was Beaten to Death, Medical Expert Concludes," *Riverfront Times*, October 11, 2016, https://www.riverfront times.com/news/bob-cassilly-was-beaten-to-death-medical-expert -concludes-3123298.
2. Laura Begley Bloom, "America's 15 Safest (and Most Dangerous) Cities for 2023, According to a Report," *Forbes*, January 31, 2023, https://www.forbes.com/sites/laurabegleybloom/2023/01/31/report -ranks-americas-15-safest-and-most-dangerous-cities-for-2023/?sh =2f9b621b309a.
3. Missouri State Archives, "Crack of the Pistol: Dueling in 19th Century Missouri," https://www.sos.mo.gov/archives/education/dueling /political-duels.asp.
4. American Battlefield Trust, "Abraham Lincoln's Duel: Broadswords and Banks," January 17, 2014, https://www.battlefields.org/learn /articles/abraham-lincolns-duel.
5. Missouri State Archives, "Crack of the Pistol."
6. Jack Gienke, "The Forgotten History of Bloody Island," *MBU Timeline*, April 17, 2020, https://mbutimeline.mobap.edu/the-forgotten -history-of-bloody-island.
7. Stephen N. Kallestad, "The Territorial Militia: History of the Iowa National Guard," Iowa National Guard, August 6, 2007, https://web

.archive.org/web/20070806010154/http:/www.iowanationalguard.com
/Museum/IA_History/Territorial_Militia.htm.

8. Allison Keyes, "The East St. Louis Race Riot Left Dozens Dead, Devastating a Community on the Rise," *Smithsonian*, June 30, 2017.

9. Our Special Correspondent, "The St. Louis Bridge," *New York Times*,
May 17, 1873, https://timesmachine.nytimes.com/timesmachine/1873
/05/17/80317692.pdf.

10. Martin Magnusson, "'No Rights Which the White Man Was Bound
to Respect': The Dred Scott Decision," *American Constitution Society*, March 19, 2007, https://www.acslaw.org/expertforum/no-rights
-which-the-white-man-was-bound-to-respect.

2. The Twain Shall Meet

1. Mark Twain, *The Autobiography of Mark Twain: Volume 1* (Berkeley:
University of California Press, 2010), 65.

2. Twain, *The Autobiography of Mark Twain: Volume 1*, 159.

3. Twain, *The Autobiography of Mark Twain, Volume 1*, 16.

4. Mark Twain, *Life on the Mississippi*, 1883, https://www.gutenberg.org
/files/245/245-h/245-h.htm.

5. J. B. Smith, "Did Lovers Really Leap from Lovers Leap?" *Waco
Tribune-Herald*, http://wacohistoryproject.org/Places/loversleap
.html.

3. Route 66: Setting Out

1. National Archives, "National Interstate and Defense Highways Act
(1956)," https://www.archives.gov/milestone-documents/national
-interstate-and-defense-highways-act.

2. Harold Meyerson, "The 40-Year Slump," *American Prospect*, November 12, 2013, https://prospect.org/article/40-year-slump-d2/.

3. Candacy Taylor, "The Roots of Route 66," *Atlantic*, November 3,
2016, https://www.theatlantic.com/politics/archive/2016/11/the-roots
-of-route-66/506255.

4. Ken Burns, *Unforgivable Blackness: The Rise and Fall of Jack Johnson*,
PBS, November 7, 2018, https://www.pbs.org/kenburns/unforgivable
-blackness/mann-act.

5. History.com, "Chuck Berry Is Arrested on Mann Act Charges in St.
Louis, Missouri," November 16, 2009, https://www.history.com/this

-day-in-history/chuck-berry-is-arrested-on-mann-act-charges-in-st
-louis-missouri.

6. Olivia Goldhill, "'A Scary Time': Fear of Prosecution Forces Doctors to Choose Between Protecting Themselves or Their Patients," *STAT*, July 5, 2022, https://www.statnews.com/2022/07/05/a-scary-time -fear-of-prosecution-forces-doctors-to-choose-between-protecting -themselves-or-their-patients.

7. *Tulsa World*, "Timeline: Richard Roberts Resigns as President of ORU 15 Years Ago Today," November 23, 2022, https://tulsaworld .com/news/local/history/timeline-richard-roberts-resigns-as-president -of-oru-16-years-ago-today/collection_9395a5f8–1ee1–11eb-9c34 -db3c45f21a14.html.

8. Bonnie Parker, "Suicide Sal," 1932, All Poetry, https://allpoetry.com /Suicide-Sal.

9. Robert O'Harrow Jr. and Shawn Boburg, "During His Political Rise, Stephen K. Bannon Was a Man with No Fixed Address," *Spokesman-Review*, March 11, 2017, https://www.spokesman.com/stories/2017 /mar/11/during-his-political-rise-stephen-bannon-was-a-man/.

10. Kathleen Parker, "About That 'Nuclear Football' Selfie at Mar-a-Lago," *Denver Post*, February 14, 2017, https://www.denverpost.com /2017/02/14/about-that-nuclear-football-and-the-selfie-at-mar-a-lago/.

4. Arkansas Crime Scene

1. City of Jasper Chamber of Commerce, "Roadhouse History," https:// jaspermo.org.

2. "Weltmerism," *The British Medical Journal* 1, no. 2571 (1910): 891–92.

3. Yvonne Johnson, *Feminist Frontiers: Women Who Shaped the Midwest* (Kirksville, MO: Truman State University Press, 2010).

4. Glenn Clark, *The Man Who Talks with the Flowers* (Jersey City, NJ: Start Publishing, 2012), 17.

5. Teresa Bergen, "A Night in America's Most Haunted Hotel," Real Food Traveler, May 15, 2017, https://www.realfoodtraveler.com/a-night-in -americas-most-haunted-hotel-eureka-springs-1886-crescent-hotel.

6. Deni Kamper, "How Arkansas Became a Red State," KNWA, May 16, 2018, https://www.nwahomepage.com/news/special-report-how -arkansas-became-a-red-state.

7. Rachel Herzog, "Arkansas Ranks Last in U.S. for Voter Turnout, Registration, Report on 2020 Election Says," *Arkansas Democrat Gazette*,

September 5, 2021, https://www.arkansasonline.com/news/2021/sep
/05/arkansas-statistics-on-voting-reported.

8. Neil Vigdor, "Arkansas Violated the Voting Rights Act by Limiting
Help to Voters, a Judge Rules," *New York Times*, August 22, 2022,
https://www.nytimes.com/2022/08/22/us/politics/arkansas-voting
-lawsuit.html; Democracy Docket, "Arkansas Voter Suppression
Laws," May 19, 2021, https://www.democracydocket.com/cases
/arkansas-voter-suppression-laws.

9. Robert H. Boyle, "The Hottest Spring in Hot Springs," *Sports Il-
lustrated*, March 19, 1962, https://vault.si.com/vault/1962/03/19/the
-hottest-spring-in-hot-springs.

10. David Hill, *The Vapors: A Southern Family, the New York Mob, and the
Rise and Fall of Hot Springs, America's Forgotten Capital of Vice* (New
York: Farrar, Straus and Giroux, 2020), 150.

11. Bill Simmons, "Defendants All Acquitted in Sedition Trial," Associated Press, April 8, 1988, https://web.archive.org/web/20190113232310
/https://www.apnews.com/604c50e36bd020ac70be35445b12d059.

12. UPI, "Jury seated in sedition trial," February 17, 1988, https://
www.upi.com/Archives/1988/02/17/Jury-seated-in-sedition-trial
/1489572072400/.

13. Howard Pankratz, "Neo-Nazi Who Shot Denver Radio Host Alan
Berg Dies in Federal Prison in Pa.," *Denver Post*, August 17, 2010,
https://www.denverpost.com/2010/08/17/neo-nazi-who-shot-denver
-radio-host-alan-berg-dies-in-federal-prison-in-pa.

14. Howard Pankratz, "Bombing Plotted Earlier?" *Denver Post*, July 29,
1995, https://extras.denverpost.com/bomb/bomb327.htm.

15. Pankratz, "Bombing Plotted Earlier?"

16. Margaret Stafford, "Man Who Fatally Shot 3 at Kansas Jewish Sites
Dies in Prison," AP News, May 4, 2021, https://apnews.com/article
/kansas-shootings-race-and-ethnicity-entertainment-21775eca479ab1
be6a8d79499cf99ab4.

17. United States Department of Justice, "Joseph Hartzler to Head Oklahoma City Probe and Prosecution Team," May 22, 1995, https://www
.justice.gov/archive/opa/pr/Pre_96/May95/288.txt.html.

18. David A. Graham, "How Did the Oklahoma City Bombing Shape
Obama Supreme Court Nominee Merrick Garland?" *Atlantic*,
March 17, 2016, https://www.theatlantic.com/politics/archive/2016/03
/merrick-garland-oklahoma-city-bombing-supreme-court/474090/.

19. James Ridgeway, "Did the FBI Bury Oklahoma City Bombing

Evidence?" *Mother Jones*, July 21, 2011, https://www.motherjones.com /politics/2011/07/trentadue-fbi-oklahoma-city-bombing-evidence/.

20. Alex N. Press, "Who Is Merrick Garland's Friend Jamie Gore-lick?" Revolving Door Project, February 23, 2021, https:// therevolvingdoorproject.org/interview-who-is-merrick-garlands -friend-jamie-gorelick; Examiner Staff, "Anybody but Jamie Gore-lick for FBI Director," March 27, 2011, *SF Examiner*, https://www .sfexaminer.com/our_sections/forum/anybody-but-jamie-gorelick-for -fbi-director/article_3e43dd00-a01c-590f-bd58-e5ef6d21c995.html.

21. Scott Higham and Sari Horwitz, "American Cartel: Inside the Battle to Bring Down the Opioid Industry," *Washington Post*, July 7, 2022, https://www.washingtonpost.com/investigations/2022/07/07/american -cartel-book.

22. Austin Wright and Josh Dawsey, "Fate of Kushner's Security Clear-ance Could Ultimately Lie with Trump," *POLITICO*, July 16, 2017, https://www.politico.com/story/2017/07/16/jared-kushner-security -clearance-240575.

23. Encyclopedia of Arkansas, "Richard Wayne Snell (1930–1995)," https: //encyclopediaofarkansas.net/entries/richard-wayne-snell-11928.

24. Associated Press, "FBI Memo Reveals Drug Smuggling at Mena Air-port in 1980s," July 20, 2020, https://katv.com/news/local/fbi-memo -reveals-drug-smuggling-at-mena-airport-in-1980.

25. Julie Stewart, "Contras, Drug Smuggling Questions Remain About Arkansas Airport," Associated Press, September 24, 1991, https:// archive.is/Y4xnm.

26. Frank Snepp, "Bill Barr: The 'Cover-Up General,'" *Village Voice*, October 27, 1992, https://www.villagevoice.com/attorney-general -william-barr-is-the-best-reason-to-vote-for-clinton.

27. Sarah Kendzior, *They Knew: How a Culture of Conspiracy Keeps Amer-ica Complacent* (New York: Flatiron Books, 2022), 52.

28. Jefferson Morley, "Bob Parry RIP: The Reporter Who Broke the Iran-Contra Story," Alternet.org, January 29, 2018, https://www.alternet .org/2018/01/bob-parry-rip-reporter-who-broke-iran-contra-story.

29. Micah Morrison, "The Mena Coverup," *Wall Street Journal*, March 3, 1999, https://archive.is/7uqst.

30. Associated Press, "FBI Memo Reveals Drug Smuggling."

31. Sally Denton and Roger Morris, "The Crimes of Mena," *Pent-house*, July 1995, https://www.whatreallyhappened.com/RANCHO /POLITICS/MENA/crimes_of_mena.html.

32. Katie Connolly, "Health-Care Protest Deja Vu: Welcome to 1994," *Newsweek*, August 10, 2016, https://www.newsweek.com/health-care -protest-deja-vu-welcome-1994–211482.

33. Mary Kekatos, "US Life Expectancy Falls to Lowest Levels Since 1996 Due to COVID, Drug Overdoses: CDC," ABC News, December 21, 2022, https://abcnews.go.com/Health/us-life-expectancy-falls-lowest -levels-1996-due/story?id=95649464.

34. Mark Carter, "Bypassing Purple," *Arkansas Money and Politics*, October 2, 2019, https://armoneyandpolitics.com/bypassing-purple -arkansas-switch-blue-red.

5. The National Parks: American Daydreams

1. US National Park Service, "Quick History of the National Park Service," https://www.nps.gov/articles/quick-nps-history.htm.

2. National Parks Conservation Association, "Poll: Strong Bipartisan Support for National Parks," August 7, 2012, https://www.npca .org/resources/2566-poll-strong-bipartisan-support-for-national -parks.

3. Daniel L. Dustin, Kelly S. Bricker, Matthew T. Brownlee, and Keri A. Schwab. "The National Parks: America's Best Idea?" *Parks and Recreation Magazine*, August 1, 2016, https://www.nrpa.org/parks -recreation-magazine/2016/august/the-national-parks-americas-best -idea.

4. Sarah Kendzior, "Trump's America, Where Even Park Employees Have Become Enemies of the State," *Guardian*, https://www .theguardian.com/commentisfree/2017/jan/29/trump-america-parks -employees-enemies-of-state.

5. "Report of the Missouri House: Special Investigative Committee on Oversight," April 11, 2018, https://house.mo.gov/Billtracking/bills181 /commit/rpt1840/Special%20Investigative%20Committee%20on%20 Oversight%20Report.pdf.

6. Jonathan Romeo, "Climate Change Impacts on Mesa Verde National Park Already Apparent, Officials Say," *Durango Herald*, September 7, 2019, https://www.durangoherald.com/articles/climate-change-impacts -on-mesa-verde-national-park-already-apparent-officials-say.

7. "Visit Mesa Verde," https://www.visitmesaverde.com/media/823190 /mv2020-rackcard-final.pdf.

8. Kimon Roussopoulos and Lynn Malpas, "Exxon and the 1970s Cli-

mate Predictions That Were Ignored," *Guardian*, January 18, 2023, https://www.theguardian.com/environment/2023/jan/18/exxon-and -the-1970s-climate-predictions-that-were-ignored.

9. Denver 7, "Spring Fire Now 3rd Largest in Colorado History," July 4, 2018, https://www.denver7.com/news/local-news/spring-fire-now-the -3rd-largest-in-colorado-history-at-more-than-94–000-acres.

10. Kirk Mitchell, "Colorado's 2018 Wildfire Season Is One of the Worst on Record, and It's Not over Yet," *Denver Post*, August 18, 2018, https:// www.denverpost.com/2018/08/18/colorado-worst-wildfire-season-2018.

11. Kelly Kizer Whitt, "2022 Was 3rd Hottest Summer in US," Earthsky, September 11, 2022, https://earthsky.org/earth/2022-3rd-hottest -summer-united-states.

12. James Karuga, "Dead Horse Point: Why It's Worth Visiting Despite Its Name," *The Travel*, December 1, 2021, https://www.thetravel.com /dead-horse-state-park-history-visiting.

13. W. Paul Reese, "Marie Ogden Led Spiritual Group in San Juan County," *History Blazer*, April 1995, https://historytogo.utah.gov /marie-ogden.

14. Get Raw Milk, "List of US States with More Cows Than People, Numbers and Ratios 2020," June 23, 2021, https://getrawmilk.com /content/list-of-us-states-with-more-cows-than-people-numbers-and -ratios-2020.

15. Theodore Roosevelt, "Conservation as a National Duty," *Voices of Democracy*, May 13, 1908, https://voicesofdemocracy.umd.edu/theodore -roosevelt-conservation-as-a-national-duty-speech-text.

16. J. Weston Phippen, "'Kill Every Buffalo You Can! Every Buffalo Dead Is an Indian Gone,'" *Atlantic*, May 13, 2016, https://www.theatlantic .com/national/archive/2016/05/the-buffalo-killers/482349.

17. Sara Kettler, "Theodore Roosevelt's Mother and Wife Died Within Hours of Each Other on Valentine's Day," *Biography*, February 13, 2020, https://www.biography.com/political-figures/theodore-roosevelt -wife-mother-death.

18. Liz Posner, "Why Is a Small Montana Town a Hotbed of Far-Right Activity?" Alternet.org, December 19, 2017, https://www.alternet.org /2017/12/whitefish-montana-center-far-right.

19. Hannah Frishberg, "Glacier National Park Removes Signs Predicting Glaciers Will Be Gone by 2020," *New York Post*, January 9, 2020, https://nypost.com/2020/01/09/glacier-national-park-removes-signs -predicting-glaciers-will-be-gone-by-2020.

20. Salish-Pend d'Oreille, "Placename Signs on U.S. Highway 93," 2019, http://csktsalish.org/index.php/audio/salish-pend-d-oreille-placename-signs-on-u-s-highway-93.
21. Reuters, "Trump Thumbs-Up Photo with Orphaned Baby in El Paso Sparks Controversy," August 9, 2019, https://www.reuters.com/article/us-usa-shooting-orphan/trump-thumbs-up-photo-with-orphaned-baby-in-el-paso-sparks-controversy-idUSKCN1UZ2HQ.

Interlude: Digging Stars

1. Amy Von Lintel, "O'Keeffe to Stieglitz, May 9, 1917, Canyon, Texas," in *Georgia O'Keeffe's Wartime Texas Letters* (College Station: Texas A & M University Press, 2020).
2. Amy Von Lintel, "O'Keeffe to Stieglitz, March 26, 1917, Canyon, Texas."
3. Amy Von Lintel, "O'Keeffe to Stieglitz, April 13, 1917, Canyon, Texas."

6. Route 66: Coming Home

1. Timothy Bella, "Missouri Lawmaker Mike Moon Suggests 12-Year-Olds Should Be Able to Marry," *Washington Post*, April 14, 2023, https://www.washingtonpost.com/politics/2023/04/14/missouri-children-marriage-transgender-care/.
2. Mike O'Brien, "Artist Lowell Davis Laid to Rest in Rural Missouri Village He Recreated Near Carthage," *Springfield News-Leader*, November 16, 2020, https://www.news-leader.com/story/news/local/ozarks/2020/11/16/missouri-red-oak-ii-village-artist-lowell-davis-laid-rest/6315523002.
3. Nathan Gunter, "Haunted Bridge, Living Mystery," *Oklahoma Today*, https://web.archive.org/web/20190108152533/http:/www.oklahomatoday.com/oklahomatoday/MAGAZINE/Routes/ND11_-_Haunted_Bridge,_Living_Mystery.html.
4. American Indian Alaska Native Tourism Association, "American Indians and Route 66," 2016, https://www.aianta.org/wp-content/uploads/2020/03/American_Indians_Route66.pdf.
5. Daniel D. Chacon, "De Vargas Statue Removed; Overnight Attempt to Move Plaza Obelisk Fails," *Santa Fe New Mexican*, June 18, 2020, https://www.santafenewmexican.com/news/local_news/de-vargas-statue-removed-overnight-attempt-to-move-plaza-obelisk-fails/article_f10f20f0-b169-11ea-8203-2722abef3f0d.html.

6. Hannah Dreier, "As Migrant Children Were Put to Work, U.S. Ignored Warnings," *New York Times*, April 17, 2023, https://www.nytimes.com/2023/04/17/us/politics/migrant-child-labor-biden.html; Gloria Oladipo, "Native American Communities Lashed by Covid, Worsening Chronic Inequities," *Guardian*, December 13, 2021, https://www.theguardian.com/us-news/2021/dec/13/pandemic-challenges-native-american-communities.

7. Margalit Fox, "Chester Nez, 93, Dies; Navajo Words Washed from Mouth Helped Win War," *New York Times*, June 5, 2014, https://www.nytimes.com/2014/06/06/us/chester-nez-dies-at-93-his-native-tongue-helped-to-win-a-war-of-words.html.

8. Alice George, "Will Rogers Was One of a Kind," *Smithsonian*, August 5, 2020, https://www.smithsonianmag.com/smithsonian-institution/will-rogers-was-one-kind-180975472.

9. George, "Will Rogers."

10. Ivie E. Cadenhead, "Will Rogers: Forgotten Man," *Midcontinent American Studies Journal* 4, no. 2 (1963): 49–57, http://www.jstor.org/stable/40640601.

11. Jay Clarke, "In His Hometown, Will Rogers Won't Soon Be Forgotten," *Orlando Sentinel*, July 24, 2005, https://www.orlandosentinel.com/2005/07/24/in-his-hometown-will-rogers-wont-soon-be-forgotten/.

12. H. Allen Anderson, "Alanreed, TX," Texas State Historical Association, https://www.tshaonline.org/handbook/entries/alanreed-tx.

13. NPR Staff, "Decades-Old Housing Discrimination Case Plagues Donald Trump," NPR, September 29, 2016, https://www.npr.org/2016/09/29/495955920/donald-trump-plagued-by-decades-old-housing-discrimination-case.

14. James Ridgeway, "Did the FBI Bury Oklahoma City Bombing Evidence?" *Mother Jones*, July 21, 2011, https://www.motherjones.com/politics/2011/07/trentadue-fbi-oklahoma-city-bombing-evidence.

7. The National Parks: New Nightmares

1. Sophia Tareen and Michael Biesecker, "In 1993, Trump Promised to Make Gary, Indiana, Great Again—It Never Happened," Associated Press, September 21, 2016, https://www.businessinsider.com/trumps-spotty-casino-history-in-gary-indiana-2016-9.

2. US Department of the Interior, "Dorothy R. Buell," http://npshistory.com/brochures/indu/dorothy-buell.pdf.

3. J. Ronald Engel, *Sacred Sands: The Struggle for Community in the Indiana Dunes* (Middletown, CT: Wesleyan University Press, 1983), 254.

4. Stephen Starr, "Overtourism Is Stressing Our National Parks. Here's How Visitors Can Help," *National Geographic*, October 4, 2019, https://www.nationalgeographic.com/travel/article/avoid-overtourism-indiana-dunes-gateway-arch.

5. Margaret L. Coit. *John C. Calhoun: American Portrait* (Boston: Houghton, Mifflin), 52.

6. Shannon Reed, "The Least-Visited National Parks—and Why They're Worth a Look," *Far & Wide*, August 24, 2023, https://www.farandwide.com/s/least-visited-national-parks-6d041f66ebc4432e.

7. US National Park Service, "People in the Floodplain," https://www.nps.gov/cong/learn/historyculture/history-culture.htm.

8. Robert Greene II, "Congaree National Park: Gateway to a Historical Legacy," *Metropole*, January 9, 2018, https://themetropole.blog/2018/01/09/congaree-national-park-gateway-to-a-historical-legacy.

9. Sammy Fretwell, "Big Spiders Invade National Park in South Carolina," *Miami Herald*, December 12, 2016, https://www.miamiherald.com/news/nation-world/national/article120211088.html.

10. Sammy Fretwell, "Climate Change Ushers Voracious Spiders (1.5 inches long!) into Central SC," *Charlotte Observer*," October 8, 2019, https://www.charlotteobserver.com/news/local/article120354058.html.

11. Christopher Walton, "Jim Harrison Had Profound Love for Northern Michigan," *Detroit Free Press*, March 27, 2016, https://www.freep.com/story/entertainment/arts/2016/03/27/jim-harrison-had-profound-love-northern-michigan/82322488.

12. Larry Buhl, "The Myth of the Cuyahoga River Fire," *Science History Institute*, May 28, 2019, https://www.sciencehistory.org/stories/distillations-pod/the-myth-of-the-cuyahoga-river-fire.

13. US National Park Service, "Carl B. Stokes and the 1969 River Fire," https://www.nps.gov/articles/carl-stokes-and-the-river-fire.htm.

14. Zenobia Jeffries, "In Detroit, People Know What It's Like to Live Without Running Water," *Grist*, May 14, 2017, https://grist.org/culture/in-detroit-people-know-what-its-like-to-live-without-running-water.

15. Mark Urycki, "50 Years Later: Burning Cuyahoga River Called Poster Child for Clean Water Act," NPR, June 18, 2019, https://www.npr.org/2019/06/18/733615959/50-years-later-burning-cuyahoga-river-called-poster-child-for-clean-water-act.

16. Gerald Ford Presidential Library, "1974/12/27 HR7077 Cuyahoga Valley National Recreation Area Ohio," December 24, 1974, https://www.fordlibrarymuseum.gov/library/document/0055/1668842.pdf.

17. Mark Twain, "The Letters of Mark Twain, Vol. 1," http://www.fullbooks.com/The-Letters-Of-Mark-Twain-Vol-12.html.

18. Jesus Jimenez, "Strong Winds Moved a Lake in Death Valley Two Miles," *New York Times*, March 8, 2024, https://www.nytimes.com/2024/03/08/us/death-valley-lake-manly-wind.html.

19. Melody Petersen, "Solar Project to Destroy Thousands of Joshua Trees in the Mojave Desert," *Los Angeles Times*, May 31, 2024, https://www.latimes.com/environment/story/2024–05–31/solar-project-to-destroy-thousands-of-joshua-trees.

8. A Cave State of Mind

1. Holly V. Hays, "Letters to Santa Claus (Indiana): Send a Note and Get a Response from Hoosier 'Elves,'" *Indianapolis Star*, November 8, 2021, https://www.indystar.com/story/news/2021/11/08/letters-santa-claus-indiana-what-you-need-know/6289628001.

2. Hays, "Letters to Santa Claus (Indiana)."

3. Joe Coscarelli, "Kellyanne Conway Admits 'Bowling Green Massacre' Error," *New York Times*, https://www.nytimes.com/2017/02/03/us/politics/bowling-green-massacre-kellyanne-conway.html.

4. Josh Nathan-Kazis, "Which Side Were We On? Kentucky Slavery, Mine Wars and Segregation," *Forward*, June 28, 2015, https://forward.com/culture/310910/which-side-were-we-on-kentucky-slavery-mine-wars-and-segregation.

5. Alexander Clark Bullitt, *Rambles in the Mammoth Cave, During the Year 1844, by a Visiter* (Louisville: Morton and Griswald, 1845), https://www.gutenberg.org/files/16220/16220-h/16220-h.htm.

6. US National Park Service, "Mat Bransford," https://www.nps.gov/people/mat-bransford.htm.

7. Mary Beth Sallee, "The Bransfords of Mammoth Cave," *Hart County News-Herald*, March 28, 2021, https://www.jpinews.com/2021/03/28/the-bransfords-of-mammoth-cave/

8. US National Park Service, "Ed Hawkins," https://www.nps.gov/people/ed-hawkins.htm.

9. Eliza McGraw, "How the Kentucky Cave Wars Reshaped the State's Tourism Industry," *Smithsonian*, July 25, 2023, https://www

545545

.smithsonianmag.com/history/how-the-kentucky-cave-wars-reshaped-the-states-tourism-industry-180982585.

10. "Kentucky Cave Men Revert to War for Tourist Business," *Wilkes-Barre Times Leader*, October 28, 1928, https://www.newspapers.com/newspage/395943920.

11. History Channel, "Guerillas Massacre Residents of Lawrence, Kansas," November 13, 2009, https://www.history.com/this-day-in-history/guerillas-massacre-residents-of-lawrence-kansas.

12. Wes Swietek, "Lost River Has Unique History, Role as 'Urban Oasis,'" *Bowling Green Daily News*, April 3, 2016, https://www.bgdailynews.com/news/lost-river-has-unique-history-role-as-urban-oasis/article_8bc6e351-d582-5e49-874c-bcc1df112aae.html.

13. Roger Ebert, "The Assassination of Jesse James by the Coward Robert Ford Movie Review," October 4, 2007, https://archive.is/Ktupd.

14. Tobin T. Buhk, "The Least Successful Train Robber in America (1910)," *Dark Corners of History*, October 2, 2015, https://www.darkcornersofhistory.com/the-least-successful-train-robber-in-america-1910.

15. Sydney Stallworth, "'Zombie Road' Is One of America's Most Haunted Roads," KSDK, October 4, 2022, https://www.ksdk.com/article/features/zombie-road-wildwood-st-louis-county/63-539520e9-8247-43ba-8f9a-22b44481a024.

16. "Discover the History of the Caverns," americascave.com, https://www.americascave.com/history.

17. Bob Ruark, "It Was Bigelow," *Wilmington News*, July 11, 1949, Star-News-Google News Archive Search, https://news.google.com/newspapers?nid=1454&dat=19490711&id=cG5gAAAAIBAJ&sjid=6nENAAAAIBAJ&pg=3606,2857936.

18. Frank O. Hall, "Jesse James Is Alive! In Lawton," *Lawton Constitution*, May 19, 1948.

19. Emily Baron Cadloff, "Yes, the Government Really Does Stash Billions of Pounds of Cheese in Missouri Caves," *Modern Farmer*, May 25, 2022, https://modernfarmer.com/2022/05/cheese-caves-missouri.

20. Henry Schoolcraft, *Rude Pursuits and Rugged Peaks: Schoolcraft's Ozarks Journal 1818–1819* (Fayetteville: University of Arkansas Press, 1996), 139.

21. The Branson Tourism Center, "Before 'Branson' or the 'Baldknobbers' There Was the 'Bald Knobbers,'" https://www.bransontourismcenter

.com/info/2014/10/24/before-branson-or-the-baldknobbers-there-was
-the-bald-knobbers.

22. Wanetta L. and Kevin V. Bright, *Smallin Civil War Cave* (Ozark, MO: Ozark Caves & Caverns Publishers, 2013), 89.

23. Elizabeth Davis, "Lester Dill and Meramec Caverns," *Columbia Daily Tribune*, May 19, 2020, https://www.columbiatribune.com /story/lifestyle/columns/2020/05/19/lester-dill-meramec-caverns /1182322007.

24. Mark Twain, *The Adventures of Tom Sawyer*, 1876, https://www .gutenberg.org/cache/epub/74/pg74-images.html.

25. Amanda Blanco, "After 20 Years of Searching, the Former Director of the Mark Twain House Discovers Samuel Clemens' Signature in a Missouri Cave," *Hartford Courant*, September 25, 2019.

26. Mark Twain, *Life on the Mississippi*, 1883, https://www.gutenberg.org /files/245/245-h/245-h.htm.

27. Victoria Cosner and Lorelei Shannon, *Missouri's Mad Doctor McDowell* (Charleston, SC: History Press, 2015), 118–19.

28. Luke Ritter, "Anatomy, Grave-Robbing, and Spiritualism in Antebellum St. Louis," *Confluence*, Spring/Summer 2021, https:// digitalcommons.lindenwood.edu/cgi/viewcontent.cgi?article=1081 &context=confluence_2009.

29. Stephen Logsdon, "Joseph Nash McDowell, the St. Louis Legend," Becker Medical Library, Washington University in St. Louis, February 10, 2012, https://becker.wustl.edu/news/joseph-nash-mcdowell -the-st-louis-legend.

30. Rebecca Leung, "A Diet of Lead," CBS News, July 9, 2003, https:// www.cbsnews.com/news/a-diet-of-lead.

31. Chad Garrison, "Smelterville," *Riverfront Times*, January 16, 2008, https://www.riverfronttimes.com/news/smelterville-2454617.

32. Leung, "A Diet of Lead."

33. Danny Wicentowski, "Flooded Missouri Mine Is Proving Ground for Thrill Seeker, Subterranean Kayaker," *Riverfront Times*, January 7, 2015, https://www.riverfronttimes.com/news/flooded-missouri-mine -is-proving-ground-for-thrill-seeker-subterranean-kayaker-2601465.

About the Author

Sarah Kendzior is the bestselling author of *The View from Flyover Country*, *Hiding in Plain Sight*, and *They Knew*. She lives with her husband and children in St. Louis, Missouri.